The Idea of Idolatry and the Emergence of Islam

From Polemic to History

In this book G. R. Hawting supports the view that the emergence of Islam owed more to debates and disputes among monotheists than to arguments with idolaters and polytheists. He argues that the 'associators' (*mushrikūn*) attacked in the Koran were monotheists whose beliefs and practices were judged to fall short of true monotheism and were portrayed polemically as idolatry. In commentaries on the Koran and other traditional literature, however, this polemic was read literally, and the 'associators' were identified as idolatrous and polytheistic Arab contemporaries and neighbours of Muhammad. Adopting a comparative religious perspective, the author considers why modern scholarship generally has been willing to accept the traditional image of the Koranic 'associators', he discusses the way in which the idea of idolatry has been used in Islam, Judaism and Christianity, and he questions the historical value of the traditional accounts of pre-Islamic Arab religion. The implications of these arguments for the way we think about the origins and nature of Islam should make this work engaging and stimulating for both students and scholars.

G. R. HAWTING is Senior Lecturer in the History of the Near and Middle East at the School of Oriental and African Studies, University of London. His publications include *The First Dynasty of Islam* (1986) and (with A. A. Shereef) *Approaches to the Qur'an* (1993).

Cambridge Studies in Islamic Civilization

Titles in the series

STEFAN SPERL, *Mannerism in Arabic Poetry: A Structural Analysis of Selected Texts, 3rd Century AH/9th Century AD–5th Century AH/11th Century AD* 0 521 35485 4

PAUL E. WALKER, *Early Philosophical Shiism: The Ismaili Neoplatonism of Abū Yaʿqūb al-Sijistānī* 0 521 44129 3

BOAZ SHOSHAN, *Popular Culture in Medieval Cairo* 0 521 43209 X

AMY SINGER, *Palestinian Peasants and Ottoman Officials: Rural Administration around Sixteenth-century Jerusalem* 0 521 45238 4 (hardback) 0 521 47679 8 (paperback)

TARIF KHALIDI, *Arabic Historical Thought in the Classical Period* 0 521 46554 0 (hardback) 0 521 58938 X (paperback)

REUVEN AMITAI-PREISS, *Mongols and Mamluks: the Mamluk–Īlkhānid War, 1260–1281* 0 521 46226 6

LOUISE MARLOW, *Hierarchy and Egalitarianism in Islamic Thought* 0 521 56430 1

JANE HATHAWAY, *The Politics of Households in Ottoman Egypt: The Rise of the Qazdağlis* 0 521 571103

THOMAS T. ALLSEN, *Commodity and Exchange in the Mongol Empire: A Cultural History of Islamic Textiles* 0 521 58301 2

DINA RIZK KHOURY, *State and Provincial Society in the Ottoman Empire: Mosul, 1540–1834* 0 521 59060 4

THOMAS PHILIPP AND ULRICH HAARMANN (EDS.), *The Mamluks in Egyptian Politics and Society* 0 521 59115 5

PETER JACKSON, *The Delhi Sultanate: A Political and Military History* 0 521 40477 0

KATE FLEET, *European and Islamic Trade in the Early Ottoman State: The Merchants of Genoa and Turkey* 0 521 64221 3

TAYEB EL-HIBRI, *Reinterpreting Islamic Historiography: Hārūn al-Rashīd and the Narrative of the ʿAbbasid Caliphate* 0 521 65023 2

EDHEM ELDEM, DANIEL GOFFMAN AND BRUCE MASTERS, *The Ottoman City between East and West: Aleppo, Izmir, and Istanbul* 0 521 64304 X

ŞEVKET PAMUK, *A Monetary History of the Ottoman Empire* 0 521 44197 8

RUDOLPH P. MATTHEE, *The Politics of Trade in Safavid Iran: Silk for Silver, 1600–1730* 0 521 64131 4

The Idea of Idolatry and the Emergence of Islam

From Polemic to History

G. R. HAWTING
School of Oriental and African Studies,
University of London

CAMBRIDGE
UNIVERSITY PRESS

PUBLISHED BY THE PRESS SYNDICATE OF THE UNIVERSITY OF CAMBRIDGE
The Pitt Building, Trumpington Street, Cambridge, United Kingdom

CAMBRIDGE UNIVERSITY PRESS
The Edinburgh Building, Cambridge, CB2 2RU, UK http://www.cup.cam.ac.uk
40 West 20th Street, New York, NY 10011-4211, USA http://www.cup.org
10 Stamford Road, Oakleigh, Melbourne 3166, Australia

First published 1999

Typeset in 10/12 pt Monotype Times New Roman in QuarkXPress™ [SE]

A catalogue record for this book is available from the British Library

Library of Congress cataloguing in publication data

Hawting, G. R. (Gerald R.), 1944–
The idea of idolatry and the emergence of Islam : from polemic to history / by G. R. Hawting.
p. cm. – (Cambridge studies in Islamic civilization)
Includes bibliographical references.
ISBN 0 521 65165 4 (hardback)
1. Islam – Origin. 2. Idolatry. 3. Civilization, Arab.
I. Series.
BP55.H39 1999
297′.09′021 – dc21 99-11039 CIP

ISBN 0 521 65165 4 hardback

Transferred to digital printing 2002

for
Mary Cecilia († 30.3.99) and Ernest James Hawting († 30.9.83)
and
Mabel and William Eddy

Idols and images
   Have none in usage
(Of what mettel so ever they be)
   Graved or carved;
My wyle be observed
   Or els can ye not love me.

From: William Gray of Reading (first half of sixteenth century), 'The Fantassie of Idolatrie', quoted by Eamon Duffy, *The Stripping of the Altars. Traditional Religion in England 1400–1580*, New Haven and London 1992, 408–9

In vain with lavish kindness
   The gifts of God are shewn;
The heathen in his blindness
   Bows down to wood and stone.

Reginald Heber (1783–1826) Bishop of Calcutta

Contents

Preface

In the prologue to his *Studying Classical Judaism,* Jacob Neusner identifies what he sees as the most significant recent theoretical development in the study of the emergence of Judaism (and Christianity) during roughly the first six centuries AD. Dealing with the spread of such study from the seminary to the secular university, and with the involvement in it there of believing Jews and Christians of different sorts, he selects as most important a rejection of the simple 'debunking' which he thinks was characteristic of the early modern study of religion. 'What scholars [in the second half of the twentieth century] have wanted to discover is not what lies the sources tell but what truth they convey – and what kind of truth' (J. Neusner, *Studying Classical Judaism. A Primer*, Louisville, Ky. 1991, esp. 20–1).

It is clear that Neusner has in mind a diminution of the importance of questions such as 'what really happened?' and 'do we believe what the sources tell us happened?', questions which he describes as 'centred upon issues of historical fact'. In their place he finds a growing interest in questions about the world-view that the religious texts and other sources convey: 'how these documents bear meaning for those for whom they were written – and for those who now revere them'. Part of this process is a realisation that 'scriptures are not true or false, our interpretations are what are true or false'.

The contrast Neusner sets up cannot be an absolute one. If scriptures are not true or false, interpretations are rarely necessarily or demonstrably the one or the other. While historians of religion are not usually interested in debunking as such, if the significance of a text or a story for a particular religious group is to be understood, then attention has to be paid to historical questions such as the circumstances in which the text or story came into existence, and those questions have implications for the way we understand what the text or story tells us.

The relevance of these reflexions for the present work is that it aims to take seriously the character of Islam as a part of the monotheist religious tradition, not merely to question the widely accepted view that Islam arose initially as an attack on Arab polytheism and idolatry. That Islam is indeed related to Judaism and Christianity as part of the Middle Eastern, Abrahamic or

Semitic tradition of monotheism seems so obvious and is so often said that it might be wondered why it was thought necessary to repeat it. The reason is that although it is often said, acceptance of Islam as a representative of the monotheist religious tradition is not always accompanied by willingness to think through the implications of the statement. Part of the reason for that is that Islam's own account of its origins seems to undercut it.

Islam's own tradition portrays the religion as originating in a rather remote part of Arabia, practically beyond the borders of the monotheistic world as it existed at the beginning of the seventh century AD. Initially, according to the tradition, it arose as the result of a revelation made by God to the Prophet Muḥammad and its first target was the religion and society within which Muḥammad lived. That society's religion is described as polytheistic and idolatrous in a very literal and crude way. Only after the Arabs had been persuaded or forced to abandon their polytheism and idolatry was Islam able to spread beyond Arabia into lands the majority of the people of which were at least nominally monotheists.

It will be argued in the introduction that that account of its genesis seems to set Islam apart from other versions of monotheism (notably Rabbinical Judaism and Christianity). That is so even in those non-Muslim reworkings that interpret the initial revelation as, for example, a psychological or physiological experience, or seek to introduce economic, social and political explanations. Other forms of the monotheist religious tradition may be understood historically – at one level – as the outcome of debates and conflicts within the tradition: idealistically, as the result of developing awareness of the implications and problems of the deceptively simple idea that there is one God. In contrast, Islam by its own account seems to emerge within a society that is overwhelmingly polytheistic and idolatrous, and remote from the contemporary centres of monotheist religion. It is as if the initial emergence of monotheism, now also including knowledge of much of monotheist history and tradition, occurred independently for a second time. Setting Islam apart from the rest of monotheism in this way can be a source of strength or of weakness in situations of religious polemic.

On the one hand, to present Islam as originating in the way tradition describes it underlines the importance of the revelation and the Prophet and counters any suggestion that it was merely a reworking of one or more existing forms of monotheism. It might be argued that since Mecca, the crucible of the new religion, was virtually devoid of Christianity, Judaism or any other type of monotheism, Islam could not have originated as a result of influences or borrowings from other monotheists. Those things that Islam shares with other forms of monotheism are not evidence, according to this view, that it evolved out of one or more of those forms, or as a result of historical contact; rather they are elements of the truth that other forms of monotheism happen to have preserved in the midst of their corruption of the revelation with which they too began. That revelation was repeated to Muḥammad, and his followers, unlike those of Moses, Jesus and other prophets, preserved it intact and in its pristine form. (This understanding of the value to Islam of its own account of its origins is supposition: I do not know of any statement in Muslim sources which makes the argument explicit. On the other hand, there is – especially Christian – polemic against Islam which portrays it as a Christian heresy. That earlier prophets had been given the same revelation as Muḥammad but that the communities of those earlier prophets had either rejected the revelation completely, or accepted it but then corrupted it, is a commonplace of Muslim tradition.)

Against that, however, non-Muslim monotheists have been able to use the Muslim traditional account to deny Islam a status equal to that of their own version of the common tradition. Islam could be presented as a version of the truth adapted to the needs of pagan Arabs and bearing within it some of the marks of the idolatrous and pagan society within which it originated. In this version, it is often said that the Koran and Islam contain mistaken and erroneous versions of the common monotheistic ideas and stories because the Prophet had either deliberately or unconsciously misapprehended them when taking them from his sources. These views are common in pre-modern and modern accounts (many of them not overtly polemical) of Islam by non-Muslims and the impression they give is that Muslims follow a somewhat crude and backward version of the truth.

This book questions how far Islam arose in arguments with real polytheists and idolaters, and suggests that it was concerned rather with other monotheists whose monotheism it saw as inadequate and attacked polemically as the equivalent of idolatry. It is this, it is assumed here, which explains that emphasis on monotheism, the need constantly to struggle to preserve it and prevent its all too easy corruption, that has been a constant theme of Islam. Naturally, it is not impossible that such an emphasis could result from an initial struggle with a real idolatry, but 'idolatry' is a recurrent term in polemic between monotheists and by the time of the emergence of Islam monotheism, in one form or another, was the dominant religious idea in the Middle East.

To come back to Neusner: he defines the fundamental question facing the student of early Judaism as, *What do we know and how do we know it?* A necessary preliminary to that is to ask, *What did we think we knew and why did we think we knew it?*

I am conscious of many who influenced me and helped in the writing of this book. For several years the Hebrew University of Jerusalem Institute of Asian and African Studies has held regular colloquia on the theme 'From Jahiliyya to Islam', in which many of the leading scholars of early and medieval Islam have participated. Although I am sure may of them will disagree with my arguments, I owe a great debt to those who have organized and invited me to those colloquia and to those colleagues in the field who have presented papers there relevant to the theme of this book. If I do not mention individuals here or below, that is partly because many of them will appear in my footnotes and bibliography, but mainly not to discourage review editors from inviting them to review this book. A version of parts of chapter 4 of this book was given as a paper at the 1996 colloquium and was published in *JSAI*, 21 (1997), 21–41.

An earlier version of chapter 3 was written at the invitation of the editors of *Israel Oriental Studies*, 17 (1997), an issue devoted to Jews and Christians in the world of classical Islam, and appeared there as pp. 107–26. I am very grateful for their invitation and the opportunity it offered.

Another opportunity to try out some of the arguments used here was provided by a conference held at Victoria College, University of Toronto, in May 1997, entitled 'Reverence for the Word: Scriptural Exegesis in Medieval Judaism, Christianity and Islam'. It is hoped that a book arising from that conference will appear shortly. Again, I thank the organisers for the opportunity offered and for their generous hospitality.

More generally, I am aware that many of the suggestions made here arise from contact over several years with Professor John Wansbrough. In his *Sectarian Milieu* he isolated idolatry as one of the topoi of monotheist sectarian polemic, and in *Quranic Studies* remarked that 'the growth of a polemical motif into a historical fact is a process hardly requiring demonstration'. It was his stress on the importance of Islam for western culture and for the monotheistic religious tradition that first inspired my own interest in the study of Islam.

To my colleagues at the School of Oriental and African Studies I am also grateful, for their continuing support and stimulation and especially for allowing me a period of study leave in 1993–4 when I was able to formulate some of the arguments put forward here.

Drafts of parts or the whole were read by my wife, Joyce, the Rev. Paul Hunt, Dr Helen Speight, Dr Norman Calder whose death on 13 February 1998 was both a personal and a scholarly loss, Dr Tamima Bayhom Daou, and Professor Michael Cook. The last also served, coincidentally, as one of the two professional readers asked to evaluate the work by the Cambridge University Press, and he responded with a list of expectedly acute remarks and criticisms; the other reader, still unknown to me, also made many helpful suggestions and comments. To all of these I am indebted; they have all contributed to improve, I hope, what was once an even more imperfect text.

Finally, I am grateful to Marigold Acland of Cambridge University Press for help and encouragement.

Needless to say, faults, mistakes, infelicities, etc., are my own responsibility.

Note on transliteration and dates

The transliteration generally follows the *Encyclopaedia of Islam* system with the two modifications customary in works in English (i.e., *q* instead of *ḳ* and *j* instead of *dj*).

In names, 'b.' is short for 'ibn' = 'son of'.

Dates are usually given according to both the Islamic (Hijrī) and the Christian (or Common) calendars; e.g., 206/821–2 = 206 AH (Anno Hijrae) corresponding to parts of 821–2 AD. When not thus given, it should be clear from the context which calendar is intended.

Abbreviations

AIPHOS	*Annuaire de l'Institut de Philologie et d'Histoire Orientales et Slaves*
AKM	*Abhandlungen für die Kunde des Morgenlandes*
AO	*Acta Orientalia*
AR	*Archiv für Religionswissenschaft*
Aṣnām-Atallah	W. Atallah, *Les idoles de Hicham ibn al-Kalbī*
Aṣnām K-R	Rosa Klinke-Rosenberger, *Das Götzenbuch. Kitâb al-Aṣnâm des Ibn al-Kalbî*, Leipzig 1941
BIFAO	*Bulletin de l' Institut Français d' Archéologie Orientale*
BMGS	*Byzantine and Modern Greek Studies*
BSOAS	*Bulletin of the School of Oriental and African Studies*
CIS	*Corpus Inscriptionum Semiticarum*
EI, EI1, EI2	*Encyclopaedia of Islam (1st, 2nd edition)*
EJ	*Encyclopaedia Judaica*, Jerusalem 1971–
GAS	F. Sezgin, *Geschichte des arabischen Schrifttums*
GS	Ignaz Goldziher, *Gesammelte Schriften*
ERE	*Encyclopaedia of Religion and Ethics*, ed. James Hastings
IJMES	*International Journal of Middle East Studies*
IOS	*Israel Oriental Studies*
IS	*Islamic Studies*
Isl.	*Der Islam*
JAAR	*Journal of the American Academy of Religion*
JJS	*Journal of Jewish Studies*
JNES	*Journal of Near Eastern Studies*
JRAS	*Journal of the Royal Asiatic Society*
JSAI	*Jerusalem Studies in Arabic and Islam*
JSS	*Journal of Semitic Studies*
MTSR	*Method and Theory in the Study of Religion*
MW	*Muslim World*
PSAS	*Proceedings of the Seminar for Arabian Studies*
RB	*Revue Biblique*
REA	*Répertoire Chronologique d'Épigraphie Arabe*

REI	*Revue des Études Islamiques*
REJ	*Revue des Études Juives*
RES	*Répertoire d'Épigraphie Sémitique*
RHR	*Revue de l'Histoire des Religions*
RSR	*Recherches de Science Religieuse*
Ryckmans, *NP*	G. Ryckmans, *Les Noms Propres Sud-Sémitiques*
Ryckmans, *RAP*	G. Ryckmans, *Les Religions Arabes Préislamiques*
SI	*Studia Islamica*
SWJA	*South West Journal of Anthropology*
Ṭab., Tafsīr (Bulaq)	Ṭabarī, *Jāmiʿ al-bayān fī taʾwīl āy al-Qurʾān*, Bulaq 1323–8 AH
Ṭab., Tafsīr (Cairo)	Ṭabarī, *Jāmiʿ al-bayān fī taʾwīl āy al-Qurʾān*, Cairo 1954–
VOJ	*Vienna Oriental Journal*
Wellhausen, *Reste*	J. Wellhausen, *Reste arabischen Heidentums*, 2nd edition
ZDMG	*Zeitschrift der Deutschen Morgenländischen Gesellschaft*

Introduction

In broad terms this work is concerned with the religious setting within which Islam emerged. More specifically, it asks what it means if we describe the primary message of the Koran as an attack upon polytheism and idolatry. It questions the commonly accepted view that the opponents attacked in the Koran as idolaters and polytheists (and frequently designated there by a variety of words and phrases connected with the Arabic word *shirk*) were idolaters and polytheists in a literal sense. This introduction, directed primarily at non-specialists, aims to elucidate these issues and to indicate some of the starting-points of the discussion. A reconsideration of the nature and target of the koranic polemic, together with a discussion of why and how it has been commonly accepted that it was directed at Arabs who worshipped idols and believed in a plurality of gods, will have some consequences for the way we envisage the origins of Islam.

Muslim tradition tells us that, insofar as it is a historically distinct form of monotheism, Islam arose in central western Arabia (the Ḥijāz) at the beginning of the seventh century AD as a result of a series of revelations sent by God to His Prophet, Muḥammad.[1] The immediate background, the setting in which Muḥammad lived and proclaimed his message, is known generally in tradition as the *jāhiliyya*. That Arabic word may be translated as 'the age, or condition, of ignorance' although the root with which it is connected sometimes has significations and colourings beyond that of 'ignorance'. The word is sometimes used, especially among modern and contemporary Muslims, in an extended sense to refer to any culture that is understood to be unislamic,[2]

[1] The expression 'Muslim tradition' refers to the mass of traditional Muslim literature, such as lives of the Prophet (*sīras*), commentaries on the Koran (*tafsīrs*), and collections of reports (*ḥadīths*) about the words and deeds of the Prophet. Such works are available to us in versions produced from about the end of the second/eighth century at the earliest. From that time onwards the number of them multiplied rapidly and they have continued to be written until modern times. The tradition is extensive and, within certain boundaries, diverse. The Koran is a work *sui generis* and is usually regarded as distinct from the traditional literature.

[2] Muḥammad Quṭb, brother of the better-known Sayyid (executed 1966), published a book with the title (in Arabic) 'The *Jāhiliyya* of the Twentieth Century' (*Jāhiliyyat al-qarn al-ʿishrīn*, Cairo 1964). In it he defined *jāhiliyya* as 'a psychological state of refusing to be guided by God's

but more narrowly refers specifically to the society of the Arabs of central and western Arabia in the two or three centuries preceding the appearance of Islam. It is not normally used to include, for instance, the civilisation that flourished in south Arabia (the Yemen) in the pre-Christian and early Christian era, or the north Arabian polities such as those based on Palmyra or Petra (the Nabataean kingdom) which existed in the early Christian centuries.

The characterisation of the *jāhiliyya* is a recurring theme in Islamic literature. The word itself, with its connotations of ignorance, indicates the generally negative image that tradition conveys of the society it sees as the background and opposite pole to Islam. Although it has to be allowed that there is some ambiguity in Muslim attitudes, and that certain features of the *jāhiliyya*, such as its poetry, could be regarded with a sense of pride,[3] in the main it was portrayed as a state of corruption and immorality from which God delivered the Arabs by sending them the Prophet Muḥammad. A salient characteristic of it in Muslim tradition is its polytheistic and idolatrous religion, and with that are associated such things as sexual and other immorality, the killing of female children, and the shedding of blood.[4]

It should be remembered that Muslim tradition is virtually our only source of information about the *jāhiliyya*: it is rather as if we were dependent on early Christian literature for our knowledge of Judaism in the first century AD. In spite of that, modern scholars have generally accepted that, as the tradition maintains, the *jāhiliyya* was the background to Islam and that the more we know about it the better position we will be in to understand the emergence of the new religion.

Footnote 2 (*cont.*)
guidance and an organisational set-up refusing to be regulated by God's revelation': see Elizabeth Sirriyeh, 'Modern Muslim Interpretations of *Shirk*', *Religion*, 20 (1990), 139–59, esp. 152. The eponym of the Wahhābī sect which provided the religious ideology for the development of the Saudi kingdom in Arabia, Muḥammad b. ʿAbd al-Wahhāb (d. 1206/1792), drew up a list of 129 issues regarding which, he asserted, the Prophet opposed the people of the *jāhiliyya* (*Masāʾil al-jāhiliyya* in *Majmūʿat al-tawḥīd al-najdiyya*, Mecca 1391 AH, 89–97). Generally, the list is not specific to the pre-Islamic Arabs, but refers to beliefs and practices which in the author's view are inconsistent with true Islam, and many of them presuppose the existence of Islam.

3 For some reflexions on the transmissions and collection of so-called *jāhilī* poetry and its importance in early Islam, see Rina Drory, 'The Abbasid Construction of the Jahiliyya: Cultural Authority in the Making', *SI*, 83 (1996), 33–49.

4 For a traditional characterisation of the *jāhiliyya*, see below, pp. 99–100. See also *EI2* s.v. 'Djāhiliyya'. For discussion of the wider connotations of the term, see I. Goldziher, 'What is meant by 'al-Jāhiliyya'', in his *Muslim Studies*, 2 vols., London 1967, I 201–8 (= I. Goldziher, *Muhammedanische Studien*, 2 vols., Halle 1889, I, 219–28); F. Rosenthal, *Knowledge Triumphant*, Leiden 1970, esp. 32ff.; S. Pines, 'Jāhiliyya and ʿIlm', *JSAI*, 13 (1990), 175–94. Wellhausen, *Reste*, 71, n.1 suggested a Christian origin for the term: he saw it as an Arabic translation of Greek *agnoia* (Acts 17:30 – 'the times of this ignorance'), used by Paul to refer to the state of the idolatrous Athenians before the Christian message was made known to them. The same Greek word occurs in a context perhaps even more suggestive of the Muslim concept and use of *al-jāhiliyya* in the Jewish Hellenistic work, The Wisdom of Solomon, 14:22 (see further below, p. 99).

The present work does not share that approach. It treats the image of the *jāhiliyya* contained in the traditional literature primarily as a reflexion of the understanding of Islam's origins which developed among Muslims during the early stages of the emergence of the new form of monotheism. It questions how far it is possible to reconstruct the religious ideas and practices of the Arabs of pre-Islamic inner Arabia on the basis of literary materials produced by Muslims and dating, in the earliest forms in which we have them, from at least 150 years after the date (AD 622) that is traditionally regarded as the beginning of the Islamic (Hijrī) era.

According to Muslim tradition, however, the Prophet Muḥammad was sent to a people who were idol worshippers and morally debased. The tradition identifies this people for us as the Arabs (of the tribe of Quraysh) of the Prophet's own town, Mecca, those of the few neighbouring towns and oases (such as Ṭā'if and Yathrib), as well as the nomads of the region generally. Although Muḥammad's move (*hijra*) to Yathrib (later called Medina) in AD 622 is said by tradition to have brought him into contact with a substantial Jewish community which lived there together with the pagan Arabs, even in the ten years he passed in that town he is portrayed as continuing to struggle against the still pagan Meccans and the Arabs of the surrounding region at the same time as he was concerned with his relationship with the Jews. Of the Koran's 114 chapters (*sūra*s), 91 are marked in the most widely used edition as having been revealed in Mecca before the *hijra*.[5]

The tradition often refers to these pagan Arabs of the Ḥijāz, whom it sees as the first targets of the koranic message, using the terms *mushrikūn* (literally 'associators') and *kuffār* ('unbelievers'). These and related expressions occur frequently too in the Koran itself with reference to the opponents who are the main object of its polemic. Those opponents are accused of the sins of *shirk* and *kufr*. The latter offence is only loosely understood as 'unbelief' or 'rejection of the truth', and is sometimes taken to apply to Jews and Christians as well as to the idolatrous Arabs. *Shirk*, however, is conceived of somewhat more precisely: it refers to the association of other gods or beings with God, according them the honour and worship that are due to God alone. Hence it is frequently translated into European languages by words indicating 'polytheism' or 'idolatry'.[6]

The traditional Muslim material – the lives of Muḥammad, the commentaries on the Koran, and other forms of traditional Muslim literature –

[5] Since the chapters traditionally assigned to the Medinese period of the Prophet's career are generally longer than those assigned to Mecca, this figure is not a precise indication of the traditionally accepted proportion of Meccan to Medinese material. The tradition's stress on the priority (in time and importance) of the Prophet's attack on Arab paganism compared with his criticism of Jews and Christians generated reports in which the pagans complain about his greater hostility to them: e.g., Muhammad b. Aḥmad Dhahabī, *Ta'rīkh al-Islām*, ed. Tadmurī, 38 vols., Beirut 1994, I, 186, citing Mūsā b. ʿUqba (d. 141/758).

[6] See Muhammad Ibrahim H. Surty, *The Qur'anic Concept of al-Shirk (Polytheism)*, London 1982, 23: '*Shirk* in *shariʿah* means polytheism or idolatry. Since a man associates other creation with the Creator he has been regarded as polytheist (Mushrik)'.

frequently explicitly identifies the *mushrikūn* or *kuffār* referred to in a particular koranic passage as the pagan Meccans and other Arabs. When that material is put together it appears to supply us with relatively abundant information about the idols, rituals, holy places and other aspects of the opponents' polytheism. The nature and validity of the identification of the koranic opponents with idolatrous Meccans and other Arabs, the extent to which traditional material about them is coherent and consistent with the koranic material attacking the *mushrikūn*, is one of the main themes of this work.

As an example of the way in which the tradition gives flesh to the anonymous and sometimes vague references in the text of scripture, we may consider the commentary on Koran 38:4–7. That passage contains some problematic words and phrases but seems to tell us of the amazement of the opponents that the 'warner' sent to them should claim that there is only one God, and of their accusation against him that he was a lying soothsayer, not a true prophet:

And they are amazed that there has come to them a Warner from among themselves. Those who reject the truth (*al-kāfirūna*) say, 'This is a lying sorcerer. Has he made the gods one god? Indeed this is a strange thing!' The leaders among them go off [saying], 'Walk away and hold steadfastly to your gods. This is something intended. We have not heard of this in the last religion.[7] This is nothing but a concoction.'

The major koranic commentator Ṭabarī (d. 311/923), who drew widely on the tradition of commentary as it had developed by his own day, glossed this passage in a way to make it clear that these opponents were Meccan polytheistic and idolatrous enemies of Muḥammad: 'Those *mushrikūn* of Quraysh were surprised that a warner came to warn them . . . from among themselves, and not an angel from heaven . . . Those who denied the unity of God . . . said that Muḥammad was a lying soothsayer.' One of the traditions Ṭabarī cited to support his gloss explains: 'Those who called Muḥammad a lying soothsayer said: "Has Muḥammad made all of the beings we worship (*al-maʿbūdāt*) into one, who will hear all of our prayers together and know of the worship of every worshipper who worships him from among us!" Ṭabarī gave a number of traditions which say in different versions that the reason why the *mushrikūn* said what God reports of them is that Muḥammad had proposed to them that they join him in proclaiming that there is no god but God (*lā ilāha illā 'llāh*) – that is what occasioned their surprise and made them say what they did. Their response was to tell Muḥammad's uncle Abū Ṭālib that his nephew was reviling their gods and to ask that he stop him.[8]

This is typical of many such amplifications of the koranic text in the com-

[7] Some commentators see this problematic expression (*al-milla al-akhira*) as referring to Christianity.

[8] *Tafsīr* (Bulaq), XXI, 78 ff. The suggestion that the opponents would have accepted the warner if he were 'an angel from heaven' sits, it might be thought, uncomfortably with the idea that they were idolatrous pagans. Some other accounts seeking to contextualise the question 'Has he made the gods one God?' refer to the custom of the pagan Arabs of stroking or rubbing against their domestic idols before leaving for a journey.

mentaries; other examples will be given in the course of this work. Generally, they are concerned to provide a relatively precise historical context for koranic verses which in themselves give few if any indications of such, and to identify individuals and groups who, in the text itself, are anonymous. One of the most obvious result of them, and of material in the literature that provides details for us about the gods and idols of the Arabs, is to establish the common image of Islam as something beginning in a largely polytheistic milieu. The exegetical amplifications of the Koran lead us to understand Islam as, in the first place, an attack on the idolatry and polytheism of the Arabs of central western Arabia.

This traditional material has both a religious and a geographical aspect. It is not only that Islam is presented as having emerged as an attack on polytheism and idolatry, but that the polytheism and idolatry concerned was specific to the Arabs of central and western Arabia. The present work is mainly concerned with the religious aspect of the traditional image. It may be possible to reassess that without rejecting the Ḥijāz as the geographical locus of the Koran, but in tradition the background is so strongly identified as a specifically inner Arabian form of polytheism and idolatry that to question whether we are concerned with polytheists and idolaters in a real sense may be thought to have geographical implications too. This will be discussed further shortly.

First, however, why do we think that the traditional accounts might or should be reassessed, and what is the purpose of doing so?

Some answers to those questions are, I hope, made clear in the main chapters of this book. To anticipate the arguments pursued there, the identification of the *mushrikūn* as pre-Islamic idolatrous Arabs is dependent upon Muslim tradition and is not made by the Koran itself; the nature of the koranic polemic against the *mushrikūn* does not fit well with the image of pre-Islamic Arab idolatry and polytheism provided by Muslim tradition; the imputation to one's opponents of 'idolatry' – of which *shirk* functions as an equivalent in Islam – is a recurrent motif in monotheist polemic (probably most familiar in the context of the Reformation in Europe) and is frequently directed against opponents who consider themselves to be monotheists; the traditional Muslim literature which gives us details about the idolatry and polytheism of the pre-Islamic Arabs of the *jāhiliyya* is largely stereotypical and formulaic and its value as evidence about the religious ideas and practices of the Arabs before Islam is questionable; and, finally, the commonly expressed view that the traditional Muslim reports about Arab polytheism and idolatry are confirmed by the findings of archaeology and epigraphy needs to be reconsidered.

Underlying those arguments is the view that the traditional understanding of Islam as arising from a critique of local paganism in a remote area of western Arabia serves to isolate Islam from the development of the monotheistic tradition in general. At least from before the Christian era until about the time of the Renaissance it seems, the important developments within the monotheist tradition have occurred as a result of debates and arguments among adherents of the tradition rather than from confrontation with opponents outside it. Those debates and arguments have often involved charges that one party or another which claimed to be monotheistic in fact had beliefs or practices that – in the view of their opponents – were incompatible with, or a perversion of, monotheism.[9]

The two major forms of the monotheist tradition other than Islam – Rabbinical Judaism and Christianity – each emerged from a common background in ancient Judaism, and their subsequent history, for example the development of Karaism and of Protestantism, has been shaped primarily by intra- and inter-communal debates and disputes. Of course, for some centuries both Jews and Christians had to face the reality of political domination by a power – the Roman Empire – associated with a form of religion that the monotheists regarded as idolatrous and polytheistic. Sometimes they were subject to persecution and physical oppression by it, and sometimes they had to enter into debate and argument with representatives of the pagan religion. There is little, however, to suggest that the monotheists took the Graeco-Roman polytheism seriously enough to regard it as a challenge at the religious level, or to respond to it in the same way that they did, for example, to Manichaeism. The gospels contain polemic against Jews, not against Graeco-Roman religion. Notwithstanding the fact that some Rabbinical texts continued to count idolatry as one of the greatest sins and incompatible with being a Jew, others indicate that the tendency of Jews towards idolatry had passed away in the time of the first temple.[10] Long before Graeco-Roman polytheism was outlawed by the (by then Christian) Roman emperors, at a learned level it had come to present itself in terms comprehensible to monotheists. Judaism and Christianity had themselves adapted Hellenistic concepts and vocabulary, but long before the seventh century the balance of power was decisively in favour of monotheism.[11]

[9] In the real world monotheism and polytheism are often subjective value judgements, reflecting the understandings and viewpoints of monotheists, rather than objectively identifiable forms of religion. We are not concerned in this book to evaluate the claims of any particular group to be monotheists: 'monotheism' here covers all those groups that have originated within the Abrahamic tradition, but not groups outside that tradition even though they might legitimately be described as monotheistic. Cf. the view of Peter Hayman that 'it is hardly ever appropriate to use the term monotheism to describe the Jewish idea of God', argued in his 'Monotheism – a Misused Word in Jewish Studies?', *JJS*, 42 (1991), 1–15.

[10] For repudiation of idolatry as the essence of being a Jew, see, e.g., Babylonian Talmud, Megillah, fo. 13 a (Eng. trans. London 1938, 44); for the view that idolatry was no longer a threat to Jews, Midrash Rabba on Song of Songs, 7:8 (Eng. trans. 1939, 290 f.). See further Saul Lieberman, 'Rabbinic Polemics against Idolatry' in his *Hellenism and Jewish Palestine*, 2nd edn. New York 1962, 115–27; *EJ*, s.v. 'Idolatry', 1235a.

[11] For the strength of monotheism in the Middle East by the time of the rise of Islam, see especially Garth Fowden, *Empire to Commonwealth. Consequences of Monotheism in Late Antiquity*, Princeton 1993.

According to the traditional accounts Islam was not born in the same way – not as a result of disputes among monotheists but from a confrontation with real idolaters. Furthermore, whereas other major developments within monotheism occurred in regions where that tradition of religion was firmly established if not always completely dominant (Palestine, Iraq, northern Europe and elsewhere), Islam is presented as having arisen in a remote region which could be said to be on the periphery of the monotheistic world, if not quite outside it. None of this is impossible but it does seem remarkable and is a reason for suggesting that the traditional account might be questioned.[12] It is a suggestion of the present work that as a religious system Islam should be understood as the result of an intra-monotheist polemic, in a process similar to that of the emergence of the other main divisions of monotheism.

Reference has already been made to the relatively late appearance of Arabic Muslim literature in general, and that too is important for the argument that the traditional accounts of Islam's origins may be reconsidered.

The earliest examples that we have of Muslim traditional literature have been dated to the second/eighth century.[13] These include several books and a number of texts preserved on papyrus fragments.The papyrus remains (i.e., those pertaining to such things as the life of the Prophet, the early history of the community, koranic commentary, *ḥadīth*s and Arabic grammar) are fragmentary and the dating of them is often insecure. The earliest of them, assigned by Adolf Grohmann to the early second century AH, that is, approximately the second quarter of the eighth century AD, seems to be one referring to events associated with the victory of the Muslims at Badr in the second year of the Hijra (AD 624). Grohmann's dating is apparently on stylistic grounds for the text itself is undated. That versions of Muslim traditional texts are to be found on fragments of papyrus does not in itself tell us anything

[12] J. Waardenburg, 'Un débat coranique contre les polythéistes', in *Ex Orbe Religionum: Studia Geo Widengren Oblata*, 2 vols., Leiden 1972, II, 143: 'Le surgissement d'un monothéisme qui se dresse contre une religion polythéiste est un phénomène poignant dans l'histoire des religions.'

[13] 'Muslim traditional literature' here excludes, as well as the Koran, early Arabic administrative documents and official and unofficial inscriptions. Such things as letters and poems ascribed to individuals living in pre-Islamic and early Islamic times are known to us only in versions included in later Muslim literary texts; we do not have them in their original form, if any. For example, when modern scholars discuss, as many have, a theological epistle addressed to the caliph ʿAbd al-Malik (65/685–86/705) by Ḥasan al-Baṣrī (d. 110/728), they are in fact discussing a document edited from two late (eighth/fourteenth-century) manuscripts and excerpts in an even later Muʿtazilī text (H. Rittter, 'Studien zur Geschichte der islamischen Frömmigkeit. I. Ḥasan al-Baṣrī', *Isl.*, 21 (1933), 62; *GAS*, 592). Recently, extensive excerpts of the letter have been found in two fifth/eleventh-century Muʿtazilī texts, but the relationship of the excerpts found in the Muʿtazilī tradition to the version of the eighth/fourteenth-century manuscripts is problematic. For fuller details and the development of attitudes to the authenticity of the ascription and dating of the epistle, see Josef van Ess, *Anfänge muslimischer Theologie*, Beirut 1977, 18, 27–9; Josef van Ess,, *Theologie und Gesellschaft im 2. und 3. Jahrhundert Hidschra*, 6 vols., Berlin 1992, II, 46–50; and Michael Cook, *Early Muslim Dogma*, Cambridge 1981, 117–23.

about their date since the use of papyrus as a writing material continued long into the Islamic era.[14]

The books (such as the *Muwaṭṭa'* of Mālik, d. 179/795, or the *Tafsīr* of Muqātil b. Sulaymān, d. 150/767) that have been accepted as of second/eighth-century origin are often accompanied by problems about transmission and redaction, and the manuscripts in which they have been preserved are considerably later than the scholars to whom the works have been attributed.[15]

It is not really until the third/ninth century, therefore, that we can speak with some certainty about the forms and contents of Muslim literature concerning such things as prophetic biography and koranic exegesis. Our earliest extant biography of Muḥammad is conventionally attributed to Ibn Isḥāq (d. 151/768), but we only have that work in a number of later, related but variant, recensions, the best known of which was made by Ibn Hishām, who died in 218/833 or 213/828. From the third/ninth century onwards the amount of Muslim literature increases rapidly. It is obvious, of course, that the earliest texts available to us are the end result of some generations of formation, transmission and reworking, both in an oral and a written form, but we have to work with the texts as we have them and reconstruction from them of the earlier forms of the tradition is problematic.[16]

Goldziher in the late nineteenth century argued that the *ḥadīth* literature tells us more about the circles and times that produced it – the generations preceding and contemporary with the emergence of the texts – than it does about the topics with which it is explicitly concerned. Reports about the Prophet and the earliest period of Islam in Arabia should, accordingly, be understood primarily as evidence of the concepts and debates within the formative Muslim

[14] For an introduction to Arabic papyri, see A. Grohmann, *From the World of Arabic Papyri*, Cairo 1952. For excerpts from Muslim tradition on papyrus, see Nabia Abbott, *Studies in Arabic Literary Papyri*, 3 vols., Chicago 1957–72. For the apparently early second-century papyrus, see A. Grohmann, *Arabic Papyri from Ḫirbet al-Mird*, Louvain 1963, 82, no. 71, and for a reassessment of the event to which it refers, see Patricia Crone, *Meccan Trade and the Rise of Islam*, Princeton 1987, 228–9.

[15] For a radical argument regarding the dating of the work known as the *Muwaṭṭa'* of Mālik, see Norman Calder, *Studies in Early Muslim Jurisprudence*, Oxford 1993, 20–38; for counter arguments, Harald Motzki, 'Der Prophet und die Katze: zur Datierung eines *ḥadīth*', paper read at the 7th Colloquium 'From Jāhiliyya to Islam', Jerusalem, 28 July–1 August, 1996, trans. as 'The Prophet and the Cat. On Dating Mālik's *Muwatta'* and Legal Traditions', *JSAI*, 22 (1998), 18–83. For a survey of the problems associated with a number of apparently early works of *tafsīr*, including those of Muqātil, see Andrew Rippin, 'Studying Early *tafsīr* Texts', *Isl.*, 72 (1995), 310–23, esp. 318–23.

[16] For recent strong arguments that it is possible to reconstruct the earlier stages of some parts of Muslim tradition, see Harald Motzki, 'The *Muṣannaf* of ʿAbd al-Razzāq aṣ-Ṣanʿānī as a Source of Authentic *aḥādīth* of the First Century AH', *JNES*, 50 (1991), 1–21; Harold Motzki, *Die Anfänge der islamischen Jurisprudenz*, Stuttgart 1991 (reviewed by me in *BSOAS*, 59 (1996), 141–3); and Gregor Schoeler, *Charakter und Authentie der muslimischen Überlieferung über das Leben Mohammeds*, Berlin 1996. For two recent substantial attempts to to reconstruct conditions in the Ḥijāz before and in the time of Muḥammad on the basis of Muslim tradition, see Michael Lecker, *The Banū Sulaym. A Contribution to the Study of Early Islam*, Jerusalem 1989 (reviewed by me in *BSOAS*, 54 (1991), 359–62); and Michael Lecker, *Muslims, Jews and Pagans: Studies on Early Islamic Medina*, Leiden 1995.

community and of its arguments with its opponents.[17] That is the position taken here – that the traditional texts, especially those pertaining to the *jāhiliyya*, can help us to see how early Muslims understood and viewed the past but are not primarily sources of information about that past. Beyond that, furthermore, the fact of the appearance of the traditional texts from the third/ninth century onwards is interpreted as indicative of the growing stabilization of the tradition and as one of the signs that at that time Islam was taking the shape that we now see as characteristic.

Another reason for thinking that we will not make much progress in understanding the genesis of Islam simply by accepting the framework provided by the tradition and working within it is the less than convincing nature of much modern scholarship which has attempted to do that.

For the Muslim traditional scholars Islam resulted from an act of revelation made by God to an Arab prophet. In this presentation Islam was substantially in existence by the time of Muḥammad's death (AD 632) and any subsequent developments were understood as secondary elaborations.[18] The traditional scholars had no need to seek beyond that explanation although their works contain a large amount of detail which seems to relate the act of revelation to what was understood as its historical context, the early seventh-century Ḥijāz.

Modern non-Muslim scholars, unable to accept the reality of the revelation, have used some of that detail to develop theories intended to provide what they saw as more convincing explanations for the appearance of Islam, explanations that stress economic, political and cultural factors, while at the same time accepting what the tradition tells us about time and place.

Two such explanations, often used together, have been particularly widespread in modern accounts of the emergence of Islam. One of them – the evolutionary development of Islamic monotheism out of pre-Islamic Arab paganism – will be discussed in the first chapter. The other attempts to account for the origins of Islam in early seventh-century Arabia by reference to the claimed location of Mecca at the heart of a major international trade route. According to that theory, developed especially by W. Montgomery Watt and prominent in the popular biography of Muḥammad by Maxime Rodinson, the impact of trade on Mecca led to a social crisis which both generated, and ensured the success of, ideas associated with the new religion preached by the Prophet. The concept of the trade route passing through Mecca has also been useful in accounting for the penetration of monotheistic ideas and stories into the Ḥijāz.[19]

17 Goldziher, *Muslim Studies*, II, esp. 89–125 (=*Muhammedanische Studien*, II, 88–130).

18 A. J. Wensinck, *Muhammad and the Jews of Medina*, 2nd edn. Berlin 1982, 73: 'Generally, posterity was obliged to trace back to Muhammad all customs and institutions of later Islam' (cited by F. E. Peters, 'The Quest of the Historical Muhammad', *IJMES*, 23 (1991), 291–315, at 306).

19 W. M. Watt, *Muhammad at Mecca*, Oxford 1953; M. Rodinson, *Mahomet*, Paris 1961 (2nd English edn., *Muhammad*, Harmondsworth 1996).

The theory has become part of the orthodoxy of modern non-Muslim, and even some Muslim, scholarship on the origins of Islam, and is to be found elaborated in many textbooks on Islam or the history of the Arabs. The weaknesses regarding evidence and logic have been clearly presented in Patrica Crone's detailed refutation of the trade route theory, and her arguments underline the difficulties of accounting for the origins of Islam in early seventh-century central western Arabia.[20] Suggesting another such theory without fundamentally rethinking our ideas about how Islam developed is unlikely to get us very far.

Such theories, which typically emphasise the role of one man and envisage a restricted time-span and location, seem too confined in their understanding of the development of a major religious tradition. It is rather as if we were to account for the rise of Protestantism simply by discussing Martin Luther and his historical environment. But in that case at least we would not need to rely mainly on sources only available to us in versions made more than a century after Luther's death and reflecting only the understanding of Protestants.

In the case of Islam,we probably need to abandon the expectation of reconstructing its origins with any more detail or precision than we can those of Christianity or Rabbinical Judaism. In the nineteenth century Ernest Renan was able to make the well-known statement that, unlike other religions whose origins were cradled in mystery, Islam was born in the full light of history. Research since then, however, has shown that the problems concerning the evidence for the emergence of Islam are just as great as those for that of the genesis of the other major forms of monotheism. Instead we should seek general theories and models which can make sense of the evidence in different ways. The argument of this book is intended to support an approach to the origins of Islam that treats Islam in a way comparable with other developments in the monotheist tradition and which does justice to Islam as a part of that tradition.

There are a number of general ideas and theoretical starting-points underlying the argument of the following chapters. The first concerns the way in which new religions emerge within the monotheistic tradition.

One of the main themes in the sociology of religion, following on from the work of Troeltsch and Weber in the early decades of the twentieth century, has concerned the emergence and development of religious groups designated by terms such as 'sect', 'denomination' and 'church'. Sociologists, who in the main have studied the development of Christianity in modern societies, have been concerned with questions about the character of the groups thus designated, how and why sects form within larger groups, and why different groups

[20] Crone, *Meccan Trade*. One of Crone's suggestions, 196–9 (with supporting evidence), is that the trading centre and the sanctuary that Muslim tradition locates at Mecca might in fact have been situated much further north. The application, by the tradition, of the relevant material to Mecca might then be understood as part of the elaboration by early Islam of an account of its origins in the Ḥijāz.

develop in different ways. The role of charismatic leaders and founders has often figured in discussions of these processes, but equally important have been factors such as the social, economic and political circumstances connected with the emergence and development of particular groups. Recent work on the rise of new religious movements (NRMs) has also drawn attention to the problem of the terms we apply to individual religious groups and the way in which words such as 'sect' and 'cult' continue to reflect subjective value judgements and are often used polemically. It may not be possible to be precise or objective in the terms we use, but such work has drawn attention to the way in which religious movements form within the matrix of larger ones and the different trajectories possible for emerging movements.[21]

In broad terms the problem of the emergence of Islam is approached here from this direction. Beyond and bigger than the groups designated by terms such as sect, denomination and church, are institutions and systems that can be referred to as 'religions' (in the sense that Judaism, Christianity or Islam can be called a religion) and 'traditions' (in the sense that Judaism, Christianity, Islam can be understood as religions that are part of a particular tradition of monotheism). In a general way, Islam is envisaged here as arising within a larger (but perhaps not very large) monotheist group and as developing over time into a distinct and independent religion.

It may be possible, although it has proved difficult given the nature of the evidence available to us, to be more precise than that, by identifying the specific form(s) of monotheism out of which Islam emerged, analysing the role played by charismatic individuals and the social and other factors involved, and charting the various stages on its evolution into the religion we know as Islam. For present purposes, however, the general statement is sufficient to indicate that the emergence of Islam is understood here as a process involving an extended period of time and, thus, a quite wide geographical area.

To identify a religious movement or group as a 'religion' implies that it cannot be analysed adequately as a sub-group of anything smaller than the wider tradition to which it belongs. It is different in quality from a group that we might want to describe as a sect or cult. To refer to the 'religion' of a community or group of communities surely implies that it consists of ideas, rituals and institutions in forms that, although they are variants of those of the wider tradition to which it belongs, are distinctive markers of the religion in question. There will be a sufficient number of such markers and they will not exist in one form only but will be interpreted or practised variantly by sub-groups (the sects or cults) of the religion concerned. Furthermore, the number of adherents of the religion concerned plays a considerable part in our classification of it as a religion rather than a sect or cult. The development of

[21] Roland Robertson, *The Sociological Interpretation of Religion*, Oxford: 1969; Bryan Wilson, *Religion in Sociological Perspective*, Oxford 1982; Eileen Barker (ed.), *New Religious Movements: A Perspective for Understanding Society*, New York 1982.

distinctive beliefs, practices and a substantial body of adherents necessarily require an extended period of time and the process can be understood as that of the evolution from a dissident sub-group into an independent religion. There is certainly room for debate about which features are the essential ones and the point at which the religion may be said to have taken on the form that henceforth is regarded as typical; religions, like smaller cults or sects, cannot stand still but have to continue to change and adapt in order to survive.

John Wansbrough's *Quranic Studies* (1977) and *The Sectarian Milieu* (1978) have analysed the emergence of Islam as a process involving the elaboration of several distinctive versions of features that would be expected of a religion within the monotheistic tradition – a scripture, a sacred language, a body of ritual, ideas about authority and theology, etc. Included among them are accounts of the origins of the religion and of the life of its founder, the Prophet. Those accounts have to be understood as the product of the developing community, embodying its own vision of how it came into the world and seeking to associate as much as possible with the figure identified as its founder, and for that reason it is difficult for historians to use them as a source of evidence.[22] That evolution from a monotheist sect to the religion we know as Islam is likely to have taken centuries rather than decades and – in a period marked by extensive migrations, territorial expansion, and shifts in the centres of power – to have involved various geographical regions.

Much modern research has concluded that some key components of Islam, without which it is hard for us to envisage what 'Islam' was, did not achieve the form or importance they have in Islam as we know it until the third/ninth century. Schacht's development of the work of Goldziher presents Islamic law as evolving slowly from rudimentary beginnings until the end of the second/eighth century when it received its theoretical basis in the work of Shāfiʿī (d. 204/820). More recently Calder's work suggests that even Schacht's dating may anticipate the process by some two generations.[23] Crone and Hinds have underlined the crucial importance of the struggle between the caliphs and the religious scholars in the second quarter of the third/ninth century (the *Miḥna*) for securing the position of the scholars as the religious authorities within Sunnī Islam.[24] Without such features – the identification of the *sunna* with the exemplary practice of the Prophet, the theory that the *sunna* (along with the Koran) was the source of the law, and the role of the scholars in elaborating the law and relating it to its theoretical sources – it is difficult to give much content to what we refer to as Sunnī Islam, and even if we resort to expressions such as 'proto-Sunnī' it is still difficult to see what Islam may have consisted of in the second/eighth century or earlier.

Scholarly investigations of other aspects of Islam – its theological positions, the adoption of Islam as a religion by individuals and communities, the devel-

[22] See especially J. Wansbrough, *The Sectarian Milieu*, London 1978, 98–100.

[23] J. Schacht, *The Origins of Muhammadan Jurisprudence*, Oxford 1950; Calder, *Early Muslim Jurisprudence*.

[24] Patricia Crone and Martin Hinds, *God's Caliph*, Cambridge 1986.

opment of Shīʿī Islam in its various forms – confirm that many of the important features that we regard as typical, and by which we identify Islam as a distinct and independent religion within the tradition of monotheism, only became established in the third/ninth or even fourth/tenth centuries. Taken together with the problems concerning the relatively late stabilisation of the tradition in a literary form, that means that attempts to define what Islam was in, say 100/717, a time when none of the Islamic texts available to us yet existed, must be fragmentary, speculative and impressionistic.

The area in which these key developments took place was not Arabia but the wider Middle East, and in particular Syria and Iraq. Whatever religious ideas the Arabs brought with them into the lands they conquered, it is likely that it was from the social, political and religious interaction of the Arabs and the peoples over whom they ruled that Islam as we know it was formed. Both Arabs and non-Arabs must have contributed to it but it is probable that it was the originally subject population that was the more instrumental. C. H. Becker proposed that sort of model nearly a century ago.[25]

This relates to what was said earlier about the Ḥijāz as an unpromising setting for a major evolution in the monotheistic tradition. It is easier to envisage such an evolution occurring in those regions of the Middle East where the tradition of monotheism was firmly established – Syria/Palestine and Iraq – in a period of political, social and religious ferment following the establishment of Arab authority over the region. Many of the cultural and religious changes that were associated with the development of Islam had certainly begun in those regions before the Arabs had arrived.[26]

There was probably a greater diversity of religious belief and practice, including forms of the monotheism, in those regions than we now know, and the first centuries of Arab rule saw considerable movement of population, the breakdown and reformation of social groups, and communal interaction. Some of the most obvious manifestations of that are the establishment of new

[25] E.g., C. H. Becker, 'The Expansion of the Saracens' in H. M. Gwatkin (ed.), *The Cambridge Mediaeval History*, 1st edn, vol. II, Cambridge 1913, 329–90, esp. 332. Recently Rina Drory ('The Abbasid Construction of the Jahiliyya', esp. 42–3) has re-emphasised the role of those of non-Arab descent in collecting and establishing the texts of the so-called *jāhilī* poetry. The processes of arabisation and islamisation that followed the Arab conquests involved the creation of a largely Arabic-speaking and Muslim population in which descendants of the Arab conquerors and those of the conquered peoples were merged. The latter must have outnumbered the former.

[26] See Averil Cameron, 'The Eastern Provinces in the Seventh Century AD. Hellenism and the Emergence of Islam', in S. Saïd (ed.), *Hellenismos. Quelques jalons pour une histoire de l'identité grecque*, Leiden 1991; Averil Cameron, *The Mediterranean World in Late Antiquity, AD 395–600*, London 1993. The traditional accounts of the origins of Islam, with their emphasis on the revelation in the Ḥijāz, in effect present Islam as something new which disrupted the continuity of Middle Eastern history. Islam, in that presentation, owes little to the history of the pre-Islamic Middle East outside Arabia. Much recent scholarship has been concerned to reassess that aspect of the traditional accounts. Again Becker was one of the first to stress the place of Islam within the continuity of Middle Eastern history. As he expressed it in his seminal article, 'Der Islam als Problem', *Isl.*, 1 (1910), 1–21: 'So bizarr es klingt: ohne Alexander den Grossen keine islamische Zivilisation!' (15).

towns which originated as Arab garrisons, movements of cultivators into those towns and other districts to avoid taxation, the recruitment of prisoners of war as slaves and clients by the Arabs, the continuing domination of the bureaucracy by the non-Arabs, reports about and examples of interreligious polemic and debate, and a wide variety of messianic and other ideas, later often rejected as extremist, within movements of opposition to the Umayyad caliphs. In terms of time-span and of location, therefore, one might expect emergent Islam to reflect the setting of the Middle East outside Arabia following the Arab conquests more than of western Arabia in the first few decades of the seventh century. Outside Arabia intra-monotheist disputes would provide a convincing setting for the polemical exchange of charges of polytheism and idolatry.

Alternatively, of course, it is possible, and has been argued, that monotheism of various sorts was significantly stronger in the Ḥijāz and even in Mecca than the tradition suggests, and that it is therefore wrong to envisage the Prophet's milieu as on the edge of or outside the region dominated by monotheism. The traditional Muslim texts that describe or allude to conditions in the Ḥijāz at the time of the Prophet contain material, stories and details which have often been understood to indicate that monotheism of various sorts was present there. Apart from the already mentioned presence of Jews in Yathrib (Medina), for example, according to some accounts the prophethood of Muḥammad was first confirmed, after the initial revelation to him, in Mecca by Waraqa b. Nawfal, an individual described as having had knowledge of the Jewish and Christian scriptures or even, sometimes, as having adopted Christianity. There are reports that Muḥammad himself had heard the famous paragon of eloquence Quss b. Sāʿida, frequently cast as a Christian bishop of Najrān in the Yemen, preaching at the market of ʿUkāẓ near Mecca. The Kaʿba in Mecca is reported to have contained a picture of Jesus and Mary, a picture which the Prophet commanded to be preserved when he ordered the obliteration of others.[27]

Some modern scholars have thought that such details are merely the tip of the iceberg.The details and inferences have been accepted as sources of real facts about the situation in Mecca and the Ḥijāz, and one of the most common ways in modern scholarship of accounting for the emergence of Islam in Mecca at the beginning of the seventh century AD has been by postulating contacts between Muḥammad and monotheists, whether in the Ḥijāz or elsewhere.[28] Some scholarship has postulated the existence of a Christian or

[27] Waraqa b. Nawfal: Ibn Hishām, al-*Sīra al-nabawiyya*, ed. Muṣṭafā al-Saqqā et al., 2 vols., 2nd printing, Cairo 1955, I, 238 (trans. A. Guillaume as*The Life of Muhammad. A Translation of Ibn Ishaq's Sirat Rasul Allah*, Oxford 1955, 107); Quss b. Sāʿida: Abū Nuʿaym al-Iṣfahānī, *Dalāʾil al-nubuwwa*, Beirut 1988, 62; the picture in the Kaʿba: Abu ʾl-Walīd Muḥammad Al-Azraqī, *Akhbār Makka*, ed. Rushdī Malḥas, 2 vols. Beirut 1969, I, 165ff.

[28] The scholarly literature goes back at least as far as R. Dozy, *Die Israeliten zu Mekka*, Leiden 1864, and includes such well-known and divergent contributions as H. Lammens, 'Les Chrétiens à la Mecque à la Veille de l'hégire', *BIFAO*, 14 (1918), 191–230; T. Andrae, 'Der

Jewish sectarian group (e.g., the Samaritans or the Qumran sect) in the Ḥijāz and influencing the Prophet, and attention has focused too on reports which refer to the presence of Zindīqs (Manichaeans?, Mazdakites?) in pre-Islamic Mecca.[29]

Reports like these, and the way in which they have been used by modern scholars, will not be discussed in detail here. Many of those that have been taken as evidence of the presence of monotheists in the Ḥijāz at the beginning of the seventh century can be explained other than as reflections of the historical situation they appear to be describing. They might reflect polemic between Muslims, Christians and Jews at the time when the traditional biography of the Prophet was coming to be formed following the Arab conquests; they possibly issue from the idea that was developed in Muslim tradition that in the remote past Abraham had come to Mecca and established monotheism there, and that this monotheism had gradually been corrupted over the centuries but certain elements of it still survived at the time of Muḥammad; or they could be exegetical, either in the narrow sense that they have arisen from a specific koranic passage or concept, or more broadly in that, since the tradition accepts that the Koran reflects conditions in Mecca and Medina in the time of the Prophet, and since the Koran alludes to and polemicises against Jews and Christians, it seems to follow that Jews and Christians must have been present in the environment. Some of these suggestions will be taken further in chapter 1. The arguments of those modern scholars who have accepted the historical reality of many of the traditionally reported facts, stories and framework generally reflect a feeling that Muḥammad must have obtained his ideas from somewhere in the vicinity of Mecca. Frequently, too, they stem from the scholar's desire to assert the primacy of either Judaism or Christianity as the form of monotheism that influenced the emergence of Islam.

That Judaism and Christianity were established in various parts of Arabia and in adjacent regions is not in doubt. Monotheism – Jewish, Christian, and possibly indeterminate – is attested for the Yemen, al-Ḥīra on the borders between Arabia and Iraq, Abyssinia, and places in north-west Arabia, but the evidence for monotheism in Mecca is very difficult to pin down. For Christianity and Judaism, F. E. Peters concluded that 'there were Christians

Ursprung des Islams und das Christentum', *Kyrkohistorisk Arsskrift*, 1923–5 (French trans., *Les Origines de l'Islam et le Christianisme*, Paris 1955); R. Bell, *The Origin of Islam in its Christian Environment*, Edinburgh 1926; and C. C. Torrey, *The Jewish Foundations of Islam*, New York 1933.

[29] The Samaritans: J. Finkel, 'Jewish, Christian and Samaritan Influences on Arabia', *The Macdonald Presentation Volume*, Princeton 1933, 145–66. A sect related to that of Qumran: C. Rabin, *Qumran Studies*, Oxford 1957. The Zindīqs in Mecca: C. Schefer, 'Notice sur le Kitab Beïan il Edian', in his *Chrestomathie persane*, Paris 1883, I, 146 (citing Ibn Qutayba via the *Ṭabaqāt al-umam* of Ibn Saʿīd); J. Obermann, 'Islamic Origins: a Study in Background and Foundation', in N. A. Faris (ed.), *The Arab Heritage*, Princeton 1944, 60; Jawād ʿAlī, *Ta'rīkh al-ʿarab qabla 'l-Islām*, 8 vols., Baghdad 1957, VI, 287–8; M. J. Kister, 'Al-Ḥīra. Some Notes on its Relations with Arabia', *Arabica*, 15 (1968), 144–5; G. Monnot, 'L'histoire des religions en Islam: Ibn al-Kalbī et Rāzī', *RHR*, 188 (1975), 23–34.

at Gaza, and Christians and Jews in the Yemen, but none of either so far as we know at Mecca, where the Quran unfolds in what is unmistakably a pagan milieu'. To that it may be added that it is only Muslim tradition that informs us of a Jewish community in Yathrib.[30]

While it is possible that the early seventh-century Ḥijāz had been penetrated by monotheism much more than we know, I do not think that the traditional accounts offer indubitable support for that and, regarding Mecca where Islam is said to have developed and the Koran to have been revealed for about ten years before the Prophet's *hijra* to Yathrib (Medina), convincing evidence of Christian, Jewish or other monotheist presence is especially elusive. The present work argues that the polemic of the Koran against the *mushrikūn* reflects disputes among monotheists rather than pagans and that Muslim tradition does not display much substantial knowledge of Arab pagan religion. There is no compelling reason to situate either the polemic or the tradition within Arabia.

It is not easy to be precise about the group or groups at which the koranic polemic was directed. Much of the koranic material points to a dispute about intermediate beings, angels and others, as sources of power and influence with God. But a developed angelology and exchanges of accusations of angel worship are characteristic of many monotheist groups in the early Christian period. The christology of the Koran has been recognised as similar to that of Judaeo-Christian groups such as the so-called Ebionites (groups that maintained the validity of the Jewish law but accepted Jesus as a messenger of God), but there is material in the Koran and other sources which could point in other directions for identification of the relevant sectarian milieu.[31]

The following pages are not intended, therefore, to add to the already extensive literature that attempts to identify the particular monotheist group within which or in reaction to which what was to become Islam first began to develop, or which, as it is more usually expressed, influenced the ideas of the Prophet. I am more concerned with the view that Islam originated as an attack on Arab paganism and that the evidence allows us to reconstruct in some detail the paganism of the *jāhiliyya*.

Finally it is important to clarify a basic starting-point for the argument put forward here which may be unfamiliar to some readers. It concerns the historical origins of the Koran.

The traditional understanding, which has been accepted generally by most

[30] See F. E. Peters, *Muhammad and the Origins of Islam*, Albany 1994, 1. Obermann, 'Islamic Origins', 63 suggests that the 'preponderance' of the Jewish community in Medina must have been reflected in Mecca but admits that 'direct historical information about Jews and Christians in Mecca is very meager indeed'. For a survey of the evidence regarding the Jews of Yathrib, see M. Gil, 'The Origin of the Jews of Yathrib', *JSAI*, 4 (1984), 203–24. Although Gil, (203) tells us that Muslim and Jewish tradition are 'quite unanimous' in describing a Jewish population extending from southern Palestine as far as Yathrib, neither he nor, so far as I can see, any of the literature he cites in n. 1 refers to a Jewish source that mentions Jews in Yathrib.

[31] Wansbrough, *Sectarian Milieu*, esp. 39–49, 51–5, 127.

modern scholars too, is that the Koran stems from Mecca and Medina in the time of the Prophet and was fixed in writing in the form in which we have it soon, perhaps twenty years or so, after his death. This understanding is embodied in the traditional practice of referring to instances in the life of the Prophet in order to interpret the Koran, and it has led some modern scholars to refer to the Koran as a source of evidence for religious and other conditions in Mecca and Medina in the early seventh century. While recognising the difficulty of using the allusive, grammatically and lexicographically difficult, and chronologically unorganised text as evidence, modern scholars have more than once referred to it as the primary source for the life of Muḥammad. If that understanding is valid, our room for reconsideration of the origins of Islam is considerably restricted.

Arguing from the literary form of the Koran and the development of different types of commentary, however, John Wansbrough has developed a theory which envisages it as a text formed from a variety of materials, stemming from various settings in life, and which established itself as the scripture of Islam at a relatively late date. Applying to the Koran ideas and methods that are common in modern biblical scholarship, Wansbrough has argued that we should regard the fixing of the text and its elevation to the status of scripture as a part of the gradual emergence of Islam itself. Precision in fixing dates is impossible and a distinction has to be made between the existence of koranic material, the compilation of the material into a collection agreed to be fixed and unchangeable, and the elaboration of various doctrines defining and supporting the role and authority of the text in various areas of Muslim life. It is clear, however, that he envisages the process as broadly contemporary with the emergence of other types of Muslim literature. This contrasts with the traditional view which compresses the appearance of the koranic materials into the life of the Prophet himself and accepts that there was a fixed and authoritative text almost from the very beginning of Islam in the Ḥijāz.[32]

It is Wansbrough's general approach, and not necessarily his tentative suggestions about absolute or relative chronology, that is relevant here. In fact the argument put forward in the following pages could indicate a significant time-lag between the first appearance of many of the koranic passages and our earliest Islamic literature, and therefore that those koranic passages are relatively

[32] J. Wansbrough, *Quranic Studies*, London 1977. The more typical approaches to the Koran among modern non-Muslim scholars are accessible in the article 'Ḳur'ān' by Alford Welch in *EI2*. For an introduction to Wansbrough's ideas and methods, see A. Rippin, 'The Methodologies of John Wansbrough', in Richard C. Martin (ed.), *Approaches to Islam in Religious Studies*, Tucson 1985, 151–63, and for a more detailed consideration, H. Berg (ed.), special issue of *MTSR*, 9/1 (1997), *Islamic Origins Reconsidered: John Wansbrough and the Study of Early Islam*. D. A. Madigan, 'Reflections on Some Current Directions in Qur'anic Studies', *MW*, 85 (1995), 345–62, while impatient with what he sees as Rippin's 'postmodern' development of Wansbrough, and ultimately rejecting many of Wansbrough's arguments, is nevertheless generally appreciative of his work. (Thanks to Salim Yafai for drawing attention to this article.) On the dating of the Koran, see also Patricia Crone, 'Two Legal Problems Bearing on the Early History of the Qur'ān', *JSAI*, 18 (1994), 1–37.

early in the development of Islam. One possible explanation for the traditional understanding that many passages of the Koran were directed against Arabs who were idolaters and polytheists of the crudest sort, and for the creation in the Muslim literary tradition of the image of the idolatrous and polytheistic Arab society, is that the koranic polemic against *shirk* was no longer properly understood. Once the historical situation that had engendered it was left behind, the polemic of the Koran could have been misunderstood and read literally. If that is the case, it may imply that the material intended to document the idolatry of the pre-Islamic Arabs, material we find already in texts such as the *Sīra* of Ibn Isḥāq (d. 151/768) and the *Kitāb al-Aṣnām* of Ibn al-Kalbī (d. 206/821), dates from significantly later than the (koranic) texts it purports to explain.

That is not the only way of envisaging the process – it is possible that it was a much more conscious and constructive creation of tradition – but the essential point here is that Wansbrough's approach to the Koran allows room for rethinking the problem of the emergence of Islam in ways that are precluded by the traditional understanding of it. That traditional understanding does not ultimately derive from the text of the Koran itself but from the extra-koranic tradition. The Koran has been seen to contain attacks on pre-Islamic Arab idolatry and polytheism because the tradition tells us that it does. Once we can recognise and question that, and view the Koran in a different perspective, a new understanding of both it and the tradition becomes possible.[33]

One consequence of this new approach to the Koran, furthermore, is a rejection of the view that it is possible to identify a relationship between various parts of the text and stages in the career of the Prophet. The view that it is possible to identify a particular koranic passages as say 'early Meccan' or 'middle Medinan' has been shared by traditional and much modern non-Muslim scholarship on the Koran and the life of the Prophet. Individual scholars have certainly disagreed about whether a particular passage is to be ascribed to one part of the Prophet's career or to another, and about whether particular verses relate to one incident in the life of the Prophet or to another. That it is possible to make such connexions, however, has been generally accepted and continues to inform some contemporary scholarship. Wansbrough's model is incompatible with such an approach.

The theoretical and methodological presuppositions indicated here are to some extent debatable and controversial. There are several contemporary scholars who have produced evidence and arguments which they feel ought to lead to the modification or rejection of some of them, and many modern scholars have felt that it is possible to work with the traditional Muslim sources without raising major questions about their quality as evidence for historical reconstruction. It is probably the position adopted regarding the

33 For identification of idolatry as a traditional monotheist topos see Wansbrough, *Sectarian Milieu*, 44.

Koran that many readers will find most questionable and in need of justification. To discuss the possible counter-arguments and opposing views in a theoretical way at this point, however, would probably still leave most readers feeling unqualified to decide between the various positions advocated by modern scholars of early Islam.[34]

Some of the relevant evidence, arguments and theories will be discussed in the following pages. Other things being equal, the validity of an idea depends upon its explanatory potential as much as upon the theoretical arguments that have led to its formulation. Ultimately, the various and competing approaches currently used among scholars of early Islam will be judged by how far and how persuasively they can be used to make sense of the available evidence. The present work has been written in that spirit: it attempts to use and build upon the work of others whose own presuppositions, methods and conclusions seem congenial and persuasive, and it is hoped that it shows how they can further our understanding of the origins of Islam.

Although to some it may seem that the following pages are mainly critical and deconstructive, questioning what many scholars are prepared to accept as certainties and replacing 'facts' with questions and ambiguities, the message is not intended to be negative. On the contrary, it is hoped that it furthers what have been presented above as more historically persuasive approaches to the emergence of Islam as a religion. If, in the course of that, we find that we have to question some of what has hitherto been widely accepted as historical fact, and to allow room for more uncertainties and obscurities, then that is a necessary price to pay.

[34] For an attempt to analyse and classify recent methods and approaches in the study of early Islam as 'traditional' or 'revisionist' (from a committed 'revisionist' perspective), see Judith Koren and Yehuda Nevo, 'Methodological Approaches to Islamic Studies', *Isl.*, 68 (1991), 87–107.

CHAPTER 1

Religion in the *jāhiliyya*: theories and evidence

Along with the idea that Mecca was at the centre of a major international trade route, the religious situation of the Ḥijāzī Arabs around the beginning of the seventh century AD has frequently been used to help account for the emergence of Islam (identified with the activity of Muḥammad). Attention has focused on what might be called a strong element of monotheism in the predominantly pagan religion of the Arabs of central and western Arabia. However it has been accounted for, this has often been used in explanations of the appearance of Islam and of its success. The image has frequently been presented of a society in which monotheism was 'in the air' and of the Prophet as in some way building upon and directing the monotheistic ingredients already existing in his environment.

A discussion of some versions of this theory will allow us to examine their theoretical bases and the way in which they use the material available in Muslim tradition. In general it will be argued that questionable theoretical presuppositions have been combined with a less than critical approach to the information provided by Muslim tradition to produce explanations of the origins of Islam in Arabia which have been remarkably tenacious, repeated in general works and textbooks as if established facts.

It should be stressed that there is no intention here to judge the real strength of monotheism among the inhabitants of early seventh-century Arabia, or to say anything about the actual religious situation there. The argument is simply that the material in Muslim tradition that has been understood as informing us about religious conditions in and around Mecca in the time of the Prophet should not be understood primarily as a reflexion of real historical conditions. Rather it reflects two fundamental Muslim beliefs: that Islam is identical with the religion of Abraham (*dīn Ibrāhīm*), and that the Koran is a revelation made in Mecca and Medina. The former belief is mirrored in reports documenting the persistence of elements of Abrahamic religion in inner Arabia in spite of its degradation by the idolatrous Arabs; the latter leads to the view that the opponents called *mushrikūn* in the Koran must be the Arab contempories and neighbours of Muḥammad.

Muslim tradition tells us that Muḥammad lived in a society dominated by polytheism and idolatry, but it also tells us that monotheists and elements of monotheism leavened the lump of the prevalent paganism. There were individuals who had rejected the dominant heathenism and worshipped the one, true God; there were rituals that although they had been overlaid with polytheistic accretions, had originated as monotheist forms of worship; there was a sanctuary (the Kaʿba at Mecca) that, although it was now the home of idols, had been built by Abraham at God's command; and, although the vast majority of the Arabs worshipped a variety of local and tribal gods and idols, there was a general conception of a supreme god standing over and above them, called Allāh. This Allāh was associated especially with the Kaʿba, which was a sanctuary venerated by almost all the tribes and the locus of an annual pilgrimage (*ḥajj*) participated in by worshippers coming from all over Arabia.

It is against this background that the traditional charge of *shirk* is usually understood. That Arabic noun (to which are related the verbal form *ashraka* and the active participle *mushrik*), is, as already indicated, frequently understood as 'idolatry' or 'polytheism' but in a basic, non-religious sense it refers to the idea of 'making someone or something a partner, or associate, of someone or something else'. [1] Understood in the light of the traditional image of the religious situation among the Arab contemporaries of Muḥammad, the word relates to their practice of associating other beings or entities as objects of worship with God (Allāh). Although the common translations of it as 'polytheism' or 'idolatry' often reflect the way that *shirk* is used in Arabic, they risk obscuring its basic meaning. According to the traditional material, the *mushrikūn* were not simple polytheists who were ignorant of the existence of God: they knew of Allāh and on occasion prayed to and worshipped Him, but generally they associated other beings with Him and thus dishonoured Him.[2]

The tradition is full of stories and details that convey this image of the religious situation in the society to which the Prophet was sent. Numerous individuals are named (not always consistently) as *ḥanīf*s, men who had rejected the paganism of their contemporaries and adhered to a pure, non-denominational form of monotheism which is sometimes called 'the religion of Abraham'. Information is given about their spiritual development, and verses of poetry said to have been composed by them are quoted.[3] Another element is the

[1] For discussion of the possible occurrences of the root *sh-r-k* in its religious sense in Arabia before Islam and of possible precursors of the concept, see pp. 69–70, 72–4 below.

[2] See U. Rubin, 'Al-Ṣamad', *Isl.*, 61 (1984), 199:

> Allāh was well known among the pre-Islamic Arabs as the name of a divine deity [Rubin refers to Wellhausen, *Reste*, 217 ff.], which means that Muḥammad shared with the pre-Islamic Arabs the same deity. The difference of opinion between Muḥammad and his Arab contemporaries did not relate to the identity of the god who had to be worshipped, but rather to the position of this god among other objects of veneration.

[3] Ibn Hishām, *Sīra*, I, 222 ff. (trans. in Guillaume, *Life of Muhammad*, 98 ff.) is perhaps the locus classicus, discussed by A. Sprenger, *Das Leben und die Lehre des Moḥammad*, 3 vols., Berlin 1861–5, I, 80 ff. See Uri Rubin, 'Ḥanīfiyya and Kaʿba', *JSAI*, 13 (1990), for copious references to other traditional material and modern discussions.

talbiya, a verbal formula frequently repeated during the rituals connected with the *ḥajj*. It is called *talbiya* because it begins with the words *labbayka Allāhumma labbayka* ('at your service, O God, at your service'). In a completely monotheist version it is an important part of the Muslim *ḥajj* rituals, but tradition tells us that before Islam many tribes had their own versions which exhibited the distinctive mixture of polytheism and monotheism that characterised *shirk*. The words of many of these versions are transmitted in the tradition – best known and typical is that attributed to the Prophet's own tribe of Quraysh: *labbayka Allāhumma labbayka lā sharīka laka illā sharīkun huwa laka tamlikuhu wa-mā malaka* ('at your service, O God, at your service; you who have no associate apart from an associate which you have; you who have power over him and that over which he has power').[4] Again, Muḥammad's pagan grandfather, ʿAbd al-Muṭṭalib, is described praying to Allāh inside the Kaʿba, the site of an idol called Hubal, and when he discovered the well of Zamzam close by he knew that it was the well of Ishmael, the son of Abraham.[5]

The way in which the *shirk* of the pagan Arabs is construed as combining a recognition of the one God Allāh with that of other gods or idols is illustrated in the following story, which was used to explain the meaning and cause of the revelation of a verse of the Koran. It concerns an idol whose name appears with slight variants in different accounts but who, for the sake of simplicity, can be called ʿUmyānis. ʿUmyānis belonged to the tribe of Khawlān. His devotees, 'so they claimed (*bi-zaʿmihim*)', used to apportion a share of their crops and cattle between ʿUmyānis and God (Allāh). If any of what they had allotted to God became mixed in with the portion of ʿUmyānis, they would let it lie; but if any of the share of ʿUmyānis fell into the allotment of God, they would retrieve it and give it back to the idol. In other words, they gave preference to their idol over God when allocating the shares. That story is told in connexion with the revelation of Koran 6:136:

> 'They assign to God from what He has created of crops and cattle a portion saying, 'This is for God' – as they claim (*bi-zaʿmihim*) – 'and this is for our associates (*shurakāʾ*)'. What is for their associates does not reach God, but what is for God does reach their associates. How evilly they decide (the portions)!'[6]

The story, therefore, identifies the 'associate' – who is given a share in what rightly belongs to God alone (the sin of *shirk)* – in this case as an idol. The example (as well as showing how *shirk* becomes assimilated to 'idolatry') illus-

[4] See *EI1* s.v. 'Talbiya' (by G. Levi della Vida), and M. J. Kister, 'Labbayka, Allāhumma, Labbayka. . .', *JSAI*, 2 (1980), 33–57.

[5] Ibn Hishām, *Sīra*, I, 144 (=Azraqī, *Akhbār Makka*, II, 44), 154–5.

[6] Ibn Hishām, *Sīra*, I, 80–1 (trans. in Guillame, *Life of Muhammad*, 36–7); Ibn al-Kalbī, *Aṣnām*, text and German trans. in *Aṣnām K-R*, 27 (text) = 53 (trans.). This particular story does not occur in the commentary upon this verse in Ṭabarī's *Tafsīr*, but there are several reports there to the same effect even though naming no particular tribe or idol. Cf. Koran 16:56: 'They give a portion (*naṣīb*) of what We have given them as sustenance to what they do not know.'

trates the way in which the elusive and rather obscure koránic verse is given substance and meaning by interpreting it as referring to a practice of the *jāhiliyya*. It is conceivable, at least, that the story has been generated precisely to do that: that the verse inspired the story which is not a report of a real practice but an attempt to give flesh to the verse by relating it to an alleged practice in tribal Arabia.[7]

The Koran has many passages in which it attacks the *mushrikūn* for associating other beings with Allāh even though they know that He is the only true God, and these passages are consistently interpreted as referring to the *shirk* of the idolatrous Arab ancestors and contemporaries of Muḥammad. One that has often been referred to by modern scholars[8] is 29:61–5:

> 'If you ask them who created the heavens and the earth, they will say, 'God' (*Allāh*); how, then, can they devise lies? . . . If you ask them who sends down rain from the heavens and thus gives life to the dead earth, they will say, 'God'. Say, 'Praise be to God', but most of them have no understanding. . . . When they embark on a ship they call upon God, offering Him alone worship (*mukhliṣīna lahu*), but when He delivers them safely to land, they associate others with Him (*yushrikūna*).'

By understanding this as a criticism of the idolatrous and polytheistic fellow townsmen of the Prophet, the tradition gives a specific historical referent to what might seem a stereotypical monotheist theme and confirms that the Koran reflects the condition of the Ḥijāz at the time of the Prophet.[9] The tradition interprets the Koran, the Koran documents the tradition. We are frequently oblivious of the way we are predisposed to interpret the Koran in a particular way, so used are we to understanding it in the light of the tradition. If we only had the Koran, would we deduce that the polemic against the *mushrikūn* must be directed at Arab polytheists and idolaters? I think not, but discussion of that will be postponed to the next chapter.

In its fleshing out of the largely anonymous and often obscure koranic material, however, the tradition often goes beyond the text and elaborates it in ways that would not be obvious if they were merely derived from the Koran itself. One topic that receives considerably more precise and detailed elaboration in the tradition compared to its treatment in the Koran needs to be emphasised here since it is important for the remainder of this chapter and for much of what follows. It concerns the way in which the tradition answers the

[7] For discussion of Isaiah Goldfeld's arguments to the contrary, see below, p. 41.

[8] E.g., Wellhausen, *Reste*, 217; D. B. Macdonald, s.v. 'Allāh' in *EI1*; W. M. Watt, 'Belief in a 'High God' in Pre-Islamic Mecca', *JSS*, 16 (1971), 35; W. M. Watt, 'The Qur'ān and Belief in a 'High God'', *Isl.*, 56 (1979), 205. The same passage is referred to by traditional Muslim heresiographers as evidence that belief in a Creator was common even among people who were not monotheists: Abu 'l-Ma'ālī, *Kitāb bayān al-adyān* (text in C. Schefer, *Chrestomathie Persane*, Paris 1883, I, 131–203; French trans. by H. Massé in *RHR*, 94 (1926), 17–75.), 135 (text) = 21 (trans.).

[9] See the gloss in Ṭab., *Tafsīr* (Bulaq), XXI, 9: God is saying to His Prophet Muḥammad, 'If, O Muḥammad, you ask these of your people who ascribe associates to God (*hā'ulā'i 'l-mushrikīna bi'llāh min qawmika*). . .'.

question: how did the polytheism and idolatry of the *jāhiliyya* come about? It is in answering that question that the tradition explains how and why there were elements of monotheism among the pagan corruption of the pre-Islamic Arabs.

According to the tradition, monotheism had been brought to Arabia and established there by the prophet Abraham (Ibrāhīm) in the remote past. He had visited Mecca at least twice: once when he had left there his concubine Hagar and his son by her, Ishmael (Ismāʿīl), after trouble between them and his wife, Sarah, and his other son, Isaac (Isḥāq); and subsequently when he was commanded by God to go there to restore and build the Kaʿba, the 'house' (*bayt*) of God. The Kaʿba had been established there for Adam but had been damaged in the course of time, especially by the Great Flood sent to punish the people of the generation of Noah. Ishmael helped his father in building up the Kaʿba again, and at that time the rituals that take place there as a part of the Muslim pilgrimage festival (the *ḥajj*) were instituted. In effect Abraham introduced monotheism into Arabia at this time.

The tradition tells us that Ishmael remained in Mecca where he married local women and became the ancestor of one of the two great branches of the Arab people recognised by the early Muslim genealogists, the branch to which the future prophet Muḥammad was to belong. Ishmael's descendants continued to be faithful to Abrahamic monotheism as manifested chiefly in the Kaʿba and its rites until eventually they became so numerous that they had to spread out into other parts of Arabia. As they did so they took stones from Mecca to remind them of the Kaʿba and they performed rituals imitating those at the Kaʿba in the localities where they had settled. In addition they continued to make pilgrimage to the Kaʿba and participate in the ceremonies held there.

But in the course of time their monotheism began to degenerate. They forgot that their local stones and rituals were merely commemorative and symbolic, and they began to give them a worship independent of the Meccan sanctuary. Furthermore, idols were brought in to Arabia from outside, and some of them were set up at the Kaʿba itself. Gradually, therefore, the Abrahamic monotheism began to be corrupted, the Kaʿba became a centre of idolatry, its rituals given idolatrous twists, and all over Arabia the various tribes had their own sanctuaries, idols and sacred stones. But the Abrahamic monotheism was never completely obscured – vestiges of it still remained in the time of the Prophet as has been indicated above. That is why the sin of the Arabs was *shirk* rather than out-and-out idolatry and polytheism.[10]

That account is at the centre of the traditional understanding of the religious situation of the Arabs at the time the Prophet was sent to them, but because most modern non-Muslim scholars are unable to accept it its significance may not be recognised. Only some of its elements are visible in the

[10] Ibn Hishām, *Sīra*, I, 76 ff.; *Aṣnām K-R*, 3 ff. = 32 ff.(trans.); Azraqī, *Akhbār Makka*, I, 80 ff.

Koran. In 22:26, in the context of references to a pilgrimage festival (*ḥajj*) involving circumambulation and animal sacrifice, God refers to His 'assigning' (*bawwa'nā*) the place of the 'house' (*bayt*, here in the sense of 'sanctuary') to Abraham; 3:96, again in connexion with *ḥajj*, refers to the first 'house' which was established for mankind at Bakka and in which was the standing place (*maqām*, i.e., place of prayer) of Abraham; 2:125 again refers to the standing place of Abraham and to the 'house' which Abraham and Ishmael were commanded to purify; and 2:127 mentions Abraham raising the foundations of the 'house' with Ishmael.

Reading these passages as allusions to the Muslim tradition about the building of the Kaʿba at Mecca by Abraham and Ishmael involves assenting to identifications (e.g., Bakka = Makka, the 'house' = the Kaʿba, the standing place of Abraham = the stone that now bears that name at Mecca) which are problematic and not self-evident. Without discussing all of this in detail, the general point to be made is simply that the tradition goes considerably beyond what is evident from the Koran itself, even though there is no obvious contradiction between the scripture and the tradition. In particular, the Koran does not clearly refer to the concept of Abraham introducing monotheism in Arabia and its subsequent degeneration into idolatry and polytheism among the descendants of his son Ishmael. That account is probably not generated by the Koran but may be recognised as a variant, applied to an Arabian setting, of a traditional monotheist topos accounting for the origins of idolatry.[11]

The relationship between the Koran and the tradition can be seen, therefore, to be complex. Some of the stories and details in the traditional texts can be understood as developments and elaborations of koranic verses, while others seem to reflect ideas that are not clearly documented in the Koran. Many modern scholars have nevertheless simply approached both the Koran and the tradition as sources of information about conditions in Arabia, especially Mecca and Medina, at the beginning of the seventh century AD. They have accepted the traditional image of a society in which elements of monotheism existed in a predominantly pagan religion, and they have read the Koran against the background of that image. In particular it has come to be widely accepted in the scholarly literature that Allāh was held by most of the Arabs to be a deity standing over and above the other gods, just as the Kaʿba at Mecca (seen as the sanctuary of Allāh) was pre-eminent among the other sanctuaries of Arabia. What most of the non-Muslim scholars did not accept, naturally, was the tradition that Abraham built the Kaʿba at Mecca and introduced monotheism into Arabia. From this common starting-point, two main theoretical approaches to explaining the evidence provided by the Koran and the tradition developed: a straightforward evolutionary approach and one associated with the notion of primaeval monotheism (*Urmonotheismus*).

[11] See below, pp. 101–2.

For the evolutionists the monotheistic ingredients were interpreted as evidence of a development from a lower to a higher stage of religion in Arabia, and Islam was seen as the eventual outcome of that development. Assuming, as so many have done, that monotheism is a type of religion more advanced than polytheism, and that all societies will eventually evolve from a polytheistic to a monotheistic form of religion, it was argued that such an evolution was taking place in Arabia around the time of Muḥammad. Although some envisaged foreign influences at work, others seemed to regard it as an inevitable process which would have happened without external stimuli. Consequently the idea was suggested that Arab religion was undergoing a fundamental evolution which might have been completed even without Muḥammad's intervention. At any rate, it often seems, all he had to do was give a final push to overturn the decrepit edifice of Arab paganism, an idea perhaps paralleled in Muslim tradition by the image of the Prophet's toppling of the numerous idols assembled around the Kaʿba in Mecca following his conquest of his native town.[12] Thus Muḥammad was portrayed as part of an evolutionary process, the sources of his own monotheism clarified, and reasons provided for his success.

The version of this theory set out by Julius Wellhausen in his *Reste arabischen Heidentums* (first edition 1887) has been particularly influential and long lived.[13]

Wellhausen considered that the evolution from polytheism to monotheism was linked with the development of a common Arab culture transcending tribal, social and political groupings. In the chapter entitled 'Der Polytheismus und seine Auflösung' he argued that polytheism was the natural condition of a fragmented society – 'quot gentes tot dii', as he put it. By the time of Muḥammad, however, religion in Arabia was losing its ethnic and tribal basis, and certain deities and sanctuaries were taking on a pan-tribal significance. Allāh had come to dominate the other gods, and the Kaʿba, the sanctuary associated especially with Allāh, was revered by most of the Arab tribes even above their own sacred places.

The predominance of the Kaʿba, according to Wellhausen, depended on the sacred months during which fighting was prohibited and on the associated fairs held around Mecca. These provided the opportunity for peaceful intermingling and engagement in commerce and poetic competitions.

Implicit in his approach is a distinction between what he regarded as proper religion and something less than that, a distinction that is explicit in his contrast (p. 221) between the pagan 'cult' and the 'religion' of Islam. Paganism, he says, was 'superstition in the proper Latin sense of the word'. We are told (p. 220) that the main reason why the Meccans were unwilling to abandon the worship of their gods was their fear of losing trade. Furthermore, it was women and children who were attached to the pagan worship much more than

[12] Azraqī, *Akhbār Makka*, I, 120–1; note, again, the equivalence of *shirk* and 'idolatry' in this passage – see below, pp. 68–9.

[13] Second edn, 1897 (repr. with a new introduction as the 3rd edn, 1961), esp. 215–24.

the men since 'they are certainly more superstitious and set more store by magic and soothsaying'.

In accounting for the application of the name Allāh to the god who was regarded as superior to all the others, Wellhausen developed a linguistic theory reminiscent of Müller's famous 'disease of language'. Wellhausen built upon one of the etymologies of the name Allāh which is provided by Muslim tradition. According to this the name is simply a contraction of *al-ilāh*, 'the god'. Wellhausen argued that each tribe had come to refer to its own deity simply as 'the god' and this paved the way for the emergence of the idea that the tribes in fact worshipped the same god. 'Just as a king in his own lands is called 'the king' and not William [Wellhausen was a Prussian] . . . so the adherents of an Arab tribal god did not refer to him by his name but by his title. . . . As so often, language prepared the way for thought by putting forward a general concept which was then personified.'

Among the texts cited by Wellhausen as evidence for the decline of polytheism and the emergence of monotheistic tendencies were koranic passages such as the above-mentioned 29:61–5, which attack the opponents for refusing to give Allāh the recognition He alone deserves even though they really know that He is the source and controller of creation.

From Muslim tradition other than the Koran he referred to a story concerning the Meccan Abū Uḥayḥa (the Umayyad Saʿīd b. al-ʿĀṣ) who was found weeping on his deathbed, not at the prospect of his imminent death but because he was afraid that the idol al-ʿUzzā would not be worshipped after him (*akhāfu an lā tuʿbada al-ʿUzzā baʿdī*). Only after he had been reassured that the cult would continue (sc.: that someone would take his place as al-ʿUzzā's guardian?) could he die in peace.[14]

Wellhausen's analysis of the situation is clear from his comparison (p. 234) with the Scandinavian *Götterdämmerung* – 'the old in the process of dissolution, the new not yet showing forth'. It is in this context that he refers to the *ḥanīfs*, whom he portrays as a group of religious 'seekers', discontented with the old polytheism, conversant with the Torah and Gospel, but not satisfied with either Judaism or Christianity. 'These seekers are . . . the symptom of a mood which was widespread throughout Arabia in the period before Muḥammad and dominated many of the most elevated spirits. The ground was prepared for Islam.'

[14] Presumably Wellhausen cited the story from the version given in *Aṣnām K-R*, 14–15 (= trans. 41), which he would have had from Yāqūt's citations from the *Aṣnām*. Muḥammad b. ʿUmar al-Wāqidī, *Kitāb al-Maghāzī*, ed. Marsden Jones, 3 vols., London 1966, 874, has a version in which the dying man is named as Aflaḥ b. Naḍr al-Shaybānī, specified as the guardian (*sādin*) of al-ʿUzzā. It may be that Ibn Kalbī's version also envisages Abū Uḥayḥa as the guardian of the idol, since the one who reassures him of the continuation of the cult is Abū Lahab, also known by the name ʿAbd al-ʿUzzā. Wellhausen's 'evolutionary' reading of the story seems forced: the story seems to be a form of exegesis on Koran 111:1, where Abū Lahab is mentioned by name. In the story the dying *sādin*'s fear is occasioned not by his awareness of a long-term diminution of enthusiasm for the idol but by his (in Ibn Kalbī's version Quraysh's) knowledge that the Prophet was attacking polytheism.

Wellhausen's analysis has been adopted, consciously or unconsciously, by many other scholars. Theodore Nöldeke, whose article 'Arabs (Ancient)' in volume I of Hasting's *Encyclopaedia of Religion and Ethics* is a useful partial substitute for Wellhausen's work for those who cannot read German, and whose extensive review of the first edition of *Reste* resulted in significant additions and alterations to the second edition (1897), talks of the 'leading spirits' of the *jāhiliyya* having 'to some extent outgrown the old religion which, taken as a whole, was of a very low type'.[15]

Many have felt uneasy about the details of the linguistic theory behind Wellhausen's interpretation of the use of Allāh as the name of God, but there has, nevertheless, been a willingness to use (possible) linguistic fact as the basis for a reconstruction of social and religious development. The derivation of Allāh from *al-ilāh* ('the god') is the most widely accepted etymology of the name of God in Arabic, Allāh being understood as a contraction of *al-ilāh*. Modern scholars have often argued that this contraction arose because of the frequency of use of the name *al-ilāh* and that has been seen as evidence that the concept of one supreme god, more powerful than the others, had wide currency. In the words of H. A. R. Gibb, 'whether owing to the influence of Jewish and Christian infiltrations or to other causes – there was already in Arabia a general recognition of a supreme God, called vaguely Al-Ilah (or in a shortened form, Allah), "The God"'. Gibb was rather more willing than older scholars such as Wellhausen and Nöldeke to grant some positive value to pre-Islamic Arab paganism but, nevertheless, explained Muḥammad's success by reference to the inability of the old religion to satisfy an evolving religious sensibility. He talked of Muḥammad as being preceded by 'an evolution of ideas, a kind of praeparatio evangelica'.[16]

One body of evidence which was relatively neglected by Wellhausen was the so called *jāhilī* poetry, the many poems and fragments of poems cited in the Muslim literature but said to have been composed by the Arabs of pre-Islamic times and transmitted orally for several generations before being collected by the scholars of the early Islamic period. The problem of the authenticity of this material has been a running topic of debate in modern scholarship,[17] but the significance of these poems for those concerned to recreate the religious thought of the pre-Islamic Arabs is that references to the gods or other features of the pagan religion of the Arabs are notable by their scarcity. That could be interpreted merely as evidence that the Arab poets were too busy fighting, drinking and pining for beautiful women to give much thought to

[15] *ERE*, I, 659b. Nöldeke's review of Wellhausen's *Reste* was in *ZDMG*, 41 (1887), 707–26.

[16] H. A. R. Gibb, 'The Structure of Religious Thought in Islam', in Stanford J. Shaw and William R. Polk (eds.), *Studies on the Civilization of Islam*, London 1962, 187. There have been suggestions that the name Allāh for God is the result of a borrowing from Aramaic – and therefore shows the influence of Judaism or Christianity (see A. Jeffery, *The Foreign Vocabulary of the Qur'ān*, Baroda 1938, s.v. Allāh for literature), but J. Blau, 'Arabic Lexicographical Miscellanies', *JSS*, 17 (1972), 175–7, insists that it is impossible linguistically.

[17] See the discussion in Wansbrough, *Quranic Studies*, 95–6.

matters of religion – at least in their poetry. Goldziher (1889) followed Dozy in opting for this conclusion, while Nöldeke talked of the hardship of bedouin life as unfavourable to the development of religious feeling.[18] Others have linked the virtual silence of the poetry on matters of religion to the sort of evolution proposed by Wellhausen. J. W. Hirschberg (1939), for example, wrote, 'We must . . . draw the conclusion that . . . the period from which we possess the earliest poems . . . represents the decay (*Verfall*) of the old pagan religion. . . . This [poetry] was associated mainly with a 'debased paganism' consisting of belief in spirits and fetishes, sorcery and omens'.[19]

An attempt to marry the evolutionary approach of Wellhausen with the more recently prominent trade route theory as an explanation of why pre-Islamic polytheism was in decline is visible in the well-known article of the anthropologist Eric R. Wolf (1951).[20] Wolf himself referred to his approach as 'functional and historical' as well as 'evolutionary'. Like Wellhausen, he associated an evolution from polytheism to monotheism with a development from a fragmentary to a more centralized society, more specifically from one based on kinship relations to one with an 'incipient state structure' (p. 352). But whereas Wellhausen was content to see the evolutionary process as moving in an inevitable, almost Hegelian, way, Wolf stressed the importance of trade in opening up the Ḥijāz to external influences and ideas. In Wolf's analysis the Meccan leaders consciously made use of the Meccan sanctuary to build up their own authority, and they were able to do so because of their wealth derived from control of the trade route passing through their territory. 'Centralization of worship and the emergence of a deity specifically linked with the regulation of non-kin relations as the chief deity went hand in hand with the centralization of trade and the disintegration of the kinship structure.'

More recently the continuing influence of the evolutionary theory and attempts to link it with the trade route theory can be seen in the article of Walter Dostal (1991) in which the wish to build on the work of Wolf and that of Fabietti (1988), itself owing much to that of Wolf, is explicitly espoused.[21]

The second chief way of accounting for the traditionally reported monotheistic elements in the religion of the *jāhiliyya* envisages, not a gradual evolution from polytheism to monotheism, but the persistence of a primitive and original Arabian monotheism into the time of Muḥammad. This approach

[18] Goldziher, *Muhammedanische Studien*, I, 2 (Eng. trans. in *Muslim Studies*, I, 12); T. Nöldeke, 'Arabs (Ancient)', in *ERE*, I, 659b.

[19] J. W. Hirschberg, *Jüdische und christliche Lehren im vor- und frühislamischen Arabien*, Cracow 1939, 12 ff. The concept of 'debased paganism' ('das niedere Heidentum') was probably borrowed from Wellhausen, who used the same expression.

[20] Eric R. Wolf, 'The Social Organization of Mecca and the Origins of Islam', *SWJA*, 7 (1951), 329–56.

[21] Walter Dostal, 'Mecca before the Time of the Prophet – Attempt of an Anthropological Interpretation', *Isl.*, 68 (1991), 193–231; Ugo Fabietti, 'The Role Played by the Organization of the "Ḥums" in the Evolution of Political Ideas in pre-Islamic Mecca', *PSAS*, 18 (1988), 25–33 (thanks to Michael Lecker for reference to this latter article).

depended on more or less the same sort of evidence as the evolutionary approach of Wellhausen and his followers and drew virtually the same conclusions with regard to the appearance of Islam. It merely used a different scheme of religious development.

The predominant influences on this theory were those scholars of comparative religion such as Nathan Söderblom and Wilhelm Schmidt who argued that monotheism (or something like it) was the natural and original religious condition of mankind. The evidence for that argument was derived from ethnographic materials that seemed to show that various 'primitive' peoples whose religious systems had been categorised by the use of terms such as totemism and animism had, in fact, some conception of a power or god which was the source of all creation. This power or god was not usually the object of worship, unlike the lesser powers or gods over which it stood remote and aloof. Among the names given to it in scholarship were *Urheber*, *deus otiosus* and high god. In discussing the idea the modern Arab scholar Jawād ʿAlī used the expression *al-qadīm al-kull aw al-ab al-akbar*.[22]

It was Carl Brockelmann in 1922 who seems to have been the first to apply this theory to the evidence regarding the religion of the *jāhiliyya*. In the so-called *jāhilī* poetry references to Allāh are considerably more frequent than to the deities and other features of paganism and, discounting what is considered to be the work of Jewish or Christian poets, Brockelmann argued that the concept of Allāh that one finds in the poetry conforms to the type of high god identified by the scholars of comparative religion. Accordingly, we should see the all-powerful creative Allāh, not as the result of foreign monotheistic influences working to erode Arab paganism, not as the development of one particular deity into a high god, and not, as Wellhausen had suggested, as the result of an abstraction from all the local and tribal deities of pre-Islamic Arabia. Rather he is the survival of the *Urheber* figure of the ancient Arabs, probably to be explained as the consequence of a primitive attempt to understand the world.[23]

A possible consequence of such a view was that in Arabia just before Muḥammad polytheism was still struggling to emerge from the mire of whatever stage of religion is regarded as preceding it on the evolutionary ladder. For Tor Andrae (1932) on the eve of Islam the Arabs were just emerging into polytheism from the stage of polydaemonism, fetishes were developing into

[22] Jawād ʿAlī, *al-Mufaṣṣal fī Taʾrīkh al-ʿArab qabla ʾl-Islām*, 10 vols., Beirut 1968–73, VI, 36 (cf. the title of 'All Father' given to the high god of the Australian Aborigines in nineteenth-century ethnographic reports such as those of A.W. Howitt in the 1880s). For discussion of the theory see Eric J. Sharpe, *Comparative Religion: A History* , London 1975, esp. 182–7, and Jonathan Z. Smith, 'The Unknown God: Myth in History', in his *Imagining Religion*, Chicago and London 1982, 66–89.

[23] Carl Brockelmann, 'Allah und die Götzen: der Ursprung des islamischen Monotheismus', *AR*, 21 (1922), 99–121. The frequency of reference to Allāh in *jāhilī* poetry was also mentioned by Abu'l-Maʿālī, writing in 485/1092, as an argument for the pre-Islamic Arabs' knowledge of God: *Kitāb bayān al-adyān*, 136 (text) = 22 (trans.).

idols and, if the development had been allowed to take its natural course, eventually a hierarchical pantheon would have been produced.[24] For Joseph Henninger (1959) belief in a supreme being among the Arabs was coupled with animism (belief in nature spirits) and ancestor worship.[25] Marshall Hodgson (1961) did not commit himself as to whether Arab paganism was in the ascendant or in decline, although he did categorize it as 'little more than magic' with 'little higher moral challenge'. His allegiance to the high god theory was, however, explicit: 'Back of these active divinities was a vaguer figure, Allāh, 'the god' par excellence, regarded as a creator god and perhaps as guarantor of rights and agreements which crossed tribal lines. But, as with many 'high gods', he had no special cult.' A debt to Wellhausen was acknowledged but Hodgson rejected the German scholar's linguistic explanation of the rise of Allāh. Such an explanation was not necessary, he argued, 'for such figures are widespread'.[26]

In the 1970s this approach to the explication of the traditional evidence about the religion of the Arabs on the eve of Islam was revived by W. Montgomery Watt (1970, 1976, 1979).[27] Watt's arguments were derived almost entirely from a literal understanding of koranic verses such as 29:61–5 and the view that these verses were addressed to Arab opponents of Muḥammad in Mecca or Medina. At the theoretical level he referred to the work of Javier Teixidor arguing that belief in some sort of high god was common in the Graeco-Roman Near East.[28] In the course of his discussions Watt reached the same conclusions that D. B. Macdonald had reached on the basis of the same evidence in his article 'Allāh' in the first edition of the *Encyclopaedia of Islam*: the pagan Arabs against whom Muḥammad preached, or some of them at least, had the idea that the lesser deities they worshipped could mediate or intercede with Allāh. This was a view that Brockelmann had rejected and which will be discussed in more detail later in connexion with the koranic evidence concerning the nature of the religion of the *mushrikūn*.

M. J. Kister has also expressed his support for the high god theory as espoused by Brockelmann. In his already cited article on the *talbiya*s of the *jāhiliyya* (1980) Kister referred favourably to Brockelmann's article and contended that the monotheistic element observable in the *talbiya*s of the pagan Arabs, as well as other monotheistic ingredients in *jāhilī* religion were 'original Arabian concepts of monotheism which developed in the Arab peninsula'.

[24] Tor Andrae, *Mohammed, the Man and his Faith*, Eng. trans. London 1936, 13–24 and generally.
[25] J. Henninger, 'Pre-Islamic Bedouin Religion', Eng. trans. in Merlin L. Swartz (ed. and trans.), *Studies on Islam*, New York and Oxford 1981, 3–22.
[26] Marshall G. S. Hodgson, *The Venture of Islam*, 3 vols., 2nd edn, Chicago and London 1974, I, 155, 159.
[27] See note 8 above. In addition to the two articles referred to there, see W. M. Watt, 'The 'High God' in pre-Islamic Mecca', *Actes du Ve Congrès International d'Arabisants et d'Islamisants*, Brussels 1970, 499–505, and his 'Pre-Islamic Arabian Religion', *IS*, 15 (1976), 73–9.
[28] Javier Teixidor, *The Pagan God: Popular Religion in the Graeco-Roman Near East*, Princeton 1977.

Like Brockelmann, Kister was concerned to refute the idea that these elements of monotheism were the result of Jewish or Christian influence. He also cited a late article of Gibb (1962) in which the latter stressed the original character of Arabian monotheism and rejected the suggestion of influences from Judaism and Christianity.[29]

Kister's article is also interesting in the way in which it reflects the subtle interpretative shift that has occurred between the tradition and modern scholarship. Kister makes it clear that for the early traditional commentator Muqātil b. Sulaymān (d. 150/767–8) the various *talbiya*s of pre-Islamic Arabia were evidence of the way in which the pure monotheism brought to Arabia by Abraham had been corrupted in the generations that followed him. Commenting on Koran 22:30, Muqātil identifies the 'false speech' (*qawl al-zūr*) that we are there commanded to shun as that contained in the *talbiya*s of the pre-Islamic Arabs. What we must avoid, he says, is attributing a partner to God in the wording of the *talbiya* (*al-shirk fi'l-talbiya*). For the twentieth-century Muslim scholar S. M. Husain, on the other hand, the emphasis is not so much on the falsehood contained in those *talbiya*s as on the element of monotheist truth in them. Husain builds on this in a way typical of the evolutionary approach to argue that the idea of the One God was already at work among the pagan Arabs and preparing the way for the coming of Muḥammad and of Islam. The subtitle of Kister's article indicates his own allegiance to that approach: 'a monotheistic aspect of Jāhiliyya practice'. Where the early Muslim scholars saw a corruption of monotheism in Arabia before Islam, modern scholarship has generally perceived a gradual alleviation of polytheism. Where traditional scholarship saw Muḥammad as sent to restore what had once existed in Arabia, modern scholars have tended to portray him as a part of the evolutionary process.[30]

The dated and questionable nature of the theoretical suppositions underlying the interpretations discussed in the previous section hardly needs to be stressed. The evolutionary approach to religious data may still be attractive to some, but the idea of an inevitable progress from polytheism to monotheism (always supposing the two types can be satisfactorily defined and clearly differentiated), and of the moral superiority of the latter, is less obvious today than it was in the time of Wellhausen and Nöldeke. Ernest Gellner and Peter Brown have both referred to David Hume's concept of a continuous oscillation between the two opposing poles of religious thought, the 'flux and reflux' between polytheism and its opposite (called by Hume theism), although the Enlightenment philosopher did, naturally, regard polytheism as base.[31] One

[29] H. A. R. Gibb, 'Pre-Islamic Monotheism in Arabia', *Harvard Theological Review*, 55 (1962), 269–80. [30] Kister, 'Labbayka, Allāhumma, Labbayka . . .', esp. 33–4 and 34–5.

[31] E. Gellner, 'Flux and Reflux in the Faith of Men', in his *Muslim Society*, Cambridge 1981, 1–85, esp. 7–16; P. Brown, *The Cult of the Saints*, London 1981, 13 ff.

suspects too that the wish to present Islam as the culmination of a development which had been taking place before Muḥammad is another example of the need felt by many non-Muslim scholars to explain Islam (equated with the preaching of Muḥammad) in a historically acceptable way, that is, without reference to revelation or direct divine intervention in history, which are of central importance in the traditional Muslim explanation.

The *Urmonotheismus* or high god approach again reflects monotheist suppositions and premises. Much of the evidence on which this general theory was based is now considered of questionable value, reflecting either the interpretations of monotheist observers of 'primitive' religions or the impact of monotheist missionaries and rulers on the societies of which the religions were a part. At any rate, as Jonathan Z. Smith has shown, any alleged evidence that is used to support the high god theory must first be properly contextualised, and it is doubtful if we can know enough about inner Arabia before Islam to provide a proper context for any fragments of information we might have.[32]

If the theoretical framework within which the evidence is explained seems shaky, however, the evidence itself, the details and stories transmitted in Muslim tradition, remains and needs to be explained. Why does the material that has led so many scholars to accept that there was a strong element of monotheism in the paganism of the *jāhiliyya* exist? Even if there were a historical basis for it, it must have some significance for the tradition or else it would not be transmitted.

A first obvious explanation, already suggested, is that much of the material originated in the course of attempts to interpret, and supply a historical context for, the verses of the Koran. As well as arguing for interpretations by reference to lexicography and grammar, the traditional Muslim exegetes supplied interpretations of individual verses by telling us why they were revealed: the verses were referred to incidents in the life of the Prophet, to customs of the pre-Islamic Arabs, to accusations levelled at the Prophet by his opponents, etc. In this way difficult and often obscure koranic passages were provided with a meaning and, at the same time, the milieu in which the Koran was revealed was established and depicted. The very diversity of these 'occasions of revelation' (*asbāb al-nuzūl*), the variety of the interpretations and historical situations the tradition provides for individual koranic verses, is an argument for the uncertain nature of the explanations that are provided. One often feels that the meaning and context supplied for a particular verse or passage of the Koran is not based on any historical memory or upon a secure knowledge of the circumstances of its revelation, but rather reflect attempts to establish a meaning. That meaning, naturally, was established within a framework of accepted ideas about the setting in which the Prophet lived and the revelation was delivered. In that way, the work of interpretation also

[32] Smith, 'The Unknown God'.

defines and describes what had come to be understood as the setting for the revelation.[33]

For example, Koran 2:6–7 talks of the seal that God has placed over the hearts and ears of the unbelievers, and of the veil that is over their eyes: 'As for those who disbelieve (*alladhīna kafarū*), it does not matter to them whether you warn them or not – they will not believe.' Interpretation of this verse involves identification both of 'those who disbelieve' and of the 'you' who warns. The latter is, naturally, understood as the Prophet Muḥammad; the former are variously identified as the Jews of Medina or the Meccans who attacked the Prophet at the battle of Uḥud.[34]

In the present context what is important is the supposition that the Koran is to be interpreted as containing references to the religious situation of the Arabs in the *jāhiliyya*. It will be argued in chapter 3 that much of the Koran can be understood as polemic directed against a group that would have regarded itself as monotheist but which the Koran views as holding beliefs incompatible with monotheism and which it attacks polemically as polytheism or idolatry. Since Muslim tradition associated the Koran with the preaching of Muḥammad in Mecca and Medina and sought to explain it against the background of a predominantly pagan Ḥijāz in the early seventh century, however, that polemic was understood literally, as directed at opponents who were idolaters and polytheists in a real sense. Therefore, when the Koran tells us that the opponents had some limited recognition of Allāh but constantly 'associated' other entities with Him, accuses them of following the *ṭāghūt* (a word generally associated with idols and idolatry), or of worshipping gods before God, the tradition brings such abstract charges alive by referring them to the idolatrous Arabs of Mecca and the surrounding regions. The tradition tells us stories and provides us with details that underline for us the fact that the Koran (and Islam) originated in the context of the idolatry of the *jāhiliyya*, but at the same time has to take account of the nature of the charge of *shirk* – that the opponents' idolatry involved some limited and grudging acceptance of Allāh.

Consider, for instance, Ṭabarī's glossing of the already referred to Koran 29:61–5, the passage that tells us that the opponents are prepared to recognise

[33] For the argument that large parts of the traditional life of the Prophet are no more than a legendary elaboration of the Koran, see H. Lammens, 'Qoran et tradition: comment fut composée la vie de Mahomet', *RSR*, 1 (1910), 5–29. For an argument that some of the evidence on which the Meccan trade theory has been based is simply guesswork about the meaning of Koran 106:1–2, see Crone, *Meccan Trade*, 203 ff. For a discussion of the exegetical function of the *asbāb al-nuzūl* ('occasions of revelation') stories, see Andrew Rippin, 'The Function of the *asbāb al-nuzūl* in Qur'ānic Exegesis', *BSOAS*, 51 (1988), 1–20, which is a suggested modification of Wansbrough's understanding of them as put forward in *Quranic Studies*. Uri Rubin, *The Eye of the Beholder. The Life of Muḥammad as Viewed by the Early Muslims*, Princeton 1995, disputes the role of exegesis in originating stories about the life of the Prophet.

[34] E.g., Jalāl al-Dīn al-Suyūṭī, *Lubab al-nuqūl fī asbāb al-nuzūl*, Tunis 1981, on this passage. Ibn ʿAbbās is named as identifying the *kuffār* here as the Jews of Medina, while al-Rabīʿ b. Anas associates the revelation with the fighting against the *aḥzāb*.

God as the creator of the heavens and the earth, as controller of the sun and the moon, as the one who revives the earth by sending the rain, that they call on upon Him when they are aboard ship at sea, but that they commit *shirk* when He has delivered them safely to land. Ṭabarī tells us that here God is saying:

If you ask, O Muḥammad, those who associate others with God (*hā'ulā'i 'l-mushrikīna bi'llāh*), 'Who created the heavens and the earth?', etc., they will answer, 'God'. . . But in their ignorance they reckon that by worshipping the gods other than God they achieve a closeness and a nearness to God (*fa-hum li-jahlihim yaḥsabūna annahum li-'ibādatihim al-āliha dūna 'llāhi yanālūna 'inda 'llāhi zulfatan wa-qurbatan*). . . . And when these 'associators' travel on the sea in ships and fear drowning and death, they call upon God alone . . . and do not ask for help from their gods and those whom they recognize as equals of God (*ālihatahum wa-andādahum*) but from God who created them. . . . But when He brings them safely to land they appoint a partner (*sharīk*) to God in their acts of worship, praying to the gods and idols (*āliha wa-awthān*) together with Him as lords.[35]

The material in which the various interpretations and 'occasions of revelation' are elaborated is found not only in the works of explicit koranic exegesis (*tafsīr*) which have come down to us, but also in other genres of Muslim literature: lives of the Prophet, collections of material on the life and religion of the *jāhiliyya*, collections of the sayings of the Prophet (*ḥadīth*s), and other sorts of texts.

Faced in the *Sīra* or another traditional work with, for example, the story related above about the practice of the tribe of Khawlān in dividing a proportion of its agricultural produce between its idol 'Umyānis and God, we should understand it less as a reflexion of a real historical situation than as an attempt to provide a meaning and a reference for the otherwise puzzling Koran verse that attacks the opponents for giving priority to their 'associates' over God when assigning portions of their crops and cattle. We may not have a certain idea of what the koranic verse, which could be alluding to the payment of tithes or first fruits, 'really means', but that is no reason for accepting that the meanings and occasions of revelation provided by the tradition are more or less historically accurate.

Many individual stories and details, therefore, could be triggered by reading the Koran as addressing Arab polytheists and others in pre-Islamic inner Arabia, or they could be understood as attempts to establish that that was the case. In other instances, however, the tradition goes considerably beyond what might be inferred from the Koran alone. For example, the traditional accounts of Abraham's visiting Mecca and introducing monotheism there are only questionably and tenuously related to koranic passages, and there are items in the tradition, such as the reports about the *talbiya*s of the *mushrikūn*, that do not seem to be linked at all with specific verses or passages of the scripture.

[35] *Tafsīr* (Bulaq), XXI, 9.

There must, therefore, be more to explain the traditional material than mere projection of the koranic verses onto a pagan Arabian background. The most powerful idea likely to have generated stories portraying the existence, or persistence, of monothestic ideas and practices amidst the corruption of the *jāhiliyya* is that of the religion of Abraham: the idea that Islam is identical with, and the direct successor of, the pure monotheism personified in the figure of Abraham.

The traditional works are in fact quite explicit about the significance of the *talbiya*s: they are adduced to illustrate the way in which Abraham's religion had been corrupted but not completely obliterated by the time of the Prophet.

But [in spite of the idolatry and polytheism which had spread among the Arabs] there were survivals (*baqāyā*) of the time of Abraham and Ishmael which they [the Arabs] followed in their rituals – revering the sanctuary, circumambulating it, *ḥajj*, *ʿumra*, standing upon ʿArafa and Muzdalifa, offering beasts for sacrifice, and making the *ihlāl* [i.e., the *talbiya*] in the *ḥajj* and the *ʿumra* – together with the introduction of things which did not belong to it.[36]

The idea of the *ḥanīf*s alive in the time of the Prophet can be explained in the same way, although in that case there is a link with koranic material too.[37] In the Koran and in the tradition the religion of the *ḥanīf*s (the *ḥanīfiyya*) is associated with the pure monotheism of which Abraham was the supreme exemplar, evident in the equation of *al-ḥanīfiyya* with the 'religion of Abraham' (*dīn/millat Ibrāhīm*): 'The Prophet said that he [ʿAmr b. Luḥayy] was the first who . . . set up the idols around the Kaʿba and changed the *ḥanīfiyya*, the religion of Abraham.'[38]

The importance for Islam of its identification with the religion of Abraham is obvious. Claim to descent from the father of monotheism and continuity with his religion might be expected of a religion emerging from within the monotheist tradition. In early Christianity Paul had claimed that 'they which are of faith, the same are the children of Abraham' (Galatians 3:7), and had developed an argument according to which the Christians had a better right to be regarded as the legitimate descendants of Abraham than did the Jews, whom he portrayed as in bondage to the law and therefore, allegorically, only descendants of Abraham through the bondmaid Hagar.[39] It is not surprising that, *mutatis mutandis*, Islam should make the same claim to Abrahamic legitimacy. Furthermore, for a religion developing in connexion with the conquest of the Middle East by the Arabs and acquiring a strong Arab identity, ideas were already available to support the claim and to provide it with a 'historical' justification not available to Paul and the early Christians. In Jewish and Christian elaborations the biblical story of Hagar's expulsion by Abraham

[36] *Aṣnām K-R*, 4 = 33; Azraqī, *Akhbār Makka*, I, 116.

[37] For *ḥ-n-f* in the Koran, see 2:135, 3:67, 10:105, 22:31, 30:30 and 98:5; for Abraham as *ḥanīf*, esp. 3:67. Apart from Abraham, the Koran does not refer or allude to any actual *ḥanīf*s and gives no reason to think that there were people called such in the society it addresses.

[38] Azraqī, *Akhbār Makka*, I, 117. [39] Gal. 3–4.

(Genesis 21:14–21) had developed strong Arabian associations: Paran, the place where Ishmael grew up and lived (Genesis 21:21), was identified as a region of north-west Arabia, and in Paul's allegorical development of the story Hagar was identified with Mount Sinai 'which is a mountain in Arabia'. 'Ishmaelites' was a common name for the Arabs among Jews and Christians in the Middle East before Islam, and the Ishmaelites referred to in the Bible were generally identified as Arabs.[40]

It is not difficult to envisage, therefore, how accounts of Abraham visiting Mecca, of his leaving Hagar and Ishmael there, of the latter's marriages with indigenous Arab women and of his fathering thereby the major branch of the Arab people to which the Prophet and his family belonged, could have been generated. They could be understood as the historicisation of the religious claim that the emerging religion was an embodiment of true monotheism directed against similar claims espoused by other forms of that religious tradition. Nor is it hard to see that portrayals of the idolatry of the Arabs at the time of the Prophet would have had to take this Abrahamic history into account: the 'fact' of Arab idolatry and polytheism would need to be reconciled with the 'fact' of Abraham's establishment of monotheism in Arabia. It is against this background that the material about the pagan *talbiya*s and the *ḥanīf*s in Arabia around the time of the Prophet is to be understood. Their purpose is to illustrate the persistence of some elements of the monotheism brought by Abraham amidst the idolatry into which it had largely degenerated; they are more likely to be the result of Muslim ideas about the genesis of Islam than of historical recollections of conditions in the *jāhiliyya*.[41]

When and how the Prophet or the Arabs became aware of Abraham as the

[40] The name Paran subsequently occurs at Num. 13:3 and 26: Moses sends out spies 'from the wilderness of Paran' and they return 'unto the wilderness of Paran, to Kadesh'. The Targums of Onkelos and Jonathan interpret the latter phrase 'the wilderness of Pharan at Reqem' (Reqem is the Semitic name for Petra). *Jubilees* (a work originally written in Hebrew in perhaps the second century BC, but known now mainly through Ethiopic and Latin versions), 20:11–13, reworking the reports about the death of Ishmael and the fate of his descendants in Gen. 25:5–6, 12–18, tells us that the sons of Ishmael and the sons of Keturah, another wife of Abraham, 'went together and settled between Paran and the borders of Babylon, in all the land that is to the east, facing the desert. And these mingled with each other, and they were called Arabs and Ishmaelites' (H. F. D. Sparks (ed.), *The Apocryphal Old Testament*, Oxford 1984, 67). For the identification of Hagar with Mt Sinai, see Gal. 4:25. For analysis of the development of the identification of the biblical Ishmaelites with the Arabs, see further I. Eph'al, '"Ishmael" and "Arab(s)": a Transformation of Ethnological Terms', *JNES*, 35 (1976), 225–35; Fergus Millar, 'Hagar, Ishmael, Josephus and the Origins of Islam', *JJS*, 44 (1993), 23–45.

[41] A source for the idea of the sanctuary as a foundation of Abraham is less obvious. The rock in Jerusalem that was identified as the altar of the destroyed Temple was also regarded in Jewish tradition as the place where Abraham had intended to sacrifice Isaac, and the 'standing-place' (Hebrew *māqōm*) of Abraham, where Abraham had stood and addressed God, is mentioned in Gen. 19:27. In the Koran and Muslim tradition the designation *maqām Ibrāhīm* is associated with the sanctuary at Mecca, and Abraham's intended sacrifice of his son is located in the vicinity of Mecca. Rubin ('Ḥanīfiyya and Kaʿba', 107–8), following a suggestion of S. D. Goitein, proposes that the idea of Abraham as the founder of the Kaʿba may be connected with the 'house' established by Abraham and known as the 'House of Abraham' referred to in *Jubilees* 22:24 ff.

ancestor of monotheism, and developed the idea that he had founded the Kaʿba, has been a topic of scholarly debate since the mid-nineteenth century at least. Dozy held that the tradition that Abraham had built the Kaʿba already existed in Mecca before the time of the Prophet and was adopted by him there. Snouck Hurgronje, on the other hand, argued that the idea was developed by Muḥammad only in Medina when, as a result of his quarrel with the Jews there, he consciously sought to give his religion an Arab identity while still maintaining its roots in the monotheist tradition. The latter view has generally been the orthodoxy in western scholarship since the time of Snouck, although more recently there has been some criticism of it based on the argument that certain verses of the Koran referring to Abraham and counted by Snouck as Medinan should in fact be interpreted as having been revealed in Mecca.[42]

Some reversion to the older view can perhaps be discerned too in the use made by more recent scholars of a report contained in the *Ecclesiastical History* of the fifth-century AD bishop of Gaza, Sozomen, which refers to Ishmaelites (i.e., Arabs) coming into contact with Jews, learning from them of their common descent from Abraham, and their adoption of certain 'Hebraic' customs such as circumcision and the avoidance of pork.[43] Although it may be no more than a way in which Sozomen sought to account for the fact that the Arabs had customs such as circumcision which he regarded as especially 'Jewish' (a fact which had been noted before, e.g., by Josephus[44]), and although, even if historical, it relates to contacts between Arabs and Jews in Palestine rather than the Ḥijāz, the report has been seen as offering a possible scenario for the acquisition by the Arabs of the idea of their Abrahamic descent and their relationship to the Jews. If this idea had reached the Arabs of the Ḥijāz by the late sixth century, then it could be argued that the idea that Abraham had founded the Kaʿba and established monotheism in Mecca was already current in and around Mecca by the time of the Prophet.[45]

But there is no compelling reason to think that ideas about Abraham as the first monotheist (after the Flood), of him as the builder of the Kaʿba, or of the Arabs as descendants of Abraham and Ishmael, were current among the Arabs of the Ḥijāz before the time of the Arab conquest of the Middle East.

[42] See *EI2* s.v. 'Ibrāhīm' (by R. Paret) for more details.

[43] *Historia Ecclesiastica*, ed. J. Bidez and G. C. Hansen, Berlin 1960, book 6, chap. 38 (Eng. trans. by E. Walford, London 1855, 309 f. and C. D. Hartranft, *Nicene and Post-Nicene Fathers*, repr. 1976). [44] *Antiquities of the Jews*, I, 12, 2.

[45] Michael Cook, *Muhammad*, Oxford 1983, 81, 92 ; Crone, *Meccan Trade*, 190, n.104; Irfan Shahid, *Byzantium and the Arabs in the Fifth Century*, Washington D.C., 1989, 167 ff.; Rubin, 'Ḥanīfiyya and Kaʿba'. Cook and Crone do not envisage the Ḥijāz as the region in which the transfer of ideas reported by Sozomen had their influence, and only Rubin makes the connexion with the idea of Abraham as the founder of the Kaʿba: 'When knowledge of this text [i.e., *Jubilees*] reached the adherents of the "religion of Abraham" in the region of Mecca and Medina, they identified [the house of Abraham mentioned in the text] with the most prominent local sanctuary, the Kaʿba in Mecca.' See too the discussion of the passage, which is translated in full in Millar, 'Hagar, Ishmael, Josephus and the Origins of Islam', 42.

The assumption that they were reflects the view that Islam had already developed significantly in Arabia before the conquests and, of course, that the Koran originated in Mecca and Medina during the first three decades of the seventh century.[46]

The fundamental ingredients of those ideas – the descent of the Arabs from Abraham and Ishmael, and Abraham as the father of true monotheism – had been part of the common stock of monotheism in the Middle East for long before the Arab conquests and may have given rise to the more detailed and specific stories as Islam developed outside Arabia after the conquests. That is not to deny that significant numbers of Arabs, especially those in areas on the peripheries of the peninsula, had come under monotheist influence and even adopted different forms of monotheism before Islam. Presumably part of that process would involve increasing familiarity with monotheist history including (perhaps especially) the story of Abraham. But the specific way in which that story was reworked and used in Islam may also be explained as part of the emergence of Islam in the years after the Arab conquest of the Middle East had brought about a situation of proximity and polemic between various religious and ethnic groups.

In short, the material in Muslim tradition that presents the religion of the Arabs of the *jāhiliyya* as a monotheism which had been significantly, but not completely, eroded by idolatry and paganism is largely explicable as an outcome of the historicisation of the idea that Islam was identical with the religion of Abraham. It also frequently reflects ideas about the meaning of koranic verses and about the background of the Koran in general. These considerations make it unlikely, in my opinion, that the material refers to a real historical situation.

In the course of a body of work that combines description and interpretation of archaeological finds in the Negev desert with innovative and far-reaching theories about the emergence of Islam, the late Yehuda Nevo together with Judith Koren suggested that the information about the religious situation among the pre-Islamic Arabs can be made sense of, and accepted as containing a certain amount of historical reality, if it is applied to the Negev region in its later Byzantine and early Arab period rather than to the Ḥijāz and the *jāhiliyya* as traditionally understood. Nevo and Koren argued that in the Negev in the seventh century there was indeed a coexistence of pagan and monotheistic religion. They suggested that many of the archaeological

[46] The earliest external source to associate the sanctuary of the Arabs with Abraham seems to be the so-called Khuzistani Chronicle, probably dating from around AD 660–70. That refers to the Dome of Abraham at which the Arabs worshipped, but does not say where it was (Latin translation by I. Guidi, *Chronica Minora*, *Corpus Scriptorum Christianorum Orientalum*, I, *Scriptores Syri*, no. 2, p. 31; German translation by T. Nöldeke, 'Die von Guidi herausgegebene syrische Chronik übersetzt und commentiert', in *Sitzungsberichte der Akademie der Wissenschaften*, Phil.-Hist. Klasse, B 128, Vienna 1893). On this text see S. Brock, 'Syriac Sources for Seventh-Century History', *BMGS*, 2 (1976), §1, no. 13; Robert Hoyland, *Seeing Islam as Others Saw it*, Princeton 1997, 182 ff., esp. 187.

remains are to be interpreted as connected with a pagan cult, that the monotheism, as attested in a number of rock inscriptions, was a form of Judaeo-Christianity not identifiable with Judaism, Christianity or Islam, and that it was supplanted by Islam only slowly and relatively late (second–third centuries AH).

In connexion with these ideas they have proposed that some of the reports to be found in Muslim tradition relating to the Kaʿba, Mecca, the religion of Abraham, the *talbiya*s, the introduction of idolatry by ʿAmr b. Luḥayy, etc. could make sense if transposed to the Negev:

> But if the Ḥijāz was to become the original Arab heartland [as a result of the creation of a history by the early Muslim scholars], its history would have to be created by supplying a myriad of details about individuals, tribes, places, and events of the Jāhiliyyah and the rise of Islam. Some of these details are the fabrications of storytellers, but many, one may suppose, were real or mythical facts known in various circles, which were incorporated into the Grand History now being constructed.

One aspect of this was the description of the sanctuary at Mecca in the *jāhiliyya* on the model of pagan cultic centres in the Negev.[47]

It is not possible here to do justice to the evidence and ideas presented by Nevo and Koren but it seems to me that their treatment of the Muslim traditional material does not pay enough attention to its literary, religious and historical contexts. The epigraphic evidence they cite for a form of monotheism in the Negev which was not distinctively Jewish, Christian or Muslim is impressive, but what Muslim tradition tells us about the religion of Abraham in the Ḥijāz seems to me more explicable in the ways suggested above than as reflecting the Judaeo-Christianity of the later seventh-century Negev inscriptions. Equally, the paucity of archaeological evidence from the Ḥijāz from the fourth to the sixth centuries which they stress is certainly true, but the assumption that the stories concerning ʿAmr b. Luḥayy reflect a historical process taking place 'in the fringe area between the Arabian desert and the Byzantine *oikoumenē*'[48] does not necessarily follow. Those stories, and others, can be understood as the result of the need to explain the decline from Abrahamic monotheism in Arabia and to account for the origins of specific idols. Furthermore, they repeat ideas and themes common in monotheistic literature about idols.[49]

It is difficult for a non-specialist to assess the argument that many of the archaeological remains in the Negev are associated with a pagan cult (earlier researchers connected them with agriculture). In principle it is reasonable that early Muslim scholars who wished to describe the Kaʿba before Islam would draw on the physical features of sanctuaries they knew, and possibly there

[47] See especially Y. D. Nevo and J. Koren, 'The Origins of the Muslim Descriptions of the Jāhilī Meccan Sanctuary', *JNES*, 49 (1990), 23–44, in particular 39–44 (the quotation is from 43); Yehuda D. Nevo, *Pagans and Herders*, Israel: IPS Ltd., Negev 84993, 1991, in particular 125 ff.

[48] Nevo, *Pagans and Herders*, 120–1.

[49] See further, pp. 101–10 below.

were such in the Negev which would provide a suitable model, but there is no necessary reason why they should have done so and it is possible that similar cult centres existed far down into Arabia. There may have been a paganism coexisting alongside a monotheism in the seventh-century Negev, but there is little or no reason to think that the sort of details and stories that Muslim tradition presents about the *jāhiliyya* – those illustrated in this chapter – reflect conditions there. They are more likely to result from the ideas developed in early Islam about the origins and nature of the new religion and the Koran, drawing upon common monotheistic material concerning the origins of idolatry and the role of Abraham in the history of monotheism.

Two other discussions which put forward arguments defending, in a more traditional way, the historicity of the story about Khawlān and their idol ʿUmyānis, and the reports concerning the *ḥanīf*s living in and around Mecca in the time of the Prophet, deserve some consideration here.

Isaiah Goldfeld was impressed by the fact that the report about the practice of Khawlān in sharing out their agricultural produce unfairly between God and their idol mentions by name a specific sub-tribe which he thought it possible to identify as a deformation of a word found in the south Arabian inscriptions, apparently referring to agricultural serfs. Furthermore, he suggested that the name of the idol as variously given in the different versions of the story in Muslim tradition could be related to names of the moon god found in the south Arabian inscriptions. On that basis he supported an argument, developed in his doctoral thesis, that in the period before Muḥammad the tribes of Arabia customarily paid a 'temple tax' to the sanctuary of Mecca and its god, Allāh, as a sign of their submission to the Quraysh of Mecca, but that immediately before the Prophet, the authority of Quraysh had begun to decline and the tribes once again devoted their tithes to their own deities. Muḥammad's mission was to restore the crumbling authority of Mecca and Quraysh. Goldfeld was aware, of course, of the relationship between the story and the interpretations of Koran 6:137, but considered that the situation referred to in the story was in fact the real referent of the koranic verse: Koran 6: 137 was indeed an attack on the sort of practice attributed to Khawlān. He argued that the story concerns one specific example of a more widespread practice which is usually described only generally and without names in the koranic commentaries (*tafsīr*).[50]

If we put aside the general theory within which Goldfeld interpreted the evidence, we are left with the occurrence of numerous variant stories in works of koranic commentary and other traditional works which are less explicitly exegetical, presented as the context and reference for the revelation and meaning of this particular koranic verse. These stories differ regarding precise details and for the most part are unspecific as to the religious, social or tribal group under attack – whether nomadic Arabs or the people of Mecca. (The frequent

[50] Isaiah Goldfeld, "Umyānis the Idol of Khawlān', *IOS*, 3 (1977), 108–19.

references to agriculture and irrigation, necessitated by the Koran's use of the word 'tillage' (*al-ḥarth*) do not sit easily with either of those identifications.) Common to all of the reports, however, is the understanding that the verse is an attack on the polytheistic Arab opponents of the Prophet and that the 'associates' (*shurakāʾ*) who are mentioned in the verse are their gods, idols, or satans (different terms are used in different accounts). The story found in the *Sīra* about Khawlān and its idol is one, more specific, version of these exegetical stories, and its connexion with the exegesis of Koran 6:137 is clear from the fact that it contains the very same phrase – *bi-zaʿmihim* – that occurs in the verse to which it relates.

One of the features of Muslim tradition is its dislike of anonymity – stories that refer to persons, tribes or places without name often generate versions that supply (variant) names – and it might be thought that the story about the practice of Khawlān has arisen from a felt need to put some flesh on the exegetical stories. The only important argument adduced by Goldfeld for considering the Khawlān version as historical rather than a result of exegetical elaboration is the two names it provides – for the sub-tribe of Khawlān and for its idol. In fact the suggested relationship between the forms that occur in Muslim tradition and those attested in the south Arabian evidence is rather tenuous and speculative. But even if we accept the suggestions (and it is reasonable to assume that names provided in Muslim tradition often do relate to those of real people, tribes, etc.), that provides no warrant for acceptance of the concepts that the story about Khawlān and its idol supports: the identification of *shirk* with 'real' idolatry, of the *mushrikūn* with the Arabs of the *jāhiliyya,* and of their religion with a conscious attempt to do down God at the expense of idols. Those concepts in turn relate to a bigger structure which Goldfeld's wider theory regarding the relationship between Quraysh/Mecca and the other tribes and sanctuaries of Arabia reflects: the superiority of the Kaʿba at Mecca and of the God with which it was associated, Allāh, over the sanctuaries and deities/idols of the rest of Arabia. I hope that enough has been said here to indicate the source of this framework and the role it plays.

Uri Rubin's defence of the reality of the *ḥanīf*s as a phenomenon of the *jāhiliyya* was a response to the suggestion by others that they should be understood as no more than the realization of a theological concept, an outcome especially of the elaboration of the koranic material that uses the word.[51]

Rubin's defence was based upon the fact that several of the men who are

[51] Rubin, 'Ḥanīfiyya and Kaʿba'. Rubin was responding especially to W. M. Watt s.v. 'Ḥanīf' in *EI2*, and Wansbrough, *Sectarian Milieu*, 7. Note that the article predates the same scholar's *Eye of the Beholder* which is much less concerned with the question of the historicity of the traditional material. A. Rippin, 'RḤMNN and the Ḥanīfs', in W. B. Hallaq and D. P. Little (eds.), *Islamic Studies Presented to Charles J. Adams*, Leiden 1991, 153–68, although published later, seems to have been generally contemporary with Rubin's paper. Rubin and Rippin may have stimulated each other's arguments at scholarly conferences where both were present.

mentioned in the tradition as *ḥanīf*s are presented there as antagonistic towards the Prophet. He proposes that there is no conceivable reason why the Muslim scholars should have made this up, and concludes that the material must, therefore, report a historical reality. If the *ḥanīf*s of tradition were really no more than an embodiment of a religious idea, then, given the linkage in the Koran between Abraham, pure monotheism, and Islam, Rubin suggests that one would expect that all of the *ḥanīf*s would be portrayed as recognising the truth of Muḥammad and accepting his prophethood.

The documentation of figures counted as *ḥanīf*s but hostile to the Prophet is extensive and impressive. Nevertheless, Muslim tradition is complex and it is not necessary to accept the historicity of the 'facts' it transmits just because an alternative explanation of the material does not immediately present itself. To argue for the historical reality of an event or detail reported in the tradition because it is possibly embarrassing for Islam is tempting but not necessarily convincing: the same reasoning has often been used to argue for the reality of the incident of the 'satanic verses'. In his article examining the evidence for the *ḥanīf*s and the way in which it has been used by islamicists and by scholars of south Arabia, Andrew Rippin suggested that the reports highlighted by Rubin might be a reflexion, since the *ḥanīf*s are sometimes associated in tradition with Christianity, of Christian opposition to the emerging new monotheism. Whether or not that is right, it does suggest that there are alternative interpretations of such material.

Beyond the reported hostility of some of them to the Prophet, Rubin's analysis of the material on the *ḥanīf*s, including verses of poetry attributed to some of them, is a good illustration of the way in which tradition associates them with the religion of Abraham. Rubin identifies, unsurprisingly it might be thought, the essence of their religion as attachment to the Kaʿba at Mecca as the House of God established by Abraham, and he suggests that the opposition to Muḥammad on the part of some of them derived from their fear that he was a threat to the Kaʿba. This underlines what has been said above about the identification in tradition of *al-ḥanīfiyya* and the *dīn Ibrāhīm* and could support the suggestion that we should understand the phenomenon of the *ḥanīf*s in tradition as a realisation of the idea that Abraham had introduced monotheism into Arabia and that elements of it still survived in the time of the Prophet.

The articles of Goldfeld and Rubin display both the complexity of the traditional evidence and the difficulty of breaking away from the framework of interpretation elaborated by the traditional scholarship. Neither of them, in my view, establishes that the intermingling of polytheism and monotheism in pre-Islamic Arabia in the way in which it is described in the traditional texts reflects an historical situation. The story about Khawlān cheating Allāh, the reports about the *ḥanīf*s, and the pagan *talbiya*s, can be explained in part from attempts to interpret the Koran, assuming that it must relate to the situation in Arabia in the time of Muḥammad, and in part from the elaboration and historicisation of the concept of the religion of Abraham of which Islam was the embodiment. If that is so, neither the Koran nor the tradition, which partly elaborates the Koran and partly, like the Koran, reflects common monotheistic ideas and themes, should be understood as historical evidence for conditions in the *jāhiliyya*.

CHAPTER 2

Idols and idolatry in the Koran

The identification of the opponents attacked in the Koran for their *shirk* was made and documented in the Muslim traditional literature. In the commentaries on the Koran, the traditional lives of the Prophet, the collections of material describing conditions in the *jāhiliyya* and providing information about the idolatrous pre-Islamic Arab religion, and other such works, it is constantly made clear that the koranic *mushrikūn* were Arab polytheists and worshippers of idols in the Ḥijāz at the time of Muḥammad. The idea was thus established that the Koran was addressed to a society in which idolatry and polytheism were a real presence, and that idea has generally been adopted from the traditional texts by modern scholarship. Some parts of the Koran explicitly address or refer to Jews and Christians, but it has generally been understood that its primary message – its insistence on absolute monotheism – has as its chief target idolatrous and polytheistic Arab contemporaries, townsmen and neighbours, of Muḥammad.

This chapter considers how far, if we simply had the Koran without the traditional material, we would be led construct an image of the opponents similar to that contained in the traditional texts. How far is it necessary or satisfactory to view the koranic *mushrikūn* as idolators in any real sense of that word?

That last phrase indicates a large part of the problem. It has already been remarked that polytheism and idolatry are not usually neutral descriptive terms but relative, value laden and subjective. In monotheist discourse merely to refer to a religion as polytheistic or idolatrous is to reject it completely, and what an antagonist might see as polytheism or idolatry could, for the adherent, be pure monotheism.

Carlos M. N. Eire's discussion of the arguments in Reformation Europe about the use of pictures and statues in worship makes that point clear: 'In the sixteenth century, one man's devotion was another man's idolatry. It is good to keep in mind that at just about the same time that the soldiers of Charles V replaced the 'horrible idols' of the Aztecs with the 'beautiful' crosses and images of Mary and the saints in the New World, Protestant iconoclasts were wreaking havoc on these Catholic objects in lands nominally ruled by him in Europe.'[1]

What was true at the time of the Protestant Reformation in Europe has been so too at other times and places in the history of the monotheist tradition, although the accusation of idolatry can indicate much more than a struggle about the legitimacy or otherwise of figural representations in religious worship.

It is reasonable to assume that when the Protestants were attacking the Catholics as idolaters they made a distinction nevertheless between Catholic idolatry and that of the Aztecs. They may, indeed, have considered Catholic idolatry as the more abhorrent of the two but at some level presumably understood it as a decadent and perverted form of monotheism, different in kind from the religious ideas and practices of the Aztecs. The use of expressions such as 'real idolatry', therefore, is intended here to reflect such a distinction.

By some Muslims in some circumstances, Christianity has been referred to as polytheistic because of the doctrine of the Trinity and idolatrous because of its use of images and crosses, but Christians have traditionally been counted among the 'people of the Book' and a distinction in status made between their religion and that of, say, Hindus. When it is asked whether the Koran attacks real idolatry and polytheism, therefore, this is the sort of distinction to be borne in mind.

While a monotheist might refer to the religion of the Aztecs or the Hindus as polytheistic and idolatrous in at least a relatively detached or descriptive way, for a Protestant to use the same terms in relation to Catholicism, or a Muslim in relation to Christianity, is to some extent consciously polemical. An outside observer may be able to recognise that, although it is always difficult, faced with polemical language, to assess how far those engaging in it are aware of the special character of their language.

The traditional Muslim scholars, even though they were probably not involved with the same opponents as was the polemic of the Koran against the *mushrikūn*, were nevertheless not detached or neutral observers, and it is their understanding of the text that has generally been taken over by modern scholarship. Understanding of the Koran, therefore, has not generally given much emphasis to the polemical aspect of its rhetoric.

No doubt the willingness of non-Muslim scholars to accept as historical the image depicted by the traditional scholars is testimony to the persuasiveness of the latters' creation, but it may also indicate a readiness on their part to undervalue the status of Islam as an authentic expression of the monotheist tradition. That may help to account for a general lack of comparative thinking in discussions of the emergence of Islam and a willingness to agree with the tradition's own (understandable) view of Islam as something completely

[1] C. M. N. Eire, *War against the Idols*, Cambridge 1986, 5; referred to in M. Halbertal and A. Margalit, *Idolatry*, Eng. trans. Cambridge, Mass. and London, 1992, 40.

different and *sui generis*. Modern scholars have thus generally been convinced that the Koran did originate in a society in which real polytheism and idolatry prevailed and have rarely felt it necessary to think in other ways about the significance of the scripture's accusations against the *mushrikūn* that they put other gods before God.

It is assumed here, then, that the Koran contains many passages that originated as polemic and that its use of concepts such as idolatry and polytheism has to be understood in the context of polemical discourse. It may be thought that making that assumption automatically makes it difficult to controvert my argument. Assuming that the text has to be read as polemic, it may be argued, makes it possible to read the Koran, every time it levels a charge of idolatry or polytheism against its opponents, as not really meaning what it says. It is for readers to judge whether and how far the Koran is misrepresented here, but it is surely acceptable at least that the Koran's presentation of the religion of the opponents is only an image and not an objective statement of fact: what we have is the representation of the opponents from the point of view of the circles among which the koranic material developed.

One more difficulty needs to be mentioned before coming to the relevant passages. The Koran often seems to see the *mushrikūn* as a group distinct from the Jews and the Christians,[2] but the elasticity of polemic means that insults are easily transferable and one must allow for the possibility, therefore, that the material attacking opponents for their *shirk* in the Koran was not all directed against the same group.

In extra-koranic polemic, *shirk* and *mushrik* are terms used against Christians and Jews (although less often), as well as various groups of Muslims.[3] In the Koran the designation *kāfir*, the referents of which are often difficult to distinguish from those of the word *mushrik,* may be applied to the Jews and possibly to Christians and others. The context of Koran 2:161 indicates that 'those who disbelieve' (*alladhīna kafarū*) are people who, it is alleged, have received a revelation but have concealed the proofs it contains – they are to be cursed by God, the angels and mankind in general. Commentators refer that verse in a general fashion to those Jews, Christians and other religious communities (*ahl al-milal*), and to the *mushrikūn* who worship idols, who have contested the prophethood of Muḥammad.[4]

If that understanding of the verse illustrates the frequent blanket coverage of the charge of *kufr*, however, it also shows the general tendency in *tafsīr* to distinguish between the *mushrikūn* as idol worshippers, and Jews, Christians and others. Nevertheless, even that distinction is sometimes surprisingly

[2] E.g., 2:105, 98:1, 6 (unbelievers among the People of the Book distinguished from those among the *mushrikūn*); 2:96 (the Jews are even more desirous of life than those who commit *shirk*); 2:135 and elsewhere (Abraham was a *ḥanīf*, not a Jew, a Christian or one of the *mushrikūn*); 22:17 (on the day of resurrection God will separate out the believers, the Jews, the Ṣābi'ūn, the Christians, and those who have committed *shirk*). [3] See the next chapter for examples.
[4] E.g., Ṭab., *Tafsīr* (Cairo), III, 261.

blurred in *tafsīr*. Koran 2:221 orders the believers not to marry the women of the *mushrikūn* 'until they believe'. While some commentators here maintained the usual understanding of *mushrikūn* as the idolatrous Arabs of the time of the Prophet, others understood it in this particular case as referring to Jews and Christians. That is especially remarkable here because Muslim law in general *does* permit Muslim men to marry Jewish and Christian women, and the understanding of those commentators who see the verse as applying to Jewish and Christian women leads to some complex discussions about how the verse and the law may be reconciled.[5]

It seems to be true generally, nevertheless, that the *mushrikūn* are distinct from Jews and Christians in the Koran even if views imputed to the two other major forms of monotheism could be included under the category of *shirk*.[6] That distinction is generally maintained, too, in the traditional literature, where the *mushrikūn* are usually portrayed as Arab idolaters and polytheists, separate from the Jews and Christians with whom the Prophet had contacts.

Reading the Koran on its own terms, trying to interpret it without resorting to commentaries, is a difficult and questionable exercise because of the nature of the text – its allusive and referential style and its grammatical and logical discontinuities, as well as our lack of sure information about its origins and the circumstances of its composition. Often such a reading seems arbitrary and necessarily inconclusive. The intention in the following is not so much to say what the Koran 'really means' as to ask whether the traditional interpretation of its material pertaining to the concept of *shirk* is a necessary or the only possible interpretation.

To begin, it should be emphasised again that neither of the expressions used most frequently in the Koran to attack those opponents not identified specifically as Christians or Jews literally means 'polytheist' or 'idolater'.

Regarding *mushrik*, literally meaning (in the Koran) 'someone who associates something or someone with God as an object of worship', its translation as 'polytheist' comes about partly because the Koran sometimes accuses the opponents of putting gods before God or claims that they have gods other than God, and thus of 'associating' these gods with God; and partly because the extra-koranic traditional literature portrays the Arab contemporaries of the Prophet as adherents of various deities such as Allāt, al-ʿUzzā and Manāt.

It comes to be equated too with 'idolater', partly because the Koran sometimes uses words redolent of idolatry in connexion with the *mushrikūn* and

[5] Ibid., IV, 362 ff.

[6] In his article s.v. 'Shirk' in *EI2*, Daniel Gimaret discusses the identity of those attacked in the Koran as *mushrikūn*. He says that we might expect the charge of *shirk* to be levelled at all of those groups whose religious beliefs might be interpreted as 'associationism', especially the Christians, but concludes: 'The Ḳur'ānic term *mushrikūn* does not in fact denote all those who, in some manner, practise a form of associationism, but only . . . those among whom this associationism is most flagrant – i.e. the worshippers of idols (*ʿabadat al-awthān*).'

partly because the tradition portrays the Arab opponents of Muḥammad as worshippers of idols. In the traditional literature the distinction between an idol and a deity is often not clear, and neither is that between idol, stone and sanctuary. For example, Allāt is sometimes used as the name of a deity, sometimes as that of an idol or stone representing that deity or in some way associated with its worship.

Although in the traditional literature *shirk* often functions as the equivalent of both polytheism and idolatry, it is important to keep its literal sense in mind.[7]

Apart from *shirk*, the other charge frequently made against the opponents in the Koran is that of *kufr*: they are *kāfirūn* or *kuffār*, on one occasion *kafara*. All these are recognised as plurals of *kāfir*, a word often translated by 'unbeliever' or 'infidel'. The origin and precise meaning of the word are debated. Some have attempted to link it with the usage of the same root in Hebrew, Aramaic or Syriac, while others have argued for a purely Arabic development. Sometimes in the Koran it is understood to mean something like 'ungrateful'. At Koran 26:19 Pharaoh reminds Moses what he has done for him as a child and how long Moses has lived in Egypt, but 'you are one of the *kāfirīn*'. Elsewhere it often seems to have the sense of active disbelief or refusal to believe, rather than simple unbelief. At Koran 6:89 God refers to His having given the scriptures, laws and prophethood to various individuals but says that if their posterity disbelieve in them (*yakfur bihā*) He will give them instead to a people who are not *kāfirīna bihā*. It may be possible to cover several of its occurrences by postulating a meaning such as 'to reject' (a favour or a truth).[8]

The word does not itself have any necessary implication of idol worship or polytheism and in Islam is used generally to refer to any non-Muslim, monotheist or not. One of the major debates in early Muslim theology was whether a Muslim might become a *kāfir* as a result of sin, and in intra-Muslim polemic opponents have often been labelled *kuffār*. Christians and Jews within the territories of Islam, the protected *dhimmī*s, are nevertheless also *kuffār*. Various Muslim theologians have elaborated lists of the different categories of *kuffār*, the majority of them being monotheists whose monotheism is in some sense less than perfect.[9] Similarly, the rabbis applied the term *kōfēr bā-ʿiqqār* ('rejecter of the principles of the faith') not only to someone who denied the existence of God but to one who accepted His existence but whose behaviour or faith in some way fell short. According to the Tosefta cited by Urbach, the heretics (*minīm*, a word the precise significance of which is debated but often referring to monotheists, such as Christians, seen as defectors from the true religion) are worse than the idolaters because the latter deny God out of

[7] For some discussion of possible pre-Islamic use and significance of the root, see below, pp. 69–71.

[8] See *EI2* s.v. 'Kāfir' (by W. Björkman). The root can have a positive connotation if the object of the *kufr* is error or falsehood.

[9] For examples of the lists of different categories of *kuffār*, see ibid.

ignorance whereas the former know Him *but introduce other elements into their conception of Him.*[10]

In applying to the opponents terms associated with *shirk* and *kufr*, therefore, the Koran does not use vocabulary that explicitly and literally carries an accusation of polytheism or idolatry.[11]

Now, there are certainly several koranic passages that imply, or explicitly say, that the opponents worshipped or believed in a plurality of gods. Koran 37:36 says that at the Last Judgement the opponents will remember the scornful response they had previously made when faced with a proclamation that there is only one God (*lā ilāha illā ʾllāh*): 'Are we to abandon our gods for a mad poet!' According to Koran 43:58, when 'the son of Mary' is presented to them as an example to be followed, they scornfully turn away and say, 'Who is better – our gods or he?' Koran 17:42, following the command not to put any other god together with God, insists that if, as the opponents say, there were gods with God, then these other gods would have sought a way to attack the Lord of the Throne. At Koran 25:43 the opponents are made to mock the Prophet and say that, if it were not for their own steadfastness, he would have led them astray 'from our gods'. Such passages could be multiplied.

Sometimes the opponents are charged with recognising or worshipping gods or beings *min dūni ʾllāh*. The Arabic expression is slightly difficult to translate: 'without God' does not really fit; 'beneath God' would be possible but does not really match the koranic polemic accusing the opponents of worshipping gods other than and equal with God; some translators (e.g., Rodwell) select 'besides God'; it may be that it echoes the biblical injunction not to take other gods '*before* me (*ʿal-panay*)' (e.g., Deuteronomy 5:7). According to Koran 19:81, 'they have taken gods *min dūni ʾllāh* that they might be a power for them'. At Koran 10:104 the Prophet is told to proclaim, 'I do not worship those whom you worship *min dūni ʾllāh*. . .'.

Before concluding that these opponents were in fact polytheists whose religion involved recognition of a plurality of gods, however, it is necessary to consider the totality of the context in which such passages occur and their character as part of a religious polemic.

It is noticeable, for one thing, that the word 'gods' is not used consistently in those passages where the opponents are accused of putting or worshipping something 'beside' or 'before' God. Sometimes the nature of the thing thus venerated is left unspecified and anonymous in phrases such as: those who are worshipped/called upon before/other than God,[12] those who are taken as

[10] E. Urbach, *The Sages*, 2nd edn Cambridge, Mass. and London, 1979, 26 f. citing Tosefta Shabbath 13: 5 (ed. S. Lieberman, New York 1955–88, 58). The italics for emphasis are mine.

[11] While it is easy to imagine what sort of expression might have been used in the Koran to label the opponents literally as idolaters (*ʿubbād/ʿabadat al-aṣnām* would be most obvious), it is not so easy to imagine a word for polytheists. Modern Arabic would almost certainly use *mushrikūn* since the language is so influenced by the Koran. Dictionaries use cumbrous neologisms such as *al-muʾminūn bi-taʿaddud al-āliha.*

[12] E.g., 6:56; 40:68; 39:64; 11:109.

patrons/friends (*awliyā'*) before God,[13] and those who are taken as 'equals/peers' (*andād*) before God. Regarding this last word, the opponents are charged with recognising certain beings as peers of God even though He is the creator of the universe and the source of all blessings and afflictions.[14]

Furthermore, the Koran does not deny the reality or the existence of those beings that the opponents are said to worship as gods or to put on the same level as God. It denies, of course, that they are gods but not that they exist: 'He among them [i.e., among those beings who are worshipped] who says, 'I am a god besides Him', We will recompense with hell' (21:29); 'You and those whom you worship besides God are the fuel (*ḥaṣab*) of hell. . . . If these were gods, they would not go down to it [hell], but all of them shall abide in it for ever' (21:98–9);[15] 'They have taken gods besides Him which have created nothing but were themselves created' (25:3); etc.

The gods of the opponents really do exist, therefore; but they are not real gods, merely some type of inferior being.[16] This is quite in keeping with monotheistic tradition in pre- and early Christian times. While insisting that there is only one God, the reality of the beings worshipped as 'gods' by others is not usually denied in the Bible. In the Song of Moses the Israelites are reproached for sacrificing 'to demons who are not God, to gods (*elōhīm*) hitherto unknown to them', words echoed in Paul's first letter to the Corinthians in his discussion of the problem of whether it is permitted to consume food that had been offered to idols. The false gods do not exist as gods for 'there is no God but the One'; though 'for us there is only one God', 'there are *so-called gods* and plenty of lords'.[17]

What is called, in the language of monotheist polemic, the 'god' of the opponents may not be considered a god by the opponents themselves and his 'worship' may only be a form of veneration or even a (disapproved of) enthusiasm. Koran 3:64 seems to be addressed to the People of the Book but implies that they commit *shirk* by recognising some of *themselves* as 'lords' before God (*qul yā ahla 'l-kitābi ta'ālū ilā kalimatin sawā'in baynanā wa-baynakum allā na'buda illā 'llāha wa-lā nushrika bihi shay'an wa-lā yattakhidha ba'ḍunā ba'ḍan arbāban min dūni 'llāhi*). Koran 41:43 recognises that men may make a 'god' of their own fantasies: 'Have you not seen him who chooses for his god his desires (*a-ra'ayta mani 'ttakhadha ilāhan hawāyahu*)?' We are surely familiar with football idols and screen goddesses. From the koranic material is it possible to deduce anything about how the opponents viewed their 'gods'?

Most obviously, we are told that the opponents expected that they would

[13] E.g., 29:41; 36:3; 42:6. [14] E.g., 2:165; 14:30; 39:8; 41:9.
[15] Cf. Matt. 25:41: 'everlasting fire prepared for the devil and his angels'.
[16] A point made too by Alford T. Welch, 'Allah and Other Supernatural Beings: The Emergence of the Qur'anic Doctrine of *tawhid*,' *JAAR*, thematic issue, 47 (1979), no. 4 S, 733–53, esp. 736 ff. I am grateful to Andrew Rippin for access to this article, upon which see further below.
[17] Deut. 32:17; 1 Cor. 10:20, cf. 1 Cor. 8:4 ff.

intercede for them with God. On occasion this seems to refer to intercession to bring about some benefit in this life. There are denials, for example, that the beings the opponents associate with God can remove an affliction, *ḍurr*, sent by God (Koran 39:8, 38; 30:33) . More usual, however, are those references to their inability to intercede at the Last Judgement. Not that intercession (*shafāʿa*) on that occasion is ruled out; but God will only permit it by and for those whom He wishes, and the beings in whom the opponents place their trust are not among these: 'Who is he that can intercede (*yashfaʿu*) with Him except by His permission?' (2:225); 'Your Lord is God who made the heavens and the earth in six days. . . . None can intercede with Him except after His permission' (10:3); 'God it is who has created the heavens and the earth and all that is between them in six days. . . . Except for Him you shall have no patron (*walī*) and no intercessor (*shafīʿ*)' (32:4); 'Warn [the opponents] about the coming day when they will have no friend (*ḥāmīm*) and no intercessor' (40:18). If one can accept such verses at face value, the opponents already know of the sovereignty of God and, perhaps, of the final judgement, something not easily reconcilable with the traditional image of them as idol-worshipping polytheists.

Furthermore, the Koran offers us clues at least about the nature of these beings whom the opponents expected to intercede for them. Some passages seem to indicate that they were angels, whom the opponents regarded as God's offspring. Koran 43:15 ff. accuses the opponents of assigning female offspring to God and in verse 19 says that they have made the angels (*malāʾika*), who are servants of the Merciful One, females. Koran 21:26–8 is part of a passage in which it is denied twice that there are gods other than God and which then tells us that the opponents claim that God has 'taken offspring' (*ittakhadha waladan*). That *walad* is a collective plural is clear from the denial of the opponents' claim: 'No, [they are] honoured servants (*ʿibād mukramūna*) who do not speak before Him and who carry out His command . . . and they do not intercede except for whom He pleases, but tremble in fear of Him.' The exegetical tradition is surely right to identify those whom the opponents regard as offspring of God here as angels, for the imagery of the koranic passage points in that direction.[18] Compare verse 20 ('They praise Him night and day, without ceasing') with Revelation 4:8.

Other passages also support the view that the opponents expected angels to intercede for them. Sūra 53:26 denies the possibility: 'Many as are the angels in heaven, their intercession shall be of no avail'. Verses 40:7–9 and 42:3–4, while they do not use the word 'intercession' (*shafāʿa*), accept that the angels ask God for the forgiveness of the righteous on earth. Alford Welch argued that the opponents themselves did not really regard as angels the beings whom they 'worshipped': Welch accepted the traditional understanding that these beings were the deities of the pagan Meccans and suggested that the

[18] Ṭab., *Tafsīr* (Bulaq), XVII, 12.

identification of them as angels is 'a Qur'anic development' (i.e., an aspect of its polemic).[19]

Allowing for the fact that the text is polemical, however, does not mean that we need to follow the tradition in transforming the angels of the Koran into gods and idols. A highly developed angelology was a feature of several monotheist groups in Late Antiquity. Early Christian polemic against Judaism included the accusation of angel worship, partly explicable as a distortion of beliefs that gave angels a role in the transmission of revelation, notably that on Mount Sinai. Such beliefs about angels blurred the distinction between angel and prophet (both could be referred to by words indicating 'messenger'), associated them or even identified them with stars, and assigned a role to them as intercessors, at the Last Judgement or more generally. It is not at all inconceivable, therefore, that what the Koran tells us about the opponents' faith in and veneration of angels, even allowing for deliberate distortion, does reflect significant reality.[20]

In some other passages those whom the opponents expect to intercede for them are referred to as their 'associates' (*shurakā'*)[21] – apparently meaning 'those they associate with God'. While it might follow that the opponents are regarded by the Koran as holding that the angels were associates of God, there do not seem to be any passages that explicitly identify these *shurakā'* as angels. Koran 6:100 in fact says that those whom the opponents made associates of God were the *jinn*, even though God was their creator.[22] Koran 72:6 (which has the *jinn* themselves speaking) tells us that there are some of mankind who take refuge with some of the *jinn*.[23] It is possible that the distinction between angels and *jinn* is blurred. It is well known that in the Koran the Devil (Iblīs) is referred to as an angel at 2:32 but as one of the *jinn* at 18:48.

If we then consider those verses of the Koran that, like the above-mentioned 21:26–8, say that the opponents regard God as having offspring, the lack of distinction between angels and *jinn* appears again. In 21:26–8 the context

19 Welch, 'Allah and Other Supernatural Beings', 740; see further below (chap. 6).

20 Paul is sometimes said to have been confronted by angel worship among the Jewish Christians at Colossae (Col. 2:18: those who 'grovel to angels and worship them') – Henry Chadwick, *The Early Church*, Harmondsworth 1967, 34. For refutation of the charge of angel worship in Rabbinical Judaism, see, e.g., *Encyclopaedia Judaica* s.v. 'Angels and Angelology', esp. col. 971; Babylonian Talmud, Sanhedrin, 38 b (Eng. tr. 1935, i, 245–6), has a story of one of the *minim* who sought to entrap Rabbi Idith into saying that we should worship the angel Metatron, but was roundly defeated. For the association and identification of angels and stars ('the host of heaven'), see the references given in *Encyclopaedia Judaica*, s. v. 'Angels and Angelology', col. 964; by J. A. Montgomery, *The Samaritans*, Philadelphia 1907, 218; and L. Ginzberg, *The Legends of the Jews*, 7 vols., Philadelphia 1911–38 (see index, s.v. 'stars'). For interceding angels, see, e.g., Job, 33:23; the apocryphal Testament of the Twelve Patriarchs (Eng. trans., in Sparks (ed.), *Apocryphal Old Testament*, 528, 565); and Montgomery, *Samaritans*, 221. For angels and prophets, see A. J. Wensinck, 'Muhammad und die Propheten', *AO*, 2 (1924), esp. 183; Wansbrough, *Quranic Studies*, 55; Günter Lüling, *Die Wiederentdeckung des Propheten Muhammad*, Erlangen 1981, esp. 77 ff. For koranic verses accusing the opponents of angel worship, see Paul Arno Eichler, *Die Dschinn, Teufel und Engel im Koran*, Leipzig 1928, 97 ff.

21 30:13; 6:94; 10:18. 22 *Wa-ja'alū lillāhi shurakā'a 'l-jinna wa-khalaqahum.*

23 *Ya'ūdhūna bi-rijālin mina 'l-jinn.*

implies that it is the angels whom the opponents identify as God's offspring. Other passages associate the idea of intercession with the idea of God having offspring but do not elaborate on the nature of these offspring:

None shall have the power of intercession except he who has taken a pact from God (*al-Raḥmān*). They say that God has taken offspring (*waladan*) . . . [It is enough to cause creation to tremble] that they attribute offspring to God. It is not seemly that God should take offspring. Everything in the heavens and the earth must come to God as a servant. . . . And all of them shall come to Him alone on the day of resurrection. (19:87 ff.)

Elsewhere it is imputed that the opponents regard the angels as God's *female* offspring: 'Has your Lord prepared sons for you and taken for Himself daughters from among the angels?' (17:40).

But other verses imply that the opponents identified the *jinn* as God's offspring: 'They have assigned the *jinn* to God as associates even though He created them, and ignorantly they have falsely attributed to Him sons and daughters (*banīna wa-banātin*). . . . How, when He has no consort, should He have offspring?' (6:100–1); 'They have made God kin with the *jinn*' (37:158).[24] The denial that God (often al-Raḥmān rather than Allāh in these passages) has offspring (23:91; 39:4), the implication that the opponents regard the angels as female (37:150; 42:19; 53:27) and the rejection of the idea that God should have female progeny (16:59; 37:149, 154; 43:16; 52:39; 53:21) all occur frequently in the Koran.

So far, although the material may not be sufficient to enable us to obtain a clear idea of the beliefs of the opponents, it does not portray them as polytheists of the sort depicted in Muslim exegetical and other traditional literature. The verses of the Koran mentioned above do not point to a group that worshipped a multiplicity of gods and bowed down before idols, but rather a group that shared some basic concepts of monotheism (God as creator, angels, perhaps the Last Judgment, intercession, etc.) but held views that the Koran equated with, and presented – surely polemically – as, polytheism and idolatry.

Even the one koranic passage that is usually understood as giving us explicit information about the names of three 'goddesses' worshipped by the opponents, Sūra 53:19 ff., also associates the three names with the veneration of angels and the idea that angels intercede for us. That passage mentions Allāt, al-ʿUzzā and Manāt, which the exegetical tradition identifies as the names of three goddesses worshipped by the polytheistic Meccan opponents of Muḥammad, but then goes on to imply that the opponents regarded the beings who bore these names as female offspring of God, and as angels whose intercession could be expected.[25]

[24] *Jaʿalū baynahu wa-bayna ʾl-jinnati nasaban.*

[25] Welch, 'Allah and Other Supernatural Beings', 738–9, suggests that the koranic passage has been revised and contains later interpolations, i.e., that the references to angels and intercession are additions which obscure the fundamental allusions to Meccan paganism.

These are the verses to which tradition attaches the story of the 'satanic verses', and the three names figure prominently in the traditional accounts of the gods and idols of the pagan Arabs. The verses and the story connected with them will be discussed in more detail in chapter 6, and it may merely be noted here that, apart from the occurrence of the names, which it is possible to relate to those of apparently divine beings attested in inscriptions and literature independent of the Muslim tradition, the rest of the passage with its reference to angels as the female offspring of God links with the koranic material discussed above.

As for the idolatry traditionally imputed to the opponents attacked in the Koran, when the two most common Arabic words for 'idol', *wathan* (plural *awthān*) and *ṣanam* (plural *aṣnām*), occur in the Koran, they usually relate to peoples of the past, most often in reports about Abraham's dealings with his father and his people.[26] Only slightly ambiguous is Koran 29:17 ('You only worship *awthān* before God and create a lie – those you worship before God can give you no provisions'). It is not completely obvious who is speaking to whom but the previous verse is marked as the words of Abraham and it seems that this one is too. That is the way it is understood in the traditional exegesis.[27]

Elsewhere *aṣnām* appear in connexion with the people the Children of Israel met after crossing the Red Sea (Koran 7:138). Seeing that this people cleaved to its idols (*aṣnām*), the Israelites demanded of Moses that he make them a god (*ilāh*) like the gods of the people, but he responded by charging them with 'ignorance' (*innakum qawm tajhalūna*).[28] None of this is surprising, given the biblical and other versions of these stories. In contrast to the traditional literature where the pre-Islamic Arabs are frequently described as worshipping *awthān* and *aṣnām*, therefore, the Koran seems more reticent.

There are, however, two words often associated with idols and idolatry used in the Koran apparently with reference to the contemporary situation: *ṭāghūt* and *jibt*.

Ṭāghūt appears eight times[29] and is explained in commentary in various ways. As well as to such things as sorcerors, soothsayers and satans, it is understood as referring to idols generally, to a particular idol or idols, or to places such as temples where idols were situated. It seems obvious that this is one of those words that the exegetical tradition does not really understand and which were the object of more or less plausible speculation.[30] The idea that it

[26] 6:74, 26:71, 21:51 (here a reference to 'images,' *tamāthīl*, but comparison with 26:71 indicates that it is a doublet for *aṣnām*), 21:57, 29:25, 14:35. For Ibn al-Kalbī's inconsistent and unconvincing attempts to establish a difference in meaning between *ṣanam* and *wathan*, see *Aṣnām K-R*, 21 = 47 with 33 = 58; and see A. Guillaume's rejection of a criticism made against him by R.B. Serjeant that he had failed to distinguish between different types of idols: 'Stroking an Idol', *BSOAS*, 27 (1964), 430. [27] E.g., Ṭab., *Tafsīr* (Bulaq), XX, 88.

[28] Note, again, the blurring of the distinction between idol and god.

[29] 2:256, 257; 4:51, 60, 76; 5:65; 16:36; 39:17.

[30] Ṭab., *Tafsīr* (Cairo), V, 416–20 (on Koran 2:256); E. W. Lane, *An Arabic–English Lexicon*, 8 vols., London 1863–93, s.v. '*ṭāghūt*'; T. Fahd, *Le panthéon de l'Arabie centrale à la veille de l'Hégire*, Paris 1968, 240.

indicates a singular entity, for example, Satan or the name of one particular deity or idol, is not consistent with verses where it seems to refer to a plural. In Koran 2:257, for example, the *ṭāghūt* are masculine plural: in contrast to the believers, whose patron is God who will deliver them from the darkness into the light, the unbelievers' patrons (*awliyā'*) are the *ṭāghūt*, who will cast them out of the light into the darkness. In verse 39:17 the feminine singular suffix pronoun presumably (as is normal in Arabic) stands for a masculine plural, although it is just conceivable that it could indicate that the preceding *al-ṭāghūt* could be read as a feminine singular.[31]

We are ordered to shun the *ṭāghūt* and to serve God (Koran 16:36; 39:17); those who disbelieve are accused of being friends of the *ṭāghūt* and fighting in the way of the *ṭāghūt* (4:76, 2:258); there are those who claim that they believe in what has been revealed to the Prophet and to previous prophets but nevertheless desire to be brought to judgement to the *ṭāghūt* (4:60).

Some traditional and most modern scholarship has recognised the word as non-Arabic in origin: some have favoured an Aramaic, others an Ethiopian, derivation. Abraham Geiger seems to have been the first to connect it with Aramaic *ṭ'wt,* literally 'error' but used in the Jerusalem Talmud and Midrash Rabba with connotations of idolatry or the worship of gods other than God. In the Jerusalem Talmud tractate Sanhedrin the word occurs in the context of a series of stories about the worship of Baal Peor; Genesis Rabba, commenting on the word 'clothes' (*sūtoh*) in Genesis 49:11, links it with a verb with similar radicals meaning 'to entice' (to the worship of other gods) in Deuteronomy 13:6 and explains that the Genesis verse refers to the correction of 'errors' by the Great Sanhedrin.[32] Schwally suggested a connexion with a Christian Palestinian form also meaning 'error', while Jeffery, following Suyūṭī, favoured an Abyssinian parallel with the basic meaning of 'defection from the true religion' but used where the Septuagint and the New Testament have *eidōla*. Nöldeke pointed out that the Abyssinian probably itself derived from Aramaic. Köbert has suggested a connexion with Syriac *ṭā'yā* (pl. *ṭā'aiyā*), 'planet', 'wandering star', and speculated on the word as evidence for a belief in astral deities in Arabia.[33]

The word *al-jibt*, a hapax legomenon which occurs in Koran 4:51 in conjunction with *al-ṭāghūt* ('Have you not seen those who have been brought a part of the Book? They believe in *al-jibt* and *al-ṭāghūt* and say to those who

[31] Ṭab., *Tafsīr* (Bulaq), XXIII, 131–2 (on Koran 39:17) insists that here and elsewhere it has a singular meaning and refers to Satan (*al-shayṭān*). One of the authorities he cites says that the word *ṭāghūt* itself is feminine singular and that is why the feminine singular pronoun is used even though Satan is meant. Another anonymous authority says that the pronoun is feminine because *ṭāghūt* is a plural.

[32] J. Levy, *Wörterbuch über die Talmudim und Midraschim*, 4 vols., 2nd edn, Berlin 1924, repr. Darmstadt 1963, II, 170b-171a, s.v. '*ṭ'wt*'.

[33] For full references to the various theories and data, see Jeffery, *Foreign Vocabulary,* 202–3; R. Köbert, 'Das koranische 'ṭāġūt'', *Orientalia*, n.s. 30 (1961), 415–6. For Ibn 'Abd al-Wahhāb's use of the idea of the *ṭāghūt*, see his *Fī ma'nā al-ṭāghūt wa-ru'ūs anwā'ihi*, in his *Majmū'at al-tawḥīd al-najdiyya*, Mecca 1319 AH, 117–18.

disbelieve that these are on a righter path than those who believe?'), seems to have a similar background. Interpreting it in a variety of ways similar to *ṭāghūt* in exegesis (idol, sorcerer, soothsayer, sorcery, Satan, etc.), some traditional sources explain it as of non-Arabic origin, although the majority sought an Arabic origin for it. Nöldeke suggested that it came from the Ethiopic *amlāka gebt*, a rendering of Greek *theos prosphatos* in passages such as Deuteronomy 32:17 ('They sacrificed unto devils, not to God; to gods whom they knew not, to *new gods* that came newly up'). Nöldeke suggested that *gebt* was misunderstood by Muḥammad or one of his Abyssinian adherents in the sense of 'idol' or 'idolatry'. Margoliouth suggested a connexion with the Greek *glypta* (from *glyphō*, 'to carve' or 'engrave'), with which the Septuagint translates Hebrew *pesel* ('idol', 'image') in Leviticus 26:1, but Jeffery rejected this on the grounds that a Greek word is unlikely to have passed into Arabic without leaving a trace in Syriac, and he too argued for an Ethiopic origin. [34]

Whatever the precise source of these words, it seems likely that the koranic is a development of earlier monotheistic usage and significance. They help to place the Koran in a tradition of monotheistic polemic against 'idolatry' and indicate that when trying to understand the koranic language we need to be aware of the range of (mainly transferred) meanings that 'idolatry' had come to have in the monotheistic tradition generally. While it cannot be excluded that some 'real' paganism was the object of the koranic ire, these passages in themselves tell us nothing about the nature of the 'idolatry' that was being attacked. Koran 4:51, with its reference to 'those who have been brought a part of the Book' as those who believe in *al-jibt* and *al-ṭāghūt*, strengthens the possibility that it is the 'idolatry' of fellow monotheists.

Although, as noted above, the words *awthān* and *aṣnām* (the two most common Arabic words for 'idols') nearly always occur in the Koran with reference to peoples of the past, there is at least one passage that is apparently addressed to the contemporary situation which uses *awthān*. At Koran 22:30 the reader or hearer is exhorted to avoid what is usually translated as 'the filth of idols and the words of falsehood (*al-rijs min al-awthān (wa-) . . . qawl al-zūr*)'.

The second part of that phrase is sometimes interpreted in the exegetical tradition as a reference to the polytheistic corruptions that had infected the originally monotheist *talbiya*.[35] Generally, however, the commentators do not attempt to supply material that would put the verse in a specific historical or

[34] T. Nöldeke, *Neue Beiträge zur semitischen Sprachwissenschaft*, Strasburg 1910, 47–8; Jeffery, *Foreign Vocabulary*, 99–100; R. Paret, *Der Koran: Kommentar und Konkordanz*, Stuttgart etc. 1971, 96. I am grateful to Andrew Palmer for help regarding *theos prosphatos*. He points out that the Christian Fathers used the expression when alluding to Ex. 20:3 ('Thou shalt have no other gods before me'): G. W. H. Lampe, *A Patristic Greek Lexicon*, Oxford 1961, 1183 s.v. 'προσφατος', cites Didymus Alexandrinus as quoting, 'Thou shalt have no *theon prosphaton*.' Early Christian apologists denied that Christ was a 'new god', while Arius was accused of having taught that the Son is a 'new god'.

[35] Kister, 'Labbayka, Allāhumma, Labbayka . . .', 34–5.

social context or to provide a precise 'occasion of revelation'. It is understood that we are being commanded to avoid idolatry and polytheism in a general sense.

Ṭabarī's interpretation of the first part of the koranic phrase is that it means: 'Beware of idolatry (*'ibādat al-awthān*), for worshipping idols is obedience to Satan, and that is filth (*rijs*)'. His gloss on the second part is: 'Beware of uttering lies and calumnies against God when you say with regard to the gods (*āliha*), 'We only serve them to bring us closer to God', and when you say with regard to the angels, 'They are the daughters of God', and other such things; for that is lying, falsehood (*zūr*), and associating other things with God (*shirk bi'llāh*)'.[36] Several of the traditions cited by Ṭabarī in support of his interpretation equate 'the uttering of falsehood' (*qawl* or *shahādat al-zūr*) with *shirk*, and they cite this verse 22:30 in support of that equation. Ṭabarī also knows of a prophetic *ḥadīth* making the same equation and citing the same verse in support.[37] The command to avoid *al-rijs min al-awthān* and the *qawl al-zūr* is understood, then, as an injunction against idolatry and polytheism.

One difficulty about the verse mentioned in the exegesis is the unusual grammar of *al-rijs min al-awthān*. Generally understood to mean something like 'the filth (or abomination) of idols', one might have expected a simple genitive construction (*iḍāfa*): *rijs al-awthān* just like the following *qawl al-zūr*. Ṭabarī raises the question: does the phrase mean that there is the possibility that there is something from or of the idols that is not filth? Of course he rejects that interpretation. Everything to do with them is filth, and the phrase means that we are commanded to avoid the filth that comes from the idols, that is, from the worship of them. Ibn Kathīr specifies that the *min* ('from' or 'of') in the phrase is intended to identify the nature of the filth – we must avoid the filth that the idols are (*min hāhunā li-bayān al-jins ay ijtanibū al-rijs alladhī huwa al-awthān*). Such suggestions underline the problematic nature of the phrase and possibly indicate that it is not simply an injunction against idolatry.[38]

It is difficult to obtain a clear idea of what the Koran is referring to at this point. The verse 22:30 comes in the context of a discussion, which occurs at various other places in the Koran too, about the legitimacy or otherwise of consuming or making use of animals upon which, it is implied, the opponents have put limitations or prohibitions. The verses following it state that it is permissible to benefit from and to eat cattle that have been dedicated to God at

[36] *Tafsīr* (Bulaq), XVII, 112. The justification (we only worship them to bring us closer to God) that Ṭabarī here ascribes to the opponents is found at Koran 39:3 (see below for further discussion of this); their view of the angels as the daughters of God, although the precise words used by Ṭabarī do not appear in the Koran, is implied at 16:57, 37:149–50, 43:16,19 and 52:39.

[37] For different versions of the *ḥadīth*, see too Abu 'l-Fidā' Ismā'īl b. Kathīr, *Tafsīr al-Qur'ān al-'azīm*, 6 vols., Beirut 1966, iv, 637, and A. J. Wensinck, *Concordance et indices de la tradition musulmane*, 8 vols., Leiden 1936–88, s.v. '*al-zūr*'.

[38] Ṭab., *Tafsīr*, (Bulaq) XVII, 113 (at top: *fa-in qāla qā'il wa-hal min al-awthān mā laysa bi-rijs*); Ibn Kathīr, *Tafsīr*, IV, 637.

the sanctuary. The camel is specifically mentioned as one of the animals given for our use, and it should be included among the sacrificial offerings and its meat consumed. Of course it is not the flesh and blood that reach God but the devotion (*taqwā*) shown in carrying out His commands.

The suggestion that 'the filth of [which comes from?] idols' and 'the words of falsehood' refer to aspects of dietary and purity regulations can be supported not only by the context in which the warning against them occurs, but also by related koranic passages which use different phrases and by reference to Jewish and Christian scriptures. Apart from the verse (22:30) with which we are immediately concerned, the opponents are accused of arbitrarily and impiously limiting the use of certain animals and produce, whether for food or other purposes, in the passage that begins at Koran 6:136 (referred to above in connexion with the story of Khawlān and its idol). Traditional exegesis associates that passage with Koran 5:103 where the opponents are accused of inventing lies against God concerning (the livestock animals known as) the *baḥīra*, the *sā'iba*, the *waṣīla* and the *ḥām*. The commentators identify these as types of animals, especially camels, regarded by the Arab pagans as prohibited for general use because they have been dedicated to the gods or the sanctuary. The Koran rejects all such practices. We should not declare forbidden what God has allowed, and we should eat of what He has given to us (e.g., Koran 5:87–8).

Aside from such things as wine, or game which one has killed when in a state of ritual purity, the only prohibited things are those that are unclean. At Koran 5:3 these are listed as carrion, blood, pork, 'what has been dedicated to other than God', anything killed other than by having its blood shed, and anything slaughtered on the *nuṣub*. Regarding the meaning of this last word, the commentators are not unanimous but it is generally understood to refer to stones connected with idolatry – stones set up as idols, stones set up before idols for sacrificial practices, or simply the idols themselves.[39] The parallel version of this list at Koran 6:145 does not mention the *nuṣub* but adds that pork is 'filth' (*rijs*), the same word as is used in the expression 'the filth of [which comes from?] idols'.

The koranic language and the lists of prohibited things are comparable with biblical texts. Acts 15:20 and 15:29 single out as the fundamental prohibited things for gentile Christians: food sacrificed to idols, blood, strangled animals, (sexual) impurity, but not, of course, pork. Both the koranic lists and those in Acts are related to the laws of purification as set out in Leviticus chapters 11 and 17. While Acts exempts the eating of pork from prohibition (Leviticus 11:7 says that it is unclean), Koran 22:36 exempts the camel (declared unclean at Leviticus 11:4). The reasons for the abhorrence of blood, common to the lists in Acts and in the Koran, are set out in Leviticus 17:10–16. Koran 5:57 ('Do not declare as forbidden the good things which God has made allowed

[39] See Lane, *Lexicon* s.v. '*nuṣub*'.

for you') would not be out of place at Acts 10:15 where Peter is told in his dream, 'What God has made clean you have no right to call profane.'

It seems, then, that *al-rijs min al-awthān* and *qawl al-zūr* in Koran 22:30 may relate to food and purity regulations: on the one hand the opponents are wrong in arbitrarily prohibiting the consumption and use of animals either because they hold them to have been set aside in some way for religious purposes, or because they have been brought to the sanctuary for slaughter; on the other hand there is a certain limited list of foods (meat) which is prohibited, because of the manner or circumstance in which it has been killed or, in the case of pork, because it is inherently impure. Regarding the circumstances in which the meat has been slaughtered, dedication to 'something other than God' or slaughter on the *nuṣub* are prominent reasons for prohibition.

Other koranic passages discussing prohibited food use variant phrases: 'a disgusting thing (*fisq*) dedicated to something other than God' (6:145); 'what has been dedicated to something other than God . . . and what has been slaughtered on the *nuṣub*' (5:3); and 'that over which the name of God has not been mentioned . . . a disgusting thing (*fisq*)' (6:121). On the other hand Koran 6:118 tells us to eat of that 'over which the name of God has been mentioned', a command reinforced in the following verse with the reassurance that God has made clear to us what He has forbidden.

The exact nature of the practices or ideas alluded to in such verses probably cannot be known. The koranic material and its background is complex and obscure enough to justify hesitation about the significance of 'the filth of [which comes from?] idols' and 'the words of falsehood' in Koran 22:30. The possibility of polemical distortion and of the use of language and ideas that were conventional in the monotheistic tradition has to be taken account of, as does the general context of the Koran's references to 'idolatry' and *shirk*. It is not clear whether slaughtering on the *nuṣub* and dedicating to 'something other than God' are practices associated with the *mushrikūn*, whereas 'declaring prohibited what God has allowed' does seem to be associated with them. Emerging Christianity was concerned not only with the dietary and other aspects of Jewish law but also with the problems caused by necessary contacts with Graeco-Roman religion and customs. It could be that the Koran exhibits the same concerns: as well as facing the purity and food regulations of the *mushrikūn*, it may be that it had to deal with the question of the legitimacy of food from other, perhaps really idolatrous or at least non-monotheist, sources.

How far Koran 22:30 disrupts the interpretation of the *mushrikūn* presented here, therefore, is debatable. I do not want to minimise its significance but it is questionable whether it is a rejection of idolatry in general or whether, rather, it is concerned with an issue distinct from the argument with the *mushrikūn*, the specific issue of food from outside sources regarded as idolatrous. A condemnation of idolatry generally might be thought superfluous because the *mushrikūn* also abhorred it – that is why it is such a potent ingredient in the polemic.

Occasionally the Koran hints at the sort of defence the opponents might make. Sūra 6:148 tells us that the *mushrikūn* claim that they and their ancestors would not have practised *shirk* had God not wished it (*law shā'a 'llāhu mā ashraknā wa-lā abā'unā wa-lā ḥarramnā min shay'in*). (Note that this verse again connects *shirk* with declaring things forbidden for normal consumption or use.) The force of that defence is not really clear but at face value it indicates that the opponents accepted that God could control everything they did.[40] According to 39:3, 'those who have taken patrons (*awliyā'*) besides Him' claim that they 'worship' the *awliyā'* only in order that they might bring them closer to God (*mā na'buduhum illā li-yuqarribūnā ilā 'llāhi zulfā*). Again this hardly supports the image of a real form of polytheism.[41]

This last verse occurs in the context of a demand that men practise *ikhlāṣ* in their worship: 'Worship God *mukhliṣan lahu 'l-dīn*; is not *al-dīn al-khāliṣ* due to God?' This concept of *ikhlāṣ* appears to mean a pure form of monotheism, free from any taint of *shirk*. In Islam the first part ('I testify that there is no god but God') of the testimony of faith, the *shahāda*, is often referred to as the *kalimat al-ikhlāṣ*, and Sūra 112 of the Koran, which is a short statement of pure monotheism, insisting that God is one, that He does not beget and is not begotten, and that He has no equal, is known as *Sūrat al-Ikhlāṣ*. In the koranic treatment of the sea journey topos, when the opponents are accused of calling upon God in their fear of the storm but of reverting to *shirk* when they reach land safely, it is clearly *ikhlāṣ* that is the opposite of *shirk*: 'When they embark on the ship they call on God *mukhliṣīna lahu 'l-dīn*, but when He brings them to land, lo they practise *shirk*' (29:65; cf. 10:22 and 31:32). This contrast between *shirk* and *ikhlāṣ* is also evident in polemic within Islam, for example in the writings of Ibn 'Abd al-Wahhāb.[42]

The opposite of the *shirk* of the opponents in the Koran, therefore, is not simply monotheism (*tawḥīd*), but the pure and intense type of monotheism indicated by *ikhlāṣ*. This strengthens the argument that their *shirk* was not literal polytheism, but a failure (in the eyes of their opponents) to maintain a full and proper form of monotheism. It is precisely this, as will be illustrated in the next chapter, that has usually been meant when monotheists have accused one another of idolatry.

It is not possible to reconstruct the religion of the opponents from the

[40] Cf. the parallel passage at Koran 16:35. Where 6:148 has 'we would not have committed *shirk*', 16:35 has 'we would not have worshipped anything apart from Him' (*mā 'abadnā min dūnihi min shay'in*). Unsurprisingly, Ṭabarī's commentary on both passages identifies 'those who have committed *shirk*' (*alladhīna ashrakū*) as idolaters – 'those *mushrikūn* of Quraysh who put the idols on a level with God' (*al-'ādilūna bi'llāh al-awthān wa'l-aṣnām*), 'those who made associates with God and worshipped idols apart from Him' (*alladhīna ashrakū bi'llāh wa-'abadū al-awthān wa'l-aṣnām min dūnihi*), etc.

[41] Koran 39:3 is quoted also by Abu'l-Ma'ālī as evidence that some of the Arab idolaters, like the Persian fire worshippers and other non-monotheists, were familiar with the one God whom the Arabs called Allāh (*Kitāb bayān al-adyān*, 136 (text) = 22–3 (trans.)).

[42] See H. Laoust, *Essai sur les doctrines sociales et politiques de Taḳī-d-Dīn Aḥmad b. Taimīya*, Cairo 1939, 531.

koranic attacks upon it, but it may be asked how far the Koran is consistent with the traditional material which portrays these opponents as Arab idol worshippers and polytheists in a crude and literal sense. From the perspective of the Koran the *mushrikūn* may, on account of their beliefs and practices, have seemed no better than polytheists and idolaters, but that does not mean that they themselves would have admitted to a belief in a plurality of gods or to the worship of idols. The gist of the koranic criticism is that although the opponents know that God is the creator and regulator of the universe, and although they appeal to Him in times of distress, regularly they fall back into something that it views as less than total monotheism. They 'associate' other beings, sometimes identified as angels or *jinn*, with God, they expect these beings to intercede for them with God, and they adopt them as patrons (*awliyāʾ*). Even the appearance at Koran 53:18–19 of the three names that tradition identifies as those of goddesses does not support the conclusion that the opponents were gross polytheists and idolaters if they are read in context.

In the previous chapter it was argued that the tradition's elaboration of the koranic material in its description of the polytheist and idolatrous Arab contemporaries of Muḥammad, together with the influence of the idea that Abraham had introduced monotheism into Arabia, has led many modern scholars, taking the traditional material as a reflexion of historical fact, to develop theories about the persistence or rise of monotheistic ideas among the pagan Arabs before Islam. Unlike the Koran, which merely provides obscure hints about and allusions to the *shirk* it attacks, much of the traditional literature is quite explicit in its portrayal of the Arab paganism. It is mainly owing to that explicitness and detail that the traditional account of the historical and social setting to which the Koran was addressed has been so widely accepted by non-Muslim scholars.

Nevertheless, the tension between, on the one hand, the religious ideas of the opponents as they are alluded to in the koranic verses and, on the other, the image of Arab paganism found in Muslim tradition is sometimes obvious even in traditional texts. Muslim scholars such as Masʿūdī (d. 345/956) and Shahrastānī (d. 548/1153) attempted to provide general accounts of the religious ideas of, among other peoples, the pre-Islamic Arabs. These accounts set out the traditional material about the pre-Islamic idolatry of the Arab contemporaries of Muḥammad together with categories constructed on the basis of individual koranic verses, and it is then that the tension between them become noticeable. For instance Masʿūdī describes, among others, a group of pre-Islamic Arabs who accepted the Creator and the fact of the creation, a resurrection and a future life, but denied the prophets and were attached to idols (*aṣnām*); they made pilgrimage to the idols, performed sacrifices to them, and accepted rules about things licit and things prohibited. These are those who say, according to Koran 39:3, that they have taken patrons other than God merely that those patrons may bring them closer to God (*wa'lladhīna 'ttakhadhū min dūnihi awliyāʾa mā naʿbuduhum illā li-yuqarribūnā ilā 'llāhi zulfā*).

Another group is described as worshipping angels, claiming that they are the daughters of God, and believing that they had the power to intercede with God for their followers. These are the ones referred to in Koran 16:57 ('they assign daughters to Allāh . . . and what they desire to themselves') and 53:19 ff. (the verses that refer to Allāt, al-ʿUzzā and Manāt imply that the opponents regarded them as female offspring of God, and insist that God only allows the power of intercession to those whom He wishes).[43]

Another of the hybrids that evolved from the attempt to cross the koranic material with the image of Arab paganism was the idea that wealthy Arabs had their camels slaughtered above their tombs so that they could ride them on the day of resurrection and thus obtain an advantage over those who had been revived only as pedestrians.[44]

Probably the clearest understanding from within Islam that the koranic attacks on the *mushrikūn* and *kuffār* were directed at people who regarded themselves as monotheists is manifested in the writings of Ibn ʿAbd al-Wahhāb (d.1206/1792). In a commentary upon the first part of the *shahāda* ('there is no god but God'), the founder of the Wahhābī school argued that the *kuffār* against whom the Prophet fought were monotheists but imperfect ones. Their monotheism was only *tawḥīd al-rubūbiyya* whereas proper monotheism consists of *tawḥīd al-ulūhiyya. Tawḥīd al-rubūbiyya* he defines as accepting that God is the sole creator, giver of life and sustenance. But that is not enough. In spite of their acceptance of it, and in spite of their relatively good lives – worshipping God, doing good works and observing some of the prohibited things – the Prophet still fought against those who espoused it and refused to accept them in Islam. The essence of their *kufr* was that they recognised (through prayers, sacrifices, vows and other things) intermediaries between themselves and God:

The *mushrikūn* against whom the Prophet fought used to call upon righteous beings (*ṣāliḥūn*) such as the angels, Jesus, Ezra,[45] and other patrons (*min al-awliyāʾ*). Thus they were *kuffār* in spite of their affirmation that God is the creator, the sustainer, and the director (of the cosmos). When you have understood this you have understood the

[43] Abu 'l-Ḥasan al-Masʿūdī, *Murūj al-dhahab*, ed. and French trans. Barbier de Meynard and Pavet de Courteille, 9 vols. Paris 1861–77, III, 256–7 (rev. ed. C. Pellat, 3 vols., Beirut 1966, II, 253); cf. Abu 'l-Fatḥ Muḥammad b. ʿAbd al-Karīm al-Shahrastānī, *Kitāb al-milal wa'l-niḥal*, ed. Kaylānī, 2 vols., Cairo 1961, II, 236 where groups among the Arabs are described in almost the same terms although somewhat more fully. A similar account in Abu'l-Maʿālī, *Kitāb bayān al-adyān*, 139 (text) = 28 (trans.) names Abū ʿĪsā al-Warrāq as its source. For discussion of the latter's life and works (he seems to have lived in the third/ninth century, but is difficult to date more precisely, and is credited with a *Kitāb al-maqālāt* which discussed religions and sects): see David Thomas (ed. and trans.), *Anti-Christian Polemic in Early Islam*, Cambridge 1992, 9–30.

[44] Shahrastānī, *Milal*, II, 244; Saʿīd b. Aḥmad al-Andalusī, *Kitāb Ṭabaqāt al-umam* (cited in Schefer, 'Notice sur le Kitab Beïan il Edian', 149), French trans. by R. Blachère, Paris 1935, 93 (the name of the man whose verses are cited ordering his son to slaughter his camel when he dies, appears in variant forms).

[45] A reference to Koran 9:30 – 'The Jews say that Ezra ('Uzayr) is the son of God and the Christians that Christ (al-Masīḥ) is the son of God.'

meaning of 'there is no god but God', and you have understood that whoever calls upon a prophet or an angel, grants him authority or asks him for help, such a one has gone away from Islam.

In the course of his argument Ibn ʿAbd al-Wahhāb refers to many of the koranic passages mentioned in this chapter, and he considers the defences made by the *mushrikūn* to justify their beliefs and behaviour. Of course, he is less concerned with the historical situation in which the Prophet lived than with the conditions of his own time, but even though his audience was those Muslims whose ideas and practices he wished to reform he was able to apply the koranic material to his own day without any sense of strain. Referring to his fellow Muslims, he talks of the *ahl al-shirk* 'of our own time' and attributes to them the same belief in intermediary beings (*wasāʾiṭ*) as was held by the *mushrikūn* of the time of the Prophet. He also insists that Christians were people of *kufr*:

You know that the Christians hold a special place among the *kuffār*. Some of them worship God night and day, live ascetic lives, and give charitably of what comes to them from the world, withdrawing from other people into their cells. In spite of that they are *kuffār* and enemies of God, bound for Hell on account of their belief in Jesus or some other of the *awliyāʾ*, calling upon him or making sacrifice to him, or offering him vows.[46]

Modern non-Muslim scholars also have sometimes demonstrated an awareness of the fact that the Koran's image of its opponents is not really consistent with the depiction of the idolatry of the Arabs found in tradition, but, accepting the traditional accounts of the origins of Islam in Mecca and Medina and of the Koran as addressing the idolatry of the Arabs of the Ḥijāz, they have rarely gone beyond conflation of the different sources.

Thus D. B. Macdonald, in his article s.v. 'Allāh' in the first edition of the *Encyclopaedia of Islam*, wrote: 'The religion of Mecca in Muḥammad's time was far from simple idolatry. It resembled much more a form of the Christian faith, in which saints and angels have come to stand between the worshippers and God.'

He then cited a series of koranic verses which he felt justified that statement. It seems clear that Macdonald, like the Muslim scholars just mentioned, derived from the Koran an image of the opponents' *shirk* that is not easily reconcilable with the portrayals of Arab idolatry in the traditional literature. But the interpretative framework supplied by the tradition had become so firmly established that he was content to identify this religion attacked in the Koran, a type of religion that Macdonald instinctively understood because of his comprehension of the import of the charge of 'idolatry' inside the Christian tradition, with 'the religion of Mecca in Muḥammad's time'.[47]

[46] Muḥammad b. ʿAbd al-Wahhāb, *Fī tafsīr kalimat al-tawḥīd*, in his *Majmūʿat al-tawḥīd al-najdiyya*, 105–9. I am grateful to Michael Cook for referring me to the *Majmūʿa*.

[47] Macdonald's own Protestant form of Christianity no doubt made him especially alive to an association between the idea of idolatry and the 'worship' of intermediate beings.

Brockelmann, too, regarded the references to intercession and intermediate beings in the Koran as redolent of Christianity, and he sensed a conflict between such ideas and his identification of a native Arabian monotheism, traces of which he believed still existed among the idolaters of Arabia in the time of the Prophet. He felt it necessary, therefore, to argue against Macdonald's conclusion, charging the latter with misinterpreting the evidence of the Koran.[48]

W. M. Watt has also sensed that what the Koran tells us about *shirk* and the *mushrikūn* does not lead to the conclusion that the opponents were simple polytheists and idolaters. His espousal of the high god thesis, mentioned in the previous chapter, was based almost entirely on koranic verses like those referred to above. Nevertheless, unlike Brockelmann, Watt did not feel that there is any conflict between the high god theory and the notion that the pre-Islamic Arabs believed in the intercession of intermediate beings. He suggested that passages of the Koran that deny that God has offspring should be understood (as tradition does) as attacks on the pagan Meccans' view that some of their deities were daughters of God 'unless there is a clear mention of Jesus' (when they should be taken to be an attack on Christian ideas).[49]

Alford Welch, a former student of Watt, also displays awareness of the potential dissonance between the koranic material and the traditional image of the idolatry and polytheism of the Arabs of the Prophet's time, but seeks to establish some harmony, partly by allowing for tendentious misrepresentation in the Koran of the beliefs of the Meccan opponents, but mainly by attempting to trace a development over time of the critique of the pagan religion by the Prophet and of the response to that critique by the pagan Meccans. Welch shows himself sensitive to the complexities involved in any attempt to arrange the koranic materials in a chronological sequence and frequently takes issue with the conclusions reached by both traditional and modern scholars who have tried to do so. Nevertheless, it may be felt that his own attempt, as well as being necessarily subjective, relies too much on the traditional accounts of the Prophet's life and the framework for the revelation of the Koran that it provides. The fact that a monotheist may talk of the 'gods' of his opponents does not mean that he (or they) in fact regards them as gods. Nor does the fact that he may at one time accept their existence (but not as gods) and at another say that they are merely names imply a development in understanding over time. Different responses may reflect different situations and requirements rather than a simple progression of thought.[50]

Another scholar who shows appreciation of the disparity between the koranic material and the traditional depiction of the enemies of the Prophet

[48] C. Brockelmann, 'Allāh und die Götzen', 102–3; for a summary and discussion of Brockelmann's theories, see above, pp. 30–1.

[49] W. M. Watt, *Muhammad at Medina*, Oxford 1956, 318. See also his 'Qur'ān and Belief in a 'High God', where Watt sees the belief in intercessory powers as a sign of the 'somewhat decadent' religious outlook of the Meccans, as well as his other presentations on the same theme referred to on p. 23 note 8 above.

[50] Welch, 'Allah and Other Supernatural Beings'.

as crude idolaters and polytheists is Jacques Waardenburg, who characterised the *shirk* imputed to the opponents in the Koran as 'the association of non-divine beings with God, *or equally the attribution of a divine quality to a being other than God*'. This *shirk* may be committed either explicitly by worshipping idols '*or by recognizing other independent representations of the sacred*'.[51]

Naturally, it is not impossible that a religion resembling Christianity was espoused by the people of Mecca at the beginning of the seventh century, but the tradition does not tell us so – it rather refers to the Meccans' 'idolatry' (*ʿibādat al-aṣnām*). Furthermore, it tells us that this idolatry was shared too by the Arabs outside Mecca; it does not distinguish between the type of idolatry followed by the Meccans and that followed elsewhere in the *jāhiliyya*, except to associate particular idols and gods with particular groups.

In addition, once one leaves the Koran and immerses oneself in the tradition the resemblances between the Arabs' idolatry and 'a form of the Christian faith' rather recede from view: except in reports relating to Koran verses, crude idol worship replaces acceptance of the power of angels to intercede with God or the view that the angels are God's offspring. To accept that the *shirk* attacked in the Koran was the religion of the people of Mecca in Muḥammad's time is to accept the framework provided by the tradition and to persist in trying to reconcile material (the Koran's attack on *shirk* and the descriptions of Arab idolatry in the tradition) which may be better understood if it is not simply conflated. To the extent that anything outside the Koran can help us understand the koranic attack on *shirk*, it is likely to be other monotheist polemic against groups perceived as falling short in their monotheism, rather than the 'historical' recreation of Arabian idolatry in Muslim tradition.

[51] Waardenburg, 'Un débat coranique', 146 (my emphases).

CHAPTER 3

Shirk and idolatry in monotheist polemic

We have seen that the attacks made in the Koran against those opponents who are accused there of practising *shirk* do not sit easily with their portrayal in Muslim tradition as adherents of crude polytheism and idolatry. Although the Koran often imputes idolatry and polytheism to the *mushrikūn*, it does not do so consistently and, from the limited indications the Koran provides about their beliefs and practices, we are hardly entitled to conclude that they were polytheists or idolaters in any sense that would be accepted outside the sphere of polemic between people regarding themselves as monotheists.

It will now be shown how the accusation of *shirk* in Islam echoes that of idolatry in forms of monotheism that use vocabulary derived from the Greek *eidōlolatreia*. Just as idolatry is frequently a charge made against individuals or groups who, by their own lights, are committed monotheists, so too in Islam the accusation of *shirk* is a term often used in polemic directed against people who would describe themselves as fully monotheistic and, frequently, as Muslims.

Since that is so, why has it been generally accepted that the *mushrikūn* of the Koran were polytheists and idolaters in a literal sense? The answer to that question is, of course, 'because Muslim tradition tells us that they were'. In chapters 4, 5 and 6 we will consider how far that tradition is convincing in what it tells us about the polytheism and idolatry of the Arabs of the *jāhiliyya* who, it says, were the object of the Koran's attack on the *mushrikūn*. If it is found not to be persuasive, then we might conclude either that the *jāhilī* Arabs were in fact monotheists whom the Koran was attacking polemically, or – and this is the alternative favoured here – that we need to rethink more drastically our ideas about when and where Islam emerged. As suggested in the introduction, the image of the *jāhiliyya*, including its geographical components, could be seen as part of early Islam's elaboration of a version of its origins that centred on the career of Muḥammad in the mainly pagan environment of the Ḥijāz.

As with 'idolatry' in Christian usage, the charge of *shirk* has been aimed by Muslims at opponents both within and outside the tradition of monotheism. In addition to groups who might with some objectivity be described as polytheistic and whose religious rituals involved some physical embodiment or representation of their deities, Muslims have frequently portrayed as *mushrikūn* those who regarded themselves as monotheists and even as Muslims. On different occasions, the charge of *shirk* has been levelled by Muslims, whether explicitly or implicity, against Christians, Jews, and other Muslims, as well as, for example, Hindus and adherents of traditional African religions.

Although etymologically *shirk* (literally, 'associationism') is not the same as idolatry or polytheism, it has not only been used in contexts similar to those where those two words of Greek derivation have been employed but has often in fact been assimilated to the idea of idolatry (literally, *ʿibādat al-aṣnām/al-awthān*).

The tendency to associate *shirk* with idolatry and polytheism is evident in the Koran itself. In the scripture, although, as has been argued, distinctive monotheistic features of the *shirk* of the opponents can be recognised in many passages, the adherents of *shirk*, the *mushrikūn*, are accused of recognising gods other than God and of worshipping beings designated by terms such as *jibt* and *ṭāghūt*, terms redolent of idols and idolatry in the language of some monotheist groups.

Outside the Koran – in the *tafsīr*, *sīra* and other types of traditional literature – the tendency to associate *shirk* with polytheism and idolatry becomes actual conflation. The koranic *mushrikūn* are consistently identified as the idolatrous and polytheistic Arab contemporaries of the Prophet, reports such as that concerning the idol of Khawlān[1] portray *shirk* as more or less crude idolatry, and the literature collects and preserves a relatively large amount of detail about the names, sites, family and tribal associations of the gods, idols and sanctuaries of the Arabs of the *jāhiliyya*.

The literature that assembles such details, the best-known example of which is the 'Book of Idols' (*Kitāb al-Aṣnām*) attributed to Hishām Ibn al-Kalbī (d. 206/821), will be discussed in some detail in later chapters, but its fundamental role in establishing the identity of the *shirk* attacked in the Koran with the idolatry of the pre-Islamic Arabs may be stressed here.

One good example of the way in which *shirk*, in spite of its etymological distinctiveness, is conflated with idolatry in the traditional material, is provided by the account of the Prophet's destruction of idols around the Kaʿba at the time of the conquest of Mecca (*al-fatḥ*) which is narrated by Wāqidī (d. 207/823):

Isāf and Nāʾila were a man and a woman . . . who committed fornication inside the Kaʿba and were changed into two stones. Quraysh took them and worshipped them, and used to perform sacrifices by them and shave their heads [at the place of the two stones] when they had finished their *ḥajj* rituals.

[When the Prophet destroyed the idols of Mecca] there came out from one of these two stones a grey haired black woman who was tearing at her face with her nails, naked, pulling at her hair and crying out in her woe. Asked about that, the Prophet said, 'This

[1] See above, pp. 22–3.

is Nāʾila who has abandoned hope that she will ever be worshipped in your land again.'

And it is said that the Devil (*Iblīs*) cried out in woe on three occasions: once when he was cursed [by God] and his form was changed from that of the angels; once when he saw the Prophet standing in prayer in Mecca; and once when the Prophet conquered Mecca and the Devil said to his progeny who had gathered to him, 'Abandon all hope that the community of Muḥammad will revert to *shirk* after this day of theirs.'[2]

Shirk thus comes to be identified with actual polytheism and idolatry.

Although both *shirk* and idolatry are terms and concepts that may be used against people outside the monotheist tradition, it is not obvious – as might at first be assumed – that that is the primary usage of the Arabic word. This chapter focuses on the use of idolatry and *shirk* as terms of polemic by monotheists against individuals and groups who understood themselves to be monotheists. Given its etymological sense of 'associationism', there is perhaps less reason to think that the charge of *shirk* was originally directed against real idolaters than is the case with *eidōlolatreia* in Jewish and Christian usage.

It has, however, been argued that the Arabic root *sh-r-k* had already been used before Islam by monotheists in south Arabia to refer to polytheism. If that is true, the suggestion that it originated in intra-monotheist polemic (and that we should look outside the Arabian peninsula for the polemic with which it was associated) would be less compelling.

The main item of evidence for the use of *sh-r-k* in pre-Islamic south Arabia, with more or less the same religious significance as it has in Islam, is a Sabaean inscription in the possession of the British Museum and published by J. H. Mordtmann and D. H. Müller in 1896. In it they read the consonants *sh-r-k* which they linked with the idea of *shirk* in the Koran and Muslim tradition and interpreted as 'attributing an associate (Beigesellung) to God, i.e., polytheism'.[3] Mordtmann suggested that Muḥammad acquired the word and the concept from south Arabia, a suggestion repeated by Ditlef Nielsen in 1927.[4]

[2] Wāqidī, *Maghāzī*, 841–2 (=Azraqī, *Akhbār Makka*, I, 122–3).

[3] I am grateful to Ms Jasna Sutara for drawing my attention to P. K. Hitti, *History of the Arabs*, 7th edn. London 1961, 105, note 5, which refers to J. H. Mordtmann and D. H. Müller, 'Eine monotheistische sabäische Inschrift', *VOJ*, 10 (1896), 265–92. There *sh-r-k* is read at p. 287 (line 3 of the inscription) and commented on at p. 290. The relevant phrase (= *CIS*, IV, no. 539) is translated 'und halte fern Beigesellung an einen Herrn, der Unheil hervorbringt und Heil stiftet'. The reading has subsequently been repeated by D. Nielsen (ed.), *Handbuch der altarabischen Altertumskunde, I. Die arabische Kultur*, Copenhagen 1927, 250, note 4, and by C. Conti Rossini, *Chrestomathia Arabica Meridionalis Epigraphica*, Rome 1931, 71, no. 61. See also C. Rabin, 'On the Probability of South Arabian Influence on the Arabic Vocabulary', *JSAI*, 4 (1984), 127, citing Jeffrey, *Foreign Vocabulary*, 186.

[4] For Nielsen, see note 3. I do not know whether it is significant that Jacques Ryckmans, a leading proponent of the idea of south Arabian influence on the development of Islam, does not refer to the inscription published by Mordtmann and Müller in an article that highlights points of contact between Islamic terms, ideas and practices and those attested in the south Arabian inscriptions (Jacques Ryckmans, 'Les inscriptions anciennes de l'Arabie du sud: points de vue et problèmes actuels', *Conférence prononcée à la societé 'Oosters Genootschap in Nederland', Le 15 mars 1973*, Leiden 1973, 79–110).

There seem to be at least two other south Arabian inscriptions (*RES*, 3318 and 3951) known in which a noun and a verbal form associated with the root *sh-r-k* occur, but in a secular context: in *RES*, 3318, line 5, we have the expression *w-sh-r-k m-l-k-w*, for which the editor, Gonzagues Ryckmans, suggested 'les associés, compagnons du roi'.[5]

It is sensible, in view of the sparse evidence and the difficulties of establishing secure readings and interpretations, to remain hesitant especially about the single example of the use of the root in a religious sense. However, it is certainly conceivable that the root *sh-r-k* was used in south, and in central and northern, Arabia before Islam with the basic sense of 'to associate with' or 'to be a companion of'. When, where and why that root should then have come to be used for the idea of 'associationism' in a religious polemic is perhaps still an open question, depending on the certainty of the reading of the text published by Mordtmann and Müller.[6]

If one turns to poetry attributed to pre-Islamic and early Islamic poets there is no sign that formations from the root *sh-r-k* were used before Islam with the religious sense that they have in the Koran and Islamic literature. In the instances of verses deploying the root in the card catalogue of the Hebrew University of Jerusalem Concordance of Early Arab Poetry, the examples using it in a religious sense all seem to be attributed to poets associated with the Prophet's time or later, while it only occurs in verses attributed to *jāhilī* poets in its 'secular' sense. An example of the latter, which of course continue into Islamic times, is attributed to the Prophet's uncle Abū Ṭālib in verses in which he criticises two ancestors of a rival Qurashī family, ʿAbd Shams and Nawfal:

> They gave a share in (*ashrakā fī*) their nobility to those without ancestry. . . .[7]

In the poetry attributed to supporters and contemporaries of the Prophet there are several instances where the root is used in connexion with the enemies of the Prophet although they rarely allow us to understand what it might signify other than a contrast with Islam and Muslims. For example, Ḥassān b. Thābit refers to God giving the followers of the Prophet victory over the *mushrikūn* at the battle of Badr, Qays b. al-Musaḥḥar makes a contrast between the (Muslim) *muhājira* and the enemy *mushrikūn* in connexion with the expedition to Mu'ta, and the Sulamī ʿAbbās b. Mirdās refers to the treading down of the *mushrikūn* by the forces of the Prophet at the battle of Ḥunayn.[8] The poet Aʿshā Maymūn, who is said to have intended going to Medina to accept Islam

[5] Jacqueline Pirenne (ed.), *RÉS*, VIII, Paris 1968, index des mots, s.v. '*sh-r-k*'.

[6] In conversation Dr Arthur Irvine remarked to me that he thought there had been questions about the reading of the text.

[7] Ibn Hishām, *Sīra*, I, 268. I am grateful to Amikam Elad for supplying me with the material regarding *sh-r-k* from the Hebrew University Concordance, the publication of which, he says, is scheduled to begin soon.

[8] Ibn Hishām, *Sīra*, I, 640, II, 383, 465.

at the hands of the Prophet but died before he could do so, is credited with accompanying a reference to God with the phrase *lā sharīka li-wajhihi*.[9] There seems no way of assessing the authenticity of such material.

In the poetry of the succeeding period there are references to *shirk* and the *mushrikūn* which are equally uninformative as to the content of *shirk* or the identity of the *mushrikūn*. Farazdaq in a eulogy of the Umayyad caliph Hishām says that those who were *mushrik* brought him taxes while those who were *muslim* were pleased with him. Ruʾba b. al-ʿAjjāj, similarly eulogising Khālid al-Qasrī, the governor of Iraq on behalf of the Umayyads, talks of his reviving the province, 'its godfearing people and its obdurate *mushrikūn*' (*taqiyyahum wa'l-mushrik al-muʿānid*).[10]

We also find, however, examples of verses that make the accusation of *shirk* against groups that, in the tradition, are treated as Muslim even though, from hostile or later perspectives, they were tainted with unorthodoxy. In 66–7/685–7 the Arab garrison town of Kufa in Iraq was controlled by Mukhtār al-Thaqafī, who is portrayed in tradition as a fount of extremism and heresy. He was supported by many non-Arabs as well as Arabs and his fighting men were referred to as his *shurṭa*, a term usually referring to the militia or police force of the governor. They sometimes called themselves the *shurṭa* of God. Some of them, it is reported, carried with them into battle a chair which they are said to have venerated in the way in which the children of Israel had venerated the Ark of the Covenant. It is in connexion with this that Ṭabarī reports verses of the poet Aʿshā Hamdān which begin:

> I testify against you that you are Sabaʾiyya,
> and I know what you are about, O *shurṭat al-shirk*.
> I swear that your chair is not a divine presence (*sakīna*),
> even if it is wrapped around with cloths,
> And that it is it not like the Ark among us,
> even though Shibām, Nahd and Khārif go around it.[11]

In 117/735 Naṣr b. Sayyār, shortly to be appointed governor of Khurāsān on behalf of the Umayyad caliphs, is said to have imputed *shirk* to the rebel Ḥārith b. Surayj and his followers in verses, apparently because of Ḥārith's reputation as an adherent of the Murjiʾite theology:

[9] Maymūn b. Qays al-Aʿshā,*Gedichte von 'Abû Basîr Maimûn ibn Qais al-'Aʿšâ*, ed. Rudolf Geyer, London 1928, no. 66, line 10.

[10] Farazdaq, *Divan de Férazdak*, ed. and trans. R. Boucher, Paris 1876, 32, line 16 (text) = 75, line 4 (trans.); Ruʾba b. al-ʿAjjāj, trans. W. Ahlwardt *Sammlungen alter arabischer Dichter. III Der Dīwān des Reğezdichters Rūba Ben El'ağğāğ*, Berlin 1903, 47, *Dīwān . . . El'ağğāğ. Aus dem Arabischen . . . übersetzt*, trans. W. Ahlwardt, Berlin 1904, 72, line 1.

[11] Ṭabarī, *Ta'rīkh*, ed. M. J. de Goeje et al., 15 vols., Leiden 1879–1901, II, 704–5. 'Saba'iyya' is a pejorative appellation traditionally applied to those holding extremist views in veneration of ʿAlī and his descendants; *sakīna*, a development of the *shekhina* of Judaism, is used and understood in a variety of ways in Islam; Shibām, Nahd and Khārif are clans of the Hamdān tribal group.

> Your [espousal of the doctrine of] *irjāʾ*
> has tied you and *shirk* together in a yoke;
> you are people of *ishrāk* . . .
> for your religion is yoked with *shirk*.[12]

The evidence of early poetry, therefore, does not appear to be incompatible with the idea that the concept of *shirk* originated in polemic between monotheists in early Islamic times. The authenticity of the verses attributed to supporters and contemporaries of the Prophet is not easily ascertainable.

If one now considers the concept rather than the Arabic root, there are at least two possible non-Arabic and pre-Islamic precursors for the concept of *shirk* in Islam.

One was suggested in 1907 by James Montgomery in his discussion of the Samaritan credal formula 'There is no god but the One'. Montgomery suggested that that formula developed polemically against the Christian doctrine of the Trinity and he supported his argument by reference to a Samaritan hymn, published by Gesenius in 1824: 'O Being of Unity, who hast no fellow, no second, nor colleague.' 'The last term, *shateph*, corresponds to the Arabic *sharik*, which with its collateral forms is frequently used in the Koran in the prohibition against 'associating' anything with God.' Montgomery noted that some later Samaritan literature written in Arabic uses *sharīk* for the Hebrew word.[13]

As Montgomery indicated too, the same root is sometimes used in talmudic literature in the same way. For example, in the Babylonian Talmud tractate Sanhedrin: Adam was created on the eve of the Sabbath lest the minim ('sectarians'; some versions have Sadducees) say that God had a partner (*shūtāf*) in the work of creation.[14]

Another Semitic root that may be linked to the Islamic concept of *shirk* is *ḥ-b-r* which often occurs in contexts indicating companionship or association. In pre-Islamic Judaism the word *ḥāvēr* (plural: *ḥavērīm*; 'member', 'associate') came to be used to refer to individuals who formed groups stringent in their observance of the law, especially that pertaining to tithing and heave-offerings and regulations regarding purity and impurity, in contrast to the common people (*ʿammē hā-ereṣ*).[15]

Although there is much obscurity about the origins and development of the class of *ḥavērīm*, it seems that by early Islamic times *ḥāvēr* had often become a title simply designating a sage or a scholar, although it may in some contexts

[12] Ṭabarī, *Taʾrīkh*, II, 1576. Murjiʾism refers to an inclusivist, catholic view on the question of whether sin can change a Muslim into a *kāfir*.

[13] Montgomery, *Samaritans*, 208; cited in R. Macuch, 'Zur Vorgeschichte der Bekenntnisformel *lā ilāha illā llāhu*', *ZDMG*, 128 (1978), 20.

[14] Sanhedrin, fo. 38 a (Eng. tr. 1935, 240); Levy, *Wörterbuch* s.v. '*shūtāf*'. The insistence on the eve of the Sabbath for Adam's creation is another way of saying that he was the last thing God created. The editor of the Soncino translation suggests that 'Sadducees' was a late substitution for '*minīm*'. A connexion between Talmudic *sh-t-f* and Arabic *sharīk* was suggested to me independently by Uri Rubin.

[15] See *EJ* s.v. 'Ḥaver', 'Ḥaverim'; Urbach, *Sages*, 583 ff.

have continued to have a more precise or technical meaning. In the Koran the plural form *aḥbār* (singular: *ḥabr*) is used to refer, apparently, to a learned or clerical group among the Jews. Translations sometimes substitute 'rabbis', although on two occasions *aḥbār* appears in tandem with *rabbāniyyūn.*[16] In tradition an early Muslim convert from Judaism is known as Kaʿb al-Aḥbār, the name usually understood as indicating that Kaʿb was 'one of the *aḥbār*'.

The root *ḥ-b-r* also occurs with the same connotations of 'association' and 'companionship' in inscriptions and documents, not always in monotheist contexts and not necessarily with a religious significance, from before Islam. On Hasmonaean coins there is often a reference to the *ḥever ha-yehūdīm* (community? council? of the Jews), frequently in conjunction with the High Priest. The full significance of the expression is disputed.[17] In an extant papyrus letter the leader of the second Jewish revolt against the Romans, Bar Kokhba, wrote to Yeshuʿa ben Gilgola 'and the men of your company (*wʾnsy ḥbrk*)'. J.-T. Milik, the editor, commented that we must read here *ḥeber* in the sense of 'company, association, or party', and saw it as a reference to the general staff of Yeshuʿa ben Gilgola, i.e., those officers jointly responsible for the decisions made by the chief.[18]

More immediately relevant here are cases where the 'association' has a religious connotation. This may be the case in the Mishnah tract Berakoth, 4:7, where *ḥever ʿīr* is usually understood to refer to the congregation or religious quorum (*minyan*) of a town. Interestingly, a similar usage appears in some of the inscriptions from the non-monotheist sites of Hatra, Palmyra and Oboda (in the Nabataean area). At those and other places, inscriptions have been read referring to 'associations' or 'fraternities', sometimes apparently religious in character. For instance, evidence from Oboda has been understood as pointing to the existence of a 'brotherhood' of Dusares, while at Hatra there seem to have been associations devoted to Semeia. At Palmyra and usually among the Nabataeans the term used is *mrzḥ(ʾ)*, while at Hatra it is formations from *ḥ-b-r*. Teixidor and Milik have drawn attention to this phenomenon: Milik refers in French to the companions as 'thiasites' and the associations as 'thiases', and he links them with Greek inscriptions from Dura Europos which refer to *hetairoi* and the *arkhetairos* (the leader of the association, the equivalent of the *rb mrzḥ*ʾ of Nabataean inscriptions).[19]

One should not theorise too much on the basis of such evidence but it at least gives some idea of the range of connotations of words indicating 'associate' or 'companion' in the Middle East before Islam, prominent among them formations from *ḥ-b-r*. What makes it possible that *sh-r-k* in Arabic continues

[16] Koran 5:44, 63 (both *al-rabbāniyyūn wa'l-aḥbār*), 9:31, 34 (both referring to the *aḥbār* of the Jews and the 'monks' (*ruhbān*) of the Christians). [17] See *EJ* s.v. 'Hever ha-Yehudim'.

[18] J.-T. Milik, 'Un lettre de Siméon Bar Kokheba', *RB*, 60 (1953), 276–94, esp. 283 where Milik provides other and earlier examples of the use of the root.

[19] J. Teixidor, 'Aramaic Inscriptions of Hatra', *Sumer*, 20 (1964), 77–80; Teixidor, *Pagan God,* 6, note 8; J.-T. Milik, *Dédicaces faites par des dieux*, Paris 1972, 392. For the use of *hetairiastas* by John of Damascus to render, apparently, Arabic *mushrikūn*, see below, p. 83–4.

and develops such connotations and vocabulary is the fact that the Koran does not limit its attack on the *mushrikūn* to their idea that heavenly mediators might intercede with God for them or share in His power. There is also criticism of the greed of those whom the *mushrikīn* made equal to, or gave preference over, God. That surely is the gist of 6:136 ff. which charges that the agricultural product and livestock that the people divide between God and the *shurakā'* all go to the latter. Furthermore, it is these *shurakā'* who have induced them to 'kill their children' and presumably they who falsely divide animals into those allowed and those prohibited, those allowed to themselves but forbidden to their wives, etc. But if the animals are carrion (*mayta*) they *all* become *shurakā'* (sharers) in it (*hum fīhi shurakā'*).[20]

It is possible, therefore, that the koranic polemic against *shirk* is a development of the ideas and vocabulary already existing before Islam. Even though *ḥ-b-r* occurs in some non-monotheist contexts, the bulk of the evidence regarding that root, and for *sh-t-p*, comes from within monotheist groups. *Sh-t-p* seems the more obvious parallel to *sh-r-k* but *ḥ-b-r* could also be an ingredient in the development of the Muslim idea of *sh-r-k*.

When used among monotheists the force of the accusation of idolatry is often that the opponents are no better than idolaters, that their beliefs or practices are inconsistent with monotheism as it ought to be understood and that the opponents, therefore, have made themselves equivalent to idolaters. In polemical language phrases such as 'no better than' or 'equivalent to' tend to be omitted.

Since the word idolatry itself is borrowed from Greek and used in other European languages, the most obvious examples occur in the history of Christianity. The Protestant accusations against Catholics of idolatry at the time of the Reformation in Europe and the Iconoclasts' use of the same term (*eidōlolatreia*) against the Iconodules in eighth-century Byzantium are the best known. The letter of Elizabeth I of England to the Ottoman sultan Murād III in which she refers to Philip II of Spain as the chief idolater shows the common cultural value of the concept. It would be interesting to know how it was translated into Turkish.[21]

In the Jewish tradition various expressions have been used which, like *shirk* in Islam, although they are not semantically equivalent to idolatry, may be said to carry the same weight. The title of the Mishnah tractate, ʿAvōdāh Zārāh, usually translated 'Idolatry', means literally 'Strange Worship', alluding to a number of biblical passages containing the word *zār* in contexts indi-

[20] The Jews and Christians too are accused of venerating their human religious authorities who are greedy and corrupt. Koran 9:31 tells us that the Jews and the Christians have taken their *aḥbār* and their monks as 'lords' (*arbāb*) before God, 9:34 that many of the *aḥbār* and the monks consume the wealth of the people.

[21] Norman Daniel, *Islam, Europe and Empire*, Edinburgh 1966, 12 (citing *Calendar of State Papers*, Foreign Series, vol. XXI, part 1, p. 508 – 9/2/1588).

cating strange forms of worship or strange gods (Leviticus 10:1, Deuteronomy 32:16, Isaiah 43:12, etc.).The tractate mainly concerns various problems arising from the contacts between Jews and adherents of Graeco-Roman religion in Palestine in the early Christian period.[22]

If that Mishnah tractate is concerned with people who, from the Jewish point of view, could be understood as idolaters in a real sense, the Karaite application of the Hebrew word *gillūlīm* to their Rabbinical opponents is an example of the discourse of idolatry used within Judaism. *Gillūlīm* literally means pieces of filth or dung and its use by the Karaites reflects the use of the same word to refer to idols in the book of Ezekiel (6:4 and throughout).[23]

However, the charge of idolatry within Christianity and Judaism was not confined to labelling one's opponents as idolaters in an abstract manner: it also involved accusing one's opponents of performing rituals or of holding beliefs that are transparently idolatrous. The rabbis charged the Samaritans with worshipping a dove in their sanctuary on Mount Gerizim,[24] while Catholics claimed that the Protestants of Zurich venerated the remains of the dead Zwingli in an idolatrous manner.[25]

The notion of idolatry was extended also to cover various forms of behaviour or belief that were disapproved of, while idolatry itself, especially in the Bible and Jewish tradition, may be referred to by metaphors relating to sexual immorality and marital infidelity (e.g., 'whoring after the gods [of the people of the land]' in Exodus 34:15–16) . Pride, anger and the love of money have been described as forms of idolatry, and in the Muslim tradition the sphere of *shirk* has been extended in a similar way.[26]

Maimonides applied the charge of idolatry to the anthropomorphic views of the common people which, he said, threatened true monotheism by endangering the concept of God as a perfect unity; Judah Halevi attached it to incorrect forms of worship; and Nachmanides to the worship of real forces which were not, however, deserving of worship.[27] Yeshayahu Leibowitz, who

[22] Halbertal and Margalit, *Idolatry*, 3–4; G. Stemberger, *Introduction to the Talmud and Midrash*, Eng. transl., 2nd edn, Edinburgh 1996, 115 (originally *Einleitung in Talmud und Midrasch*, Munich 1992).

[23] N. Wieder, *The Judaean Scrolls and Karaism*, London 1962, 151–3.

[24] H. J. Schoeps, *Theologie und Geschichte des Judenchristentums*, Tübingen 1949, 392; J. Fossum, 'Samaritan Demiurgical Traditions and the Alleged Dove Cult of the Samaritans', in R. van den Broek and M. J. Vermaseren (eds.), *Studies in Gnosticism and Hellenistic Religions*, Leiden 1981, 143–60.

[25] Eire, *War against the Idols*, 86. The accusation was a polemical development of the idea that Zwingli's heart had not been destroyed, that 'his soul goes marching on'.

[26] For pride and anger as idolatry see, e.g., Solomon Schechter, *Aspects of Rabbinic Theology* (1909), repr. New York 1961, 223–4; for pride as *shirk*, I. Goldziher, *Introduction to Islamic Theology and Law*, (1910), repr. Princeton 1981, 42. (Goldziher notes the identification made by some Muslim scholars of a 'lesser *shirk*' or a 'hidden *shirk*' [*al-shirk al-aṣghar, shirk khafī*], in Sufism the opposite of *tawakkul*.) For love of money as idolatry, see Matt. 6:24, and Karl Marx cited by Halbertal and Margalit, *Idolatry*, 243. For the sexual metaphor, ibid., 9–36.

[27] Halbertal and Margalit, *Idolatry*, 109–10, 186–90, and 190–7.

denounced the cult of the Western Wall as a golden calf, argued that anyone who regarded the holiness of Israel as a fact rather than as something that was the goal of continuous striving was guilty of idolatry: "'Holy' is an attribute that applies exclusively to God. It is therefore inapplicable to anything in the natural or historical domain. He who does so apply it is guilty of idolatry. He exalts something natural or human to the level of the divine.'[28]

All of these examples come from what may be seen as religious discourse and polemic, but the notion has been extended in many ways to refer to beliefs and practices that would not normally be regarded as within the religious sphere. Francis Bacon's analysis in his *Novum Organum* of common intellectual fallacies as the four 'idols of the mind' is well known.[29] Today we commonly talk of putting people, institutions or even ideas on a pedestal, while prominent individuals in sport or entertainment are often called idols, gods and goddesses.

Between Judaism and Christianity mutual accusations of idolatry seem to have been relatively limited. It may be that political circumstances made it necessary for Jews to be guarded in their use of language when alluding to the religion associated with their rulers, and later Jewish scholars (from Maimonides onwards) also developed ideas suggesting that what counts as idolatry for Jews does not necessarily apply to gentiles, and that Christianity and Islam have some positive value.[30] Even so, the accusation of idolatry has not been absent from polemic between Jews and Christians.

Regarding the expression *kōfēr bā-ʿiqqār*, Urbach's reference to the statement attributed to Rabbi Ṭarfon (end of the first century AD), according to which the *minīm* are effectively worse than the idolaters has already been mentioned: whereas the idolaters (i.e., adherents of Graeco-Roman religion) deny God out of ignorance, the *minīm* are familiar with the conception of the one God, but introduce other elements into it. The *minīm* here may be gnostics, but Urbach thought it more likely that they are Christians and that the allusion is to the belief in Jesus as the Son of God.[31] It is clear that Jews have seen fundamental doctrines and practices of Christianity, such as the recognition of Jesus as the Son of God or the use of icons in worship, as forms of idolatry, and sometimes that has been made explicit. Thus the thirteenth-century anthology from northern Europe of Jewish apologetic and polemic against Christianity, the *Sefer Niṣṣaḥōn Yāshān*, referred to the idols (*pesīlīm*) in the Christian houses of abomination/houses of idolatry (*bātē tarefōtām/bātē*

[28] Y. Leibowitz, *Judaism, Human Values and the Jewish State*, Cambridge, Mass. 1992, 86.

[29] Anthony Quinton, *Bacon*, Oxford 1980, 35–8, links Bacon's language with his Puritan upbringing.

[30] See, e.g., *The Encyclopaedia of Religion*, ed. Mircea Eliade, s.v. 'Polemics', (by David Berger), XI, 393.

[31] Urbach, *Sages*, 26. For the view that much of the Jewish apologetic that has sometimes been interpreted as directed against dualists should in fact be understood as directed against Christians, see *EJ*, III, col. 191, s.v. 'Apologetics'.

ʿavōdāh zārāh), and portrayed the doctrine of the Incarnation as the deification of a human being.[32]

It has been possible for Christian apologists and polemicists in turn to depict Judaism as idolatrous by referring to passages of the Hebrew Bible where the prophets accused the people of Israel of idolatry and, above all, to the the story of the Golden Calf. Chapter 7 of the Acts of the Apostles already reports Stephen's speech in which, among other accusations made against the Jews, reference is made not only to their making the idol of the Calf but also to their worshipping the host of heaven (referring to Amos 5:25, 26). In a similar vein, the twelfth-century Melkite bishop of Sidon, Paul of Antioch, in a letter claiming to be addressed to a friend among the Muslims of the town, portrays the Jews as idolaters, citing the text of Psalm 106 (105): 36–8: *wa-ʿabadū al-aṣnām . . . wa-arāqū daman zakiyan . . . alladhī dhakkaw li-manḥūtāti* [= Hebrew *ʿāṣāb*] *Kanʿān* ('and they served their idols . . . and shed innocent blood . . . which they offered to the idols of Canaan').[33]

The accusation of idolatry in many of these examples was not merely an empty or meaningless one, but was made when some aspect of the opponent's belief or practice could be portrayed as weakening the divine unity or uniqueness. Frequently the train of thought is quite obvious: there is no difficulty in understanding how the use of icons or statues in worship, or the claim that Jesus was the Son of God, could be interpreted as idolatry and polytheism by those who rejected them. (To say that they were rejected because they were seen as idolatrous and polytheistic would be to oversimplify the problem of the nature and sources of religious beliefs.)

Sometimes, on the other hand, the logical connexions involved in the imputation of idolatry to an opponent are not so simple and a certain amount of exegesis is necessary to uncover the links. An example might be the way in which the Karaites were able to portray the rabbis as the idols of their followers: those who accepted the rabbis' authority in effect made them associates, from the Karaite point of view, in the authority of God since, according to the Karaite theory, only God's revelation, the Torah, was authoritative. Men were being put on the same level as God.[34] In the case of the ascription of a dove cult to the Samaritans, one element at least seems to be a tendentious interpretation by the rabbis of Genesis 35:4, which refers to Jacob having buried certain 'strange gods' under the oak tree at Shechem, the site of the Samaritan sanctuary.[35] As for the depiction of pride as a form of idolatry or *shirk*, the reasoning seems to be that the proud man takes account of the way in which

[32] D. Berger, *The Jewish–Christian Debate in the High Middle Ages. A Critical Edition of the Nizzaḥon Vetus*, Philadelphia 1979; see, e.g., sections 67, 210 and 219. For idolatrous connexions of the cross, see also Judah Halevi, *Kitāb al-Radd*, cited below, note 62.

[33] P. Khoury, *Paul d'Antioche évêque melkite de Sidon (XIIe s.)*, Beirut: 1964, 166 (text) = 74 (trans.).

[34] Wieder, *Judaean Scrolls and Karaism*, 151–3.

[35] Schoeps, *Theologie und Geschichte*, 392; see Midrash Rabba on Genesis, 81:3 (748), and J. Talmud, ʿAvōdāh Zārāh, 5:4 (Chicago 1982, 199).

other men see him when he should pay attention only to the way he appears to God. Again it is a case of men being put on the same level as God. The rationale behind accusations of idolatry may not always be readily apparent, therefore, but in most cases there is one.

It is perhaps impossible for an outsider to decide how far the participants in these exchanges meant what they said or believed their own rhetoric. While the charges were certainly understood as in some sense true, it also seems likely that at least some of the disputants were aware of using language in a specialised sense. That awareness might vary according to the sophistication of the participants. The intellectual level of polemic would also have differed in accordance with different participants and conditions. It seems worth asking in fact whether 'polemic' is quite the right word to apply to texts such as as the critiques of the doctrine of the Trinity by Warrāq and Saʿadya Gaon. The latter prefaces his attack by saying that it is not addressed to uneducated Christians who have a corporealist and gross understanding of the doctrine, but to the educated who claim that it rests on 'rational speculation and subtle understanding'.[36]

For the outsider there must be a danger that the nature of the language will not be recognised and that it will be construed as representing a reality rather in the way that some modern scholars have sought to use the Koran as a source of evidence for conditions in Mecca and Medina in the early years of the seventh century. The problem becomes more acute once the original context of the language has been lost, and what began as polemic may come to be understood literally and then incorporated as fact in historical description. To some extent that may account for the transformation of koranic *shirk* into Arab idolatry, but it may not be a complete explanation.

Among Muslims the polemical use of *shirk* and sometimes of *kufr* parallels that of idolatry in the examples just given. Concern to defend the absolute unity and uniqueness of the divinity has been a defining feature of Islam throughout its history and it is not surprising that accusations that opponents, both inside and outside Islam, have compromised and injured that unity and uniqueness have been a recurring feature of its polemic.[37] As with the idea of idolatry in the other traditions of monotheism, so in the Islamic, *shirk* has covered a range of beliefs and practices as well as moral failings such as pride and the belief in premonitions and presentiments.

Goldziher referred to the fifth/eleventh-century mystic Samnūn al-Muḥibb

[36] Saʿadya Gaon, *Kitāb al-āmanāt waʾl-iʿtiqādāt*, trans. S. Rosenblatt as *The Book of Beliefs and Opinions*, New Haven 1948, 103. The passage is cited too in *EJ* s.v. 'Apologetics'. For the work of al-Warrāq, see Thomas (ed.), *Anti-Christian Polemic*.

[37] Cf. I Goldziher, 'Le monothéisme dans la vie religieuse des Musulmans', *RHR*, 16 (1887), 157–65 (=*GS*, II, 173–81). For illustration of the polemical use of the idea of *shirk* among modern Muslim reformers of differing sorts, see Sirriyeh, 'Modern Muslim Interpretations'.

who is said to have had qualms about associating the name of Muḥammad with that of God in the statement of Muslim faith, the *shahāda*, and this has been a theme in the mystical tradition.[38] Rabīʿa (d. 185/801) is reported to have said that her love of God left no room in her heart for the Prophet, while Abū Bakr al-Shiblī (d. 334/945), it is said, only included the name of the Prophet alongside that of God in the call to prayer, the *adhān*, because it was part of God's law. Annemarie Schimmel argues that others, perceiving a danger of antinomianism in such an attitude, stressed the importance of the second part of the *shahāda*. The extent to which anything that might deflect the believer from God could be labelled as *shirk* is evident in two other Sufi dicta cited by Schimmel: 'the essence of *shirk* is that you think you are without *shirk*'; and even Sufism may be called idolatry 'since it is the safeguarding of the heart from the vision of the other, and there is no other'.[39]

Outside the Koran, one of the earliest examples in Muslim tradition of the accusation of *shirk* made between Muslims is that said to have been directed by the Khārijites against ʿAlī, at the time of the first civil war (36–40/656–61). The accusation is presented as having arisen out of ʿAlī's agreement to appoint the two 'arbitrators' to settle his dispute with Muʿāwiya. Individuals who had previously supported ʿAlī are reported to have viewed that agreement as giving men a share in a decision that belonged to God alone, a view expressed in what became the defining slogan of the Khārijite movement within Islam: *lā ḥukma illā li'llāh* ('no one has authority but God'). They demanded, therefore, that ʿAlī repent of his *kufr*, and they recited to him Sūra 39:65: 'It has been revealed to you and to those who came before you that, if you commit *shirk* (*la-in ashrakta*), your deeds shall be of no avail and you will be one of those who are lost.'

Although this could represent a later theological reading of a clash over political power, the chain of ideas, and some of the terminology used, has parallels with Karaite polemic against the rabbis, and it may be that the reports in Muslim tradition reflect a dispute in early Islam similar to that between the Jewish groups – an argument about the relative importance as sources of authority of revelation and so-called oral law.[40]

The letters issued by the ʿAbbāsid caliph Ma'mūn in connexion with the beginning of the *Miḥna*, the struggle for authority between the caliph/imam and the traditionalist religious scholars which began in 218/833, also make

[38] I. Goldziher, 'Le culte des saints chez les Musulmans', *RHR*, 2 (1880), 262–63 (= *GS*, VI, 67–68).

[39] Annemarie Schimmel, 'The Sufis and the *shahāda*', in R. G. Hovannisian and Speros Vryonis Jr. (eds.), *Islam's Understanding of Itself*, Malibu 1983, 103–25, esp. 112 and 117.

[40] Ṭabarī, *Ta'rīkh*, I, 3363. For further discussion, see G. R. Hawting, 'The Significance of the Slogan *lā ḥukma illā lillāh* . . .', *BSOAS*, 41 (1978), 453–63. For a survey of the evidence regarding a conflict over the relative authority of scripture and oral law in early Islam, see M.A. Cook, "Anan and Islam: The Origins of Karaite Scripturalism', *JSAI*, 9 (1987), 165 ff. For some other relatively early examples (in poetry) of the charge of *shirk* in polemic between groups associated with Islam, see above, pp. 71–2.

free with charges of *shirk* and *kufr*, on this occasion against those Muslims who refused to swear that the Koran was created. Their position is compared with that of the Christians, who hold that Jesus is the uncreated Word of God. In their refusal to accept that the Koran is created, it is said, the ignorant have put God on the same level with what He has revealed; they have abandoned the truth for what is vain (*bāṭil*); they have taken an intimate (*walīja*) apart from God, who leads them into error (cf. Koran 9:16); they have fallen short in their monotheism and they are called to absolute monotheism (*ikhlāṣ al-tawḥīd*) – 'there is no *tawḥīd* in those who do not accept that the Koran is created'; 'their doctrines are pure *kufr* and clear *shirk* in the eyes of the Commander of the Faithful'.[41]

The debate in Islam about whether the Koran may be described as created or uncreated was an aspect of the theological dispute concerning the divine attributes: whether or not the divinity may be analysed in terms of attributes distinct from the divine essence. The Muʿtazilī position on this question, a refusal to envisage that God has attributes separable from His essence, was adopted in the fifth/eleventh-century Maghrib by Ibn Tumart and his Almohad followers, and the account of their polemic against their Mālikī opponents is similar to that of the Muʿtazila against the traditionalists. Although the accusation of *kufr* rather than that of *shirk* seems predominant, the charge against the opponents centres on the claim that their acceptance of eternal divine attributes independent of the divine essence in effect introduced multiplicity into the divine being. They did not, therefore, maintain true monotheism and, as *kuffār*, were subject to the *jihād*.[42]

In the polemic against the generality of their fellow Muslims by the Wahhābīs, the reform movement whose interpretation of Islam is espoused by the Saudi kingdom, *shirk* again took a central place. Behind this charge lay the doctrine of *tawḥīd al-ulūhiyya* developed by Ibn Taymiyya (d. 728/1328) and his neo-Ḥanbalī followers, the doctrine that worship must be directed to God

[41] Ṭabarī, *Taʾrīkh*, III, 1112–32, throughout. Cf. J. van Ess, *Theologie und Gesellschaft*, III, 452–6. See too I. Goldziher, 'Materialen zur Kenntniss der Almohadenbewegung in Nordafrika', *ZDMG*, 41 (1887), 68–9 (= *GS*, II, 229–30). Goldziher refers to an accusation of *shirk* made by Maʾmūn against the poet ʿAkawwak for his excessive eulogy of Abū Dulaf, an accusation that justified killing the poet and tearing out his tongue. According to the account of the poet's life by Ibn Khallikān, which was Goldziher's source, the caliph indeed told the poet that he was going to kill him for his *kufr* and *shirk* (*bi-kufrika fī shiʿrika . . . fa-ashrakta biʾllāh al-ʿaẓīm wa-jaʿalta maʿahu mālikan qādiran*): Shams al-Dīn Abu ʾl-ʿAbbās b. Khallikān, *Wafayāt al-aʿyān*, ed. Iḥsān ʿAbbās, 8 vols., Beirut n.d., III, 352–3. Ibn Khallikān's source, Ibn al-Muʿtazz, however, reads: *bi-kufrika wa-jurʾatika ʿalā ʾllāh an taqūla fī ʿabd mahīn tusawwī baynahu wa-bayna rabb al-ʿālamīn*: Abd Allāh b. al-Muʿtazz, *Ṭabaqāt al-shuʿarāʾ*, ed. ʿAbd al-Sattār Aḥmad Farrāj, Cairo 1956, 172.

[42] I. Goldziher, 'Mohammed Ibn Toumert et la théologie de l'Islam dans le maghreb au XIe siècle', introduction to J. D. Luciani (ed.), *Le Livre de Mohammed Ibn Toumert*, Algiers 1903, esp. 55–6, 61–2, 63 ff., 71–3, 79 ff; Goldziher, 'Almohadenbewegung', 69 (= *GS*, II, 230) for a poem in which Goldziher interprets *mushrikūn* as referring to non-Almohad Muslims, *ahl al-kufr* to Christians.

alone and that anything that could be interpreted as worship of any other being, whether a prophet, saint, leader of a brotherhood, or temporal ruler, was a form of idolatry.[43]

In his tract entitled *The Four Principles of the Religion which Distinguish the Believers from the Mushrikūn*, Ibn ʿAbd al-Wahhāb stressed that the essence of the *ḥanīfiyya*, the religion of Abraham, is pure monotheism. Any element of *shirk* will make all worship invalid and void, so that anyone who performs an act of worship while tainted by *shirk* is destined for hell. He urges his readers to recognise that, so that God may rescue them from the snare of *shirk*. He then proceeds to set out the four principles to which God has referred in His book:

1. It is not enough to recognise God as the Creator, the source of sustenance, the giver of life and death, the cause of everything, whether beneficial or harmful. The *kuffār* against whom the Prophet fought recognised as much, but it did not cause them to enter Islam.
2. The *mushrikūn* say, 'We have only turned to and called upon them in order to seek nearness and intercession, and we mean [nearness] to God and not to them, but by means of their intercession and drawing close to them.' God's words provide proof of (the futility of their arguments regarding both) nearness and intercession.
3. The Prophet made no distinction between the different types of *shirk* adhered to by his enemies. Some of them worshipped the sun and the moon, some of them righteous men (*al-ṣāliḥūn*), some the angels, some the prophets, and some the trees and stones, but the Prophet was commanded by God to fight them all without distinction. (As usual Ibn ʿAbd al-Wahhāb supports his argument with a series of proof texts, usually koranic. It is especially interesting that when he wishes to discuss those who worshipped trees and stones, he has recourse not to the Koran but to *sīra* material – the account of the tree called Dhāt Anwāṭ which the pagan Arabs (the *mushrikūn*) used to worship and regarding which the newly converted followers of the Prophet asked him for something similar.[44])
4. The *shirk* of the contemporaries of Ibn ʿAbd al-Wahhāb is worse than that of the original *mushrikūn*. The latter, at least, used to devote worship to God alone (*yukhliṣūna li'llāh*)[45] in times of stress even though they would

[43] Laoust, *Essai*, 472, 531; E. Peskes, *Muḥammad b. ʿAbdalwahhāb (1703–92) im Widerstreit*, Beirut 1993, esp. 15–33 (thanks to Michael Cook for the latter reference). For the concept of *shirk* among the Wahhābīs, see also Sirriyeh, 'Modern Muslim Interpretations, 142–6. For an example of Ibn ʿAbd al-Wahhāb's understanding of the contrast between *tawḥīd al-rubūbiyya* and *tawḥīd al-ulūhiyya*, see above, p. 64, n.46. Note that in his list of 129 ideas and practices that characterise the condition of *jāhiliyya* Ibn ʿAbd al-Wahhāb includes 'calling the following of Islam *shirk*' (*Majmūʿat al-tawḥīd*, no. 56). Evidently he distinguishes between true Islam and something that might claim to be Islam but which, in his view, is not.

[44] E.g., Ibn Hishām, *Sīra*, II, 442.

[45] For *ikhlāṣ* as the opposite of *shirk* in the Koran, see above, p. 61.

practise *shirk* when things were easy; the *shirk* of the contemporaries is constant, whether in hard or easy circumstances.[46]

Despite of the distinction between Jews, Christians and *mushrikūn* made in some of the passages of the Koran,[47] it is sometimes impossible to maintain it in other Muslim texts, where *kufr* and *shirk* are imputed to Jews and Christians. For example, the *Kitāb ahl al-kitābayn* in the *Muṣannaf* of ʿAbd al-Razzāq has some subheadings referring to the *mushrikīn* but the *ḥadīth*s they contain relate to Jews and Christians. Thus the chapter, the title of which indicates that it is concerned with the question of the *mushrik* who converts from one *dīn* to another, has two reports about Jews or Christians who may wish to become Zindīqs and one about a Jew or Christian who may attempt to win his descendants over to Judaism or Christianity (presumably from Islam). Conversely, the chapter that proclaims that it is concerned with the expulsion of the Jews from Medina has a tradition in which the Prophet, in his final illness, orders that the *mushrikūn* be expelled from the Arabian peninsula, followed by another in which, again on his deathbed, he commands that no Jew or Christian should remain in the Ḥijāz.[48]

Even in the Koran the distinction seems sometimes dubious. Sūra 5:72–3 accuses of *kufr*, and imputes *shirk* to, those who identify the Messiah, the son of Mary, with God or say that God is 'the third of three'. Commenting on these verses, Ṭabarī denounced both groups – those who believe that Jesus was God and those who accept the Trinity – as infidels and polytheists/idolaters (*kilāhumā kafara mushrikūn*).[49] In the context of Muslim polemic against Christians, the idea of *shirk* seems to be associated particularly with reference to the doctrines of the divine sonship of Jesus and of the Trinity, whereas the use of crucifixes and icons tends to be presented as idolatry in a more explicit way by accusing the Christians of worshipping a thing made of wood or stone.

The association of *shirk* and Christianity is evident at an early stage in the development of Islam. In the inscriptions inside the Dome of the Rock and on the east and north entrances, which date from the time of its construction under ʿAbd al-Malik (72/691),[50] *sharīk* and *mushrik* both occur once. The former is part of a statement that God has no partner (*sharīk*) in His power, the latter of a proclamation that God has sent His messenger with the guidance and the religion of truth so that He may cause it to triumph over all religion (*ʿalā ʾl-dīn kullihi*), even though the *mushrikūn* resent it. Although there is

[46] Ibn ʿAbd al-Wahhāb, *Fī arbaʿ qawāʿid al-dīn – tamīzu bayna ʾl-muʾminīna waʾl-mushrikīn*, in *Majmūʿat al-tawḥīd*, 110–12. I am grateful to Michael Cook for reference to this text. See too (in Cook's words, the 'wild and woolly') *Lamʿ al-shihāb fī sīrat Muḥammad ibn ʿAbd al-Wahhāb*, ed. A. M. Abū Ḥākima, Beirut n.d. (1967?), 187–90. [47] See above, p. 47.

[48] Al-Ṣanʿanī ʿAbd al-Razzāq, al-*Muṣannaf*, 12 vols., ed. Ḥabīb al-Raḥmān al-Aʿẓamī, Beirut 1983–7, X, 318, 358.

[49] *Tafsīr* (Cairo), X, 480–2. The description of belief in Jesus as the Son of God as *shirk* and idolatry echoes the view of Christian theologians such as Athanasius and Gregory of Nyssa that Christians would be idolators if Jesus were indeed not the Son of God.

[50] It is disputed whether that date indicates the start or the completion of the building.

no explicit linkage of Christianity to the terms, it is clear that a major part of the message contained in the inscriptions is a rejection of Christian claims regarding the status of Jesus and the doctrine of the Trinity.[51]

In his account of the rising of the tribe of Nājiya against ʿAlī in 38/658–9, a rising that was supported by many Christian Arabs in Fars, Ṭabarī gives the text of a letter sent to ʿAlī by one of his commanders reporting a victory. In it it is recounted that the leader of the rising, Khirrīt b. Rāshid, had sought help from the *mushrikūn*. It is difficult to know who this refers to, if not to the local Christians.[52]

Presentation of Christian use of the cross and icons as a form of idolatry, and of its Christology as a form of polytheism and unbelief, was common in Muslim polemic against Christianity in works of the *radd ʿalā al-naṣārā* type, even though explicit use of the terms *shirk* and *kufr* do not seem as frequent as one might expect.

> You revere the cross and the icon, you kiss them and prostrate before them, but they are man made things which cannot hear or see, can do neither good nor ill; you think that the greatest of them are those made of gold and silver, just as the people of Abraham did with their images and idols (*bi-ṣuwarihim wa-awthānihim*) . . . [The Prophet] commanded us to worship God alone, not to associate anything with Him (*allā nushrika bihi shayʾan*), not to make any god with Him, not to worship the sun, the moon, idols, a cross or an icon, and not to adopt one another as lords apart from God.[53]

Ibn Qayyim al-Jawziyya ridiculed the idea that God would deign to go through the process of gestation in the womb of a woman and suffer all the mockery and torture reported of Jesus, and he took particular exception to what he alleged the Christians said in justification of the idea of God as the father of Jesus in a real sense: that anyone who does not beget is barren and that barrenness is a defect and a shame. He retorted: 'This is their *kufr* and their *shirk* concerning the Lord of the Worlds, and their insulting of Him.'[54]

An awareness on the part of the Christians of the accusation of *shirk* is evident, it seems, in the *De Haeresibus* attributed to John of Damascus (d. c. 754) and an early ritual of abjuration for those converting to Christianity from the religion of the Saracens. The latter text must be late ninth century at the earliest in the form in which we have it, but Cumont argued that it contains materials of a date much earlier than that. In these two texts it is mentioned

[51] *RÉA*, I, nos. 9–11; C. Kessler, ''Abd al-Malik's Inscription in the Dome of the Rock, a Reconsideration', *JRAS* 1970, 2–14; O. Grabar, 'The Umayyad Dome of the Rock in Jerusalem', *Ars Orientalis*, 3 (1959), 53–5, 59; A. Elad, *Medieval Jerusalem and Islamic Worship*, Leiden 1995, 44–6. Most (but not quite all) of the inscriptions occur as passages in the Koran: the passage with *sharīk* is Sūra 17:111, that with *mushrikūn* is Sūra 9:33 and 61:9.

[52] Ṭabarī, *Taʾrīkh*, I, 3432.

[53] D. Sourdel (ed. and trans.), 'Un pamphlet musulman anonyme d'époque ʿabbāside contre les chrétiens', *REI*, 34 (1966), 29 (text) = 17 (trans.), 33 (text) = 25 (trans.).

[54] Shams al-Dīn Muḥammad b. Abī Bakr b. Qayyim al-Jawziyya, *Hidāyat al-ḥayārā fī ajwibat al-yahūd waʾl-naṣārā*, Beirut 1987, 166.

that the Ishmaelites call the Christians 'associators' (*hetairiastas*, a Greek rendition presumably of *mushrikūn*, and one that would carry connotations of prostitution) because of their view that Christ was the Son of God and God, and idolaters (*eidōlolatras*) because of the veneration of the cross.[55]

The attempted refutation of the charge in the *De Haeresibus* is based partly on an unspecific appeal to scripture and the prophets, partly on theological arguments which involve the counter-charge that the Ishmaelites are 'mutilators' (*koptas*) of God in their striving not to associate anything with Him, and partly by turning the tables and accusing them of idolatry. Other Christian apologists reject the implication of *shirk* by emphasising their own aversion to any doctrine that supports the idea of plurality in the godhead, and by stressing those koranic verses that distinguish the Christians from the *mushrikūn*. Paul of Antioch (twelfth century AD) asked, since we Christians regard as *kufr* any implication of plurality or corporeality to God, anything that leads to *shirk* or anthropomorphism (*tashbīh*), how can our opponent impute such things to us? If they charge us with *shirk* and anthropomorphism, we charge them with corporealism (*tajassum*) and anthropomorphism (because of their insistence on the literal understanding of those koranic verses in which God is described anthropomorphically). And he cited Sūras 22:17 and 5:69 in an attempt to show that the Muslims' own scripture distinguished between the Christians and the *mushrikīn*: *wa-nafā ʿannā ism al-shirk bi-qawlihi* ('God has removed from us the label of *shirk* in what He has said').[56]

Explicit accusations of *shirk* against the Jews seem less frequent than against the Christians, although they did occur. One of the main motives for the accusation of *shirk* by Muslims was, as we have seen, the view that the opponents were guilty of anthropomorphic and corporealist views of the divinity. These theological errors were in fact imputed especially to Judaism, to the extent that we find statements to the effect that 'Judaism is corporealism' (*madhhab al-Yahūd al-tajsīm*).[57] Goldziher adduced some canonical *ḥadīth* in which the association of anthropomorphism with Jews was evident, and recently van Ess has drawn attention to the way in which a *ḥadīth* that warns against *shirk* in an unspecific way appears in an Ibāḍī source in a

[55] For the text and translation of the *De Haeresibus*, see D. J. Sahas, *John of Damascus and Islam*, Leiden 1972; for the accusations of 'association' and idolatry, 134, 136 (text) = 135, 137 (trans.); B. Kotter (ed.), *Die Schriften des Johannes von Damaskos. IV Liber De Haeresibus*, Berlin and New York 1981. For arguments against the attribution of the *De Haeresibus* to John, see A. Abel, 'Le chapitre CI du Livre des Héresies de Jean Damascène: son inauthenticité', *SI*, 19 (1963), 5–25. For the abjuration formula, see E. Montet, 'Un rituel d'abjuration des musulmans dans l'église grecque', *RHR*, 53 (1906), 145–63 (the rebuttal of the 'association' charge is at p.154), and F. Cumont, 'L'Origine de la formule greque d'abjuration imposé aux musulmans', *RHR*, 64 (1911), 143–50.

[56] Khoury, *Paul d'Antioche*, text III, sections 22, 53, 54.

[57] Goldziher, 'Monothéisme', 157 (= *GS*, II, 173); I. Goldziher, 'Usages Juifs d'après la littérateur religieuse des Musulmans', *REJ*, 28 (1894), 88 (= *GS*, III, 335); see too I.Goldziher, 'Mélanges Judéo-Arabes', *REJ*, 47 (1902), 179–86 (= *GS*, IV, 416–23), esp. 182–3 (= 419–20) on polemics between Karaites and Rabbanites on the question of *tashbīh*. The Christian apologetic tract against Islam attributed to al-Kindī also associates the Jews with anthropomorphism (*Risālat ʿAbd al-Masīḥ Ibn Isḥāq al-Kindī*, London 1870, 95).

context associating *shirk* with anthropomorphism and linking anthropomorphism with Jews. In Ibn Ḥanbal's version, Abū Mūsā al-Ashʿarī cites the the Prophet's dictum, 'Fear this *shirk* for it is more secretive than the influx of ants' (*ittaqū hādha 'l-shirk fa-innahu akhfā min dabīb al-naml*) in a context that does not indicate what the word *shirk* might be referring to. In the Ibāḍī *ḥadīth* collection attributed to Rabīʿ b. Ḥabīb the saying is given, in a slightly different form, as the response of Ibn Masʿūd as he passed a Jew who was teaching that God had gone up to heaven from Jerusalem after the creation, putting His foot on the rock (that over which the Dome of the Rock was built) as He did so.[58] Elsewhere alleged Jewish anthropomorphism is designated as *kufr wāḍiḥ*.[59]

The attempt in the *De Haeresibus* to turn the tables by insisting that the Ishmaelites are themselves guilty of idolatry in their rubbing and kissing of a stone near their Khabathan, a stone which is the head of Aphrodite, appears too in the abjuration formula required of converts to Christianity and is commonly repeated in Byzantine texts.[60] The portrayal of the *ḥajj* and the sanctuary at Mecca as idolatrous institutions is frequent. The *Risāla* attributed to al-Kindī draws a parallel between the *ḥajj* and the idolatrous pilgrimages and processions of the Indians. The author is familar with ʿUmar's address to the Black Stone – that he knew that it was only a stone which could do neither good nor harm and that he would not have kissed it unless he had seen the Prophet doing so – and he uses it to substantiate the charge that the Muslim sanctuary rituals are fundamentally idolatrous.[61]

Judah Halevi, although the passage as a whole seems to allude both to Muslims and Christians, presumably had the Muslims chiefly in mind when he said that, in spite of their praising the place of prophethood in what they say, they take as their *qibla* places which had been devoted to idols (*mawāḍiʿ kānat li'l-awthān*) and continue the ceremonies of the ancient worship, the days of its *ḥajj*, and their rituals (*maʿa ibqā'ihim rusūm al-ʿibādāt al-qadīma wa-ayyām ḥajjihā wa-manāsikahum*). They have merely obliterated the

[58] Goldziher, 'Usages Juifs', 88 (= 335). The Prophet's saying in its shorter form is in Aḥmad b. Ḥanbal, *Musnad*, 6 vols., Cairo 1313, IV, 403; the version quoted by van Ess runs, 'There will be a time when *shirk* will be more clandestine than ants stepping on a black rock in dark night' (J. van Ess, "Abd al-Malik and the Dome of the Rock. An analysis of some texts', in J. Raby and J. Johns (eds.), *Bayt al-Maqdis: ʿAbd al-Malik's Jerusalem*, part 1, Oxford 1993, 94–5). Uri Rubin has pointed out to me that a version of this *ḥadīth* was cited in Edward Lane's *Arabic–English Lexicon*, s.v. '*shirk*', as an example of the use of that word as the equivalent of hypocrisy. For the anti-anthropomorphist tendency of Rabīʿ b. Ḥabīb's *Musnad*, see Cook, "Anan and Islam', 171.

[59] Ibn Taymiyya in his work (*al-Jawāb al-ṣaḥīḥ li-man baddala dīn al-Masīḥ*) against the Christians, cited by Goldziher 'Usages Juifs', 88 (= 335).

[60] E. Montet, 'Un rituel 'abjuration', 153–4. For Muslim worship of Aphrodite in Byzantine polemic generally, see A. T. Khoury, *Polémique byzantine contre l'Islam*, Leiden 1972, 275–81.

[61] *Risālat ʿAbd al-Masīḥ al-Kindī*, 104–5. For the problems of the attribution of this text, see *EI2* s.v. 'al-Kindī'. For the association of the *ḥajj* and the sanctuary with idolatry in Byzantine texts see Khoury, *Polémique byzantine*, 275–81.

representations of the idols (*al-ṣuwar allatī kānat hunāka*) without abolishing their practices (*rusūm*). He concluded by alluding to several passages in Deuteronomy which foretold the worship of 'other gods, of wood and of stone', the wood interpreted as the cross worshipped by the Christians, the stone as that worshipped by the Muslims.[62]

The imputation of idolatry to the Muslims in medieval European Christian romances and *chansons de geste* is possibly the best-known aspect of this polemical exchange of the charge of idolatry between the different traditions of monotheism. In the *Song of Roland* the Muslims ('les paien') are portrayed as serving Mahum, Apolin, and Tervagant, while other such works provide us with a total of about thirty gods.[63] The anti-Muslim accusation became such a commonplace that in English the word 'mawment', derived from the name of Muhammad, was used to mean an idol or a vain thing.[64]

In Appendix A of his *Islam and the West*, Norman Daniel discussed the imputation of idolatry to Islam in the romance and *chanson de geste* type of medieval European literature. Daniel favoured the idea of Henri Grégoire that the charge was invented as part of the propaganda of the Crusade, although possibly related to the idea that Arab idolatry had been preserved in Islam in the *ḥajj* and the Kaʿba. Grégoire had suggested that this latter idea may have come into European Christian literature via Petrus Alfonsi from rabbinic sources, although he was aware, naturally, that the charge was a topos of Byzantine polemical literature. Daniel, finally, made the point that '"idolatry" may always be correctly used to describe any mistaken idea of God that men may worship, but that it does not then mean the worship of physical idols'.[65]

This last point has been the theme of this chapter. Ideas that in European languages centre on the word 'idolatry' are polemical and part of the monotheist discourse shared by Jews, Christians and Muslims. In the Muslim tradition they are represented particularly by *shirk* and *kufr*. The related charges of idolatry and polytheism rarely seem to be made without any rationale, although it is sometimes a complicated one and difficult now to reconstruct. Because the accusation functions as polemic, it is not legitimate to infer from it that those who made it understood their opponents as idolators in a literal sense.

62 Judah Halevi, *Kitāb al-Radd wa'l-dalīl fi'l-dīn al-dhalīl (Kitāb al-Khazarī)*, ed. D. H. Baneth and prepared for the press by H. Ben Shammai, Jerusalem 1977, 162 (book 4, section 11); partial Eng. trans. by Isaak Heinemann, Oxford 1947, 115. H. Grégoire, 'Des dieux Cahu, Baraton, Tervagant . . . et de maints autres dieux non moins extravagants', *AIPHOS*, 7 (1939–44), 465.

63 R. W. Southern, *Western Views of Islam in the Middle Ages*, Cambridge, Mass. and London, 1962 (rev. repr. 1978), 32; B. Z. Kedar, *Crusade and Mission*, Princeton 1984, 88–9.

64 Susan Brigden, *London and the Reformation*, Oxford 1989, 94, cites Joan Baker of St Mary Magdalen Milk Street as wishing, in 1510, that she had never gone on pilgrimage since the images at the shrines were 'but mawments and false gods . . . idols and not to be worshipped or honoured'.

65 N. Daniel, *Islam and the West*, Edinburgh 1960, 309–13; Grégoire, 'Cahu, Baraton, Tervagant', esp. 462–6.

Much less can one infer that the religion or culture as a whole that produced the texts saw those at whom they were directed as really idolatrous – different texts were produced for different purposes and in different circumstances. Although Muslims frequently charged Christians with *shirk*, in Ṭabarī's *Tafsīr* on the opening verses of Sūra 30 (*Sūrat al-Rūm*), it is clear that some exegetes wanted to distinguish the Christian Byzantines as *ahl al-kitāb* from the Persian Magians who are variously labelled as *mushrikīn* and *ahl al-awthān*. The insistence on the status of the Byzantines as monotheists was felt important here because it was necessary to explain why the scripture says that the Believers would rejoice to hear of a Byzantine victory over the Persians. Variations in circumstances and in the purposes and intended audience of particular texts make it inadvisable to generalise about the image one group had of another, even over a relatively short period of time.[66]

Any attempt to use polemical literature to deduce the meanings, knowledge and understanding of those who produced it necessitates first a proper recognition of it as polemic.

[66] Cf. Southern, *Western Views of Islam*, which characterises the whole period until the early twelfth century as 'the age of ignorance'.

CHAPTER 4

The tradition

It is the Muslim tradition contained in biographies of the Prophet, commentaries on the Koran and other works that has created the understanding that the Koran originated among and was concerned to attack Arabs who were idolatrous and polytheistic in a full sense. It is true that discussions of pre-Islamic Arab religion take into account also the findings of archaeology and epigraphy in Arabia and the Middle East, as well as those few literary sources external to Muslim tradition that might have a bearing on the matter. But such evidence has been of secondary importance insofar as the religion of the *jāhiliyya* is concerned. The use of such sources in discussions of *jāhilī* religion has often depended on understandings derived in the first place from the Muslim tradition and has sometimes involved considerable and questionable speculation. The value of the evidence external to Muslim tradition, and the way that it has been used, will be considered further in chapters 5 and 6. The focus of this chapter is the character of the Muslim literary tradition about the idolatrous religion of the pre-Islamic Arabs.

In addition to the details about pre-Islamic Arab idolatry to be found in genres such as koranic commentary and biographies of the Prophet, there are works devoted entirely to compiling information about the gods, sanctuaries and idols of the pagan Arabs. The best known is the *Kitāb al-Aṣnām* (Book of Idols) attributed to Hishām b. Muḥammad al-Kalbī (d. 206/821). That written (apparently with the same title) by the famous litterateur and scholar Jāḥiẓ (d. 255/868) now seems to be lost, but the brief summary of its contents provided by that author in the introduction to his *Kitāb al-Ḥayawān* suggests that it may have had some points of contact with the sections in the *al-Milal wa'l-niḥal* of Shahrastānī (d. 548/1153) that discuss the religions of the Arabs of the *jāhiliyya* and the Indians.[1] Insofar as data or information about the religious ideas and practices of the pre-Islamic Arabs is concerned, there is no reason

[1] 'Amr b. Baḥr al-Jāḥiẓ, *Kitāb al-Ḥayawān*, ed. 'Abd al-Salām Muḥammad Hārīn, 7 vols. Cairo 1938–45, I, 5–6; Charles Pellat, 'Ǧāḥiẓiana III', *Arabica*, 3 (1956), no. 26; *Aṣnām-Atallah*, introduction, lvii; Shahrastānī, *Milal*, II, 232–65. Jāḥiẓ says that the work, among other things, compared Arab and Indian idolatry and explored the distinctions between various terms for 'idol': *budd*, *wathan*, *ṣanam*, *dumya* and *juththa*.

to think that the book of Jāḥiẓ would lead us to revise the image we have from those traditional works that have come down to us.[2]

Ibn al-Kalbī's book on the idols of the Arabs has been of central importance for discussions of pre-Islamic Arab religion. It was extensively cited in the *Muʿjam al-buldān* of Yāqūt (d. 626/1229) and, lacking access to any manuscript of Ibn al-Kalbī's work, Wellhausen used those citations as a main source in his *Reste arabischen Heidentums* (first edition 1887). Wellhausen's *Reste*, although it was not the first western investigation of pre-Islamic Arab religion, is undoubtedly the most important and influential and is still widely regarded as authoritative in that field. In the early years of the twentieth century the Egyptian scholar Aḥmad Zakī Pasha bought a manuscript of Ibn al-Kalbī's work in Damascus, and prepared an edition in Cairo in 1914, but only the second edition of 1924 was widely distributed. Other editions and translations followed.[3] In the present work reference is mainly to the text presented with a German translation and extensive notes by Rosa Klinke-Rosenberger.[4] Since the *Kitāb al-Aṣnām* is so central to the subject, much of the discussion here about the nature of Muslim tradition in general will refer to it: conclusions about Ibn al-Kalbī's work will affect our attitude to the tradition as a whole.

Ibn al-Kalbī's *Kitāb al-Aṣnām* is at first sight a rather random list of some of the idols and sanctuaries of the pre-Islamic Arabs, with details about their geographical situation, the tribe or tribes associated with them, and other information less consistently given, such as the way in which an individual sanctuary or idol was destroyed in the Islamic period.[5] Most of the entries are quite short and the work as a whole, in the manuscript used by Zakī Pasha, consists of only fifty-six pages (not folios) of twelve lines per side. The longest entry is devoted to the idol al-ʿUzzā, which Muslim tradition and the Koran always associate with Allāt and Manāt – these are the three 'daughters of Allāh' or 'goddesses' at the centre of the story of the 'satanic verses' and are

[2] Among other works with sections listing the idols of the Arabs are Ibn Hishām, *Sīra*, I, 76–91 (material included almost word for word in the *Aṣnām* of Ibn Kalbī), Abū Jaʿfar Muḥammad b. Ḥabīb (d. 245/859), *Kitāb al-Muḥabbar*, ed. I. Lichtenstaedter, Hyderabad Deccan 1942, 309–23, Abū Muḥammad ʿAlī b. Aḥmad b. Ḥazm (d. 456/1064), *Jamharat ansāb al-ʿarab*, ed. E. Lévi-Provençal, Cairo 1948, 457–60.

[3] On a Medina MS of the work, apparently of little value, see the editor's introduction to *Aṣnām-Atallah*, xxix–xxxi.

[4] *Aṣnām K-R*. Enquiries about Klinke-Rosenberger have yielded little information. The Leipzig office of her publisher, Otto Harrassowitz, was destroyed by bombing in World War II, and all correspondence and documentation was lost. I am grateful to Albrecht Weddigen of Harrassowitz Verlag, Wiesbaden, and to others who have responded to my enquiries. There is an English translation of the *Aṣnām* by N. A. Faris, *The Book of Idols*, Princeton 1952.

[5] The work attributed to Ibn al-Kalbī is sometimes cited with the title *Tankīs al-aṣnām* (The Overturning of the Idols). If that was in fact the title, it recalls the Syriac *On the Fall of the Idols* of Jacob of Seruj (fifth century AD), which celebrates the end of idolatry with the coming of Christ, and underlines the need to situate Ibn al-Kalbī's work in the tradition of monotheist literature on the topic.

alluded to together by name at Koran 53:19–20 (where they are not called 'goddesses'). In the *Aṣnām* these three are grouped together and discussed one after the other, as are the only other idols to be named in the Koran (71:23), the five 'gods of the people of Noah' – Wadd, Suwāʿ, Yaghūth, Yaʿūq and Nasr.[6] Elsewhere there is no obvious order in the listing, although it is occasionally possible to suggest why a particular idol or sanctuary appears where it does.[7]

The details about the idols and sanctuaries are interwoven with citations of poetry, understood as referring or alluding to the idol or sanctuary in question. The relationship between the poetry and the text, whether the verses are adduced merely for illustrative purposes or whether the work should be regarded as a commentary on, and amplification of, the verses, needs to be discussed. There are also koranic quotations but these are remarkably few, probably because, apart from the two groups of three and five names just mentioned, no explicit references to the idols and sanctuaries dealt with in the *Aṣnām* are to be found in the Koran.

The work begins with, and the list of idols and sanctuaries is in places interrupted by, accounts and explanations of how mankind in general became idolaters after knowledge of God had been revealed to Adam and his descendants, and how the Arabs became idolaters after Abraham had introduced true monotheism, the *dīn Ibrāhīm*, into Arabia. Sometimes these accounts and explanations tell us how particular idols originated. They prevent the work from being simply a list and, insofar as it has an argument, they provide it.

To what extent can we regard the work as a creation of Ibn al-Kalbī? It seems clear that the *Aṣnām* as we know it is a product of accretion, the end result of the reworking and interpolation of a transmitted text. It contains rep-

6 One other name occurs in the Koran which is sometimes treated in the tradition as a part of the polytheism of the *jāhiliyya*. Koran 53:49, part of a series of verses that emphasise the power of God, refers to God as the Lord of al-Shiʿrā, the latter name referring to Sirius, the dog star. Although the *Aṣnām* does not treat al-Shiʿrā, some commentators tell us that the star was worshipped by the tribe of Khuzāʿa and specifically by a certain Abū Kabsha, an ancestor of the Prophet. See *Aṣnām K-R*, 80, n. 56.

7 For example, the discussion of the five 'gods of the people of Noah' near the beginning of the work is separated from the sentence 'these five idols were worshipped by the people of Noah' by the apparently intrusive discussion of the sanctuary (*bayt*) at Ṣanʿāʾ called Riʾām. It is likely that the discussion of Riʾām has been put here because the account of the last of the five idols, Nasr, has involved reference to the tribal group of Ḥimyar, and Riʾām was regarded as a sanctuary which had belonged to Ḥimyar. In a similar manner the discussion of the idols Isāf and Nāʾila near the beginning of the work seems to interrupt the account of how ʿAmr b. Luḥayy distributed the five noachian idols among the Arab tribes. It is likely that Isāf and Nāʾila are treated in this place because the whole section is concerned with the theme of how idols came to be worshipped among the Arabs after Abraham and Ishmael had established true monotheism in Arabia. The story of Isāf and Nāʾila is one of the ways in which this is explained. However, the perception of such logical connexions cannot allow us to judge whether the text at this point shows sufficient coherence to indicate that the arrangement was that of Ibn al-Kalbī himself or his source. It could be that passages such as these are interpolations introduced where they are because some later editor or transmitter has decided this is a suitable place for material he wished to add.

etitions, variants and interruptions in the logical flow of the discussion (even though it should be allowed that logical connexions might sometimes exist but be invisible to the modern reader). It contains different accounts in different places of the origins of idolatry; the same idol, sanctuary or other feature of Arab paganism is sometimes treated at different places in the text in different or contradictory ways; there are two separate sections headed *al-anṣāb*; there are two distinct and varying attempts to define the difference in meaning between *wathan* and *ṣanam* at separate locations in the text;[8] the first part of the work, after the introductory *isnād*, is a continuous text which does not give the authorities for individual reports while the latter part gives a separate *isnād* for many of its reports; the same verse of Mutalammis, in which the poet swears 'by Allāt and by the *anṣāb*', is given in two different places, on the first occasion the commentator describing it as a lampoon (*hijā'*) against ʿAmr b. al-Mundhir, on the second referring to ʿAmr by his alternative name, ʿAmr b. Hind, and explaining that the lines were written 'because of what he had done to al-Mutalammis and to Ṭarafa b. ʿAbd'.

On the basis of such features, Nyberg argued that the work contains a core text, extending from the beginning to p. 47, l.4 of the Zakī Pasha edition (= *Aṣnām K-R*, 31, l.8). At that latter point (*awwalu mā ʿubidat al-aṣnām*) the topic with which the work began, 'The beginnings of idolatry', occurs again although in a different form. But Nyberg excluded from this core text p. 25, l.4 to p. 26, l.7 (= *Aṣnām K-R*, 15, l.15 – 16, l.14), a report about the destruction of al-ʿUzzā which is introduced by a shorter *isnād* than that with which the work began and one that prefaces many of the reports in the latter stages of the work as we know it.

The core text, according to Nyberg, was transmitted to Abū Bakr Aḥmad b. Muḥammad al-Jawharī (active c. 333/944–45),[9] whose name is part of the *isnād* at the beginning of the work and who is the last link in the shorter *isnād*s to be found in the latter part of the work. Jawharī then added to the core other reports he knew which were ascribed to Ibn al-Kalbī, among them the interpolated passage about the destruction of al-ʿUzzā. At an even later date two appendixes containing information on two more idols were added. Even so, it is clear that the work does not contain all the relevant material ascribed to Ibn al-Kalbī: Yāqūt, who quotes extensively from the *Aṣnām*, has material from Ibn al-Kalbī relating to the idol al-Jalsad which is not from the *Aṣnām*.[10]

This leaves the date of the core text somewhat indeterminate and it may be

[8] See above (chap. 2, p. 55, n. 26).

[9] Not the contemporaneous Abū Bakr Aḥmad b. ʿAbd al-ʿAzīz al-Jawharī who transmitted from Ibn Shabba and others and who is credited with a *Kitāb al-Saqīfa* (*GAS*, I, 322; Āgha Buzurg Tihrānī, *al-Dharīʿa ilā taṣānīf al-shīʿa*, Najaf 1936–78 s.v. 'Saqīfa').

[10] H. S. Nyberg, 'Bemerkungen zum 'Buch der Götzenbilder' von Ibn al-Kalbī', in *ΔΡΑΓΜΑ Martino P. Nilsson . . . dedicatum*, Lund 1939, 346–66, esp. 350–4. A work on Arab idolatry is listed among the writings of Ibn al-Kalbī in the *Fihrist* of Abu 'l-Faraj Muḥammad b. Isḥāq al-Nadīm (d. c. 380/990–91: *The Fihrist of al-Nadīm*, trans. Bayard Dodge, New York and London 1970, 208). For the material on al-Jalsad, see Wellhausen, *Reste*, 53 ff.

that there are more lines of cleavage than Nyberg's account allows for, but it is enough to show that Ibn al-Kalbī should probably not be regarded as the author, in any modern sense of that word, of the work as we have it, even though the material in it goes back to him and his circle. It is not impossible that the text was composed some time after Ibn al-Kalbī by the amalgamation of individual reports and items of tradition which had been transmitted on his authority.

Beyond that, it is difficult to ascertain the sources of the individual items of information. The *isnāds* (chains of authority) in the work show Ibn al-Kalbī transmitting much of the material from his father, Muḥammad b. Sā'ib al-Kalbī (d. 146/763) but the ultimate sources are only intermittently specified. The famous companion of the Prophet ʿAbd Allāh b. al-ʿAbbās is named as the authority for several of the items pertaining to the exegesis of the Koran, to the Prophet and the 'biblical' stories, but that is likely to be a conventional ascription indicating that such material was part of the great mass of similar reports ascribed to Ibn ʿAbbās in the field of koranic exegesis and *ḥadīth*.[11]

Nyberg suggested that the work contains local Arabian traditions and reports from bedouin informants, and it is true that there are a few items that are ascribed to such sources. A description of the idol Wadd at Dūmat al-Jandal in the border region between the Arabian peninsula and Syria is given on the authority of a member of the family that is said to have been its guardians. A report about the idol al-Fals is said to have reached Ibn al-Kalbī from members of the Ṭā'ī tribe to which it belonged. The second group of reports about al-Uqayṣir are prefaced by an *isnād* going back to a man of the tribe of Jarm, and subsequently an explanation of some verses relating to al-Uqayṣir mentions a dispute regarding a water source, said to have been settled by the Prophet in favour of Jarm.

Local tradition may be reflected too in some topographical details, such as that the idol Dhu 'l-Khalaṣa was now the threshold of the mosque at Tabāla, or in the peculiarly detailed information about the site of the (destroyed) sanctuary of al-ʿUzzā. Naturally, we cannot judge the accuracy or validity of such statements – local tradition does not guarantee authenticity.[12]

The sources of the *Aṣnām*, the individuals who formulated the reports Ibn al-Kalbī collected and transmitted, therefore, remain unclear. What is clear is that, in spite the fact (to be illustrated) that it is locatable within the general tradition of monotheistic criticism of idolatry, the *Aṣnām* is a specifically Muslim work. It is not only that there is a negative or hostile approach towards

[11] For a fuller discussion of the sources, and a more positive evaluation of the material attributed to Ibn al-ʿAbbās, see Asnām-Atallah, xlvii–xlix; cf. A. Rippin, 'Ibn ʿAbbās's *al-Lughat fī'l-Qur'ān*', *BSOAS*, 44 (1981), 15–25 for a more critical conclusion regarding the attribution of literary works to Ibn ʿAbbās.

[12] See *Aṣnām K-R* nn. 114 and 133 for travellers' reports of local traditions in nineteenth-century Ṭā'if which explained various stones there as idols that are listed by Ibn Kalbī and other traditional sources but without any connexion to that town.

the idolatry it depicts, but in its organisation and approach it constantly refers to specifically Muslim concerns.

The initial account of the origins of idol worship among the Arabs, who fell away from the monotheism brought by Abraham, explains it as a corruption, due to human weakness and forgetfulness, of an attachment to the Kaʿba and its rituals. The list of idols begins with those that have a koranic connexion or an association with Mecca. We are told how idols came to be erected around the Kaʿba and then of Isāf and Nāʾila[13], two Meccan idols the story of whose origin concerns both the Kaʿba and the violation of the sexual abstention imposed on those making the pilgrimage to it in Islam. There then follow the three female idols mentioned by name in the Koran and said to have been worshipped by the Meccans, and the five noachian idols, also named in the Koran. Even the apparently intrusive discussion of Riʾām, which divides these two groups, has a Meccan connexion since its destruction was credited to a south Arabian ruler whose story (not in the *Aṣnām*) involved Mecca and the Kaʿba. Next follow reports about three further idols in Mecca (none of which is mentioned in the Koran) – Hubal, Isāf and Nāʾila (again).

From this point the principles, if any, of organisation become more difficult to discern. A brief discussion of whether all pre-Islamic Arab names beginning with ʿAbd ('servant of') are theophorics as they are in Islam precedes a short account of the Prophet's destruction of the idols around the Kaʿba after his conquest of Mecca. Logically, the latter might make more sense immediately following the account of the Meccan idols while the problem regarding names with ʿAbd would link better with the brief reference to the idol Manāf (ʿAbd Manāf being an important figure in traditions about pre-Islamic Mecca) from which, in the text, it is separated by the account of the destruction of the idols around the Kaʿba.

There then follows a miscellany of topics with no obvious order of arrangement. Nevertheless, even here references to the Kaʿba and to Mecca recur. An account of domestic idols refers only to their use by Meccans, the standing stones (*anṣāb*) are shown to reflect the veneration the pre-Islamic Arabs made to the Kaʿba, and a brief sentence stressing the depths of Arab idolatry equates worshipping an idol with adopting a sanctuary other than the Kaʿba. Furthermore, a passage regarding the *jinn* is linked with the interpretation of Koran 7:193.

Even the following treatment of a series of idols and sanctuaries that have no immediate connexion with the Kaʿba or the Koran occasions a number of linkages. ʿUmyānis (see chap. 1 above) is associated with the interpretation of Koran 6:136, a key text for the notion of *shirk*. Of three kaʿbas in places in Arabia other than Mecca, two (according to the text) have nothing to do with religion and the third was never built; there would be no reason to mention them other than the connexion between their names and the Kaʿba at Mecca.

[13] On this pair, see above, p. 68–9.

A church in the Yemen called al-Qalīs (possibly a deformation of *ecclesia*) would inevitably call to mind the story of Abraha (who is said to have built it) and his attack against Mecca, a story linked in exegesis with Koran Sūra 105.

Then, at the point Nyberg regarded as the end of the core text, we begin again with accounts of how idolatry began (in the world this time, rather than just in Arabia) and some of the topics and idols of the core text are taken up again. The focus is mainly on the noachian idols, before the work ends with the Dajjāl (the Muslim version of the eschatological figure called the Antichrist in Christian tradition) and the idol al-Fals. Throughout the entire text most of the 'information' is in some way explicitly connected with Muslim concerns, whether the Meccan sanctuary, interpretation of the Koran and *ḥadīth*, or the idea of the religion of Abraham.

Why did such a work come to exist? Nyberg suggested that the koranic material was so 'concrete' that it led the Muslims to demand to know more about the religion that is attacked in it. He also referred to the romantic interest in Arab things (*Beduinromantik*) which typified, in his view, the culture of the Umayyad period (AD 661–750).[14] Although he noted that the poetry the early Islamic scholars collected from the bedouins contains remarkably few references to *jāhilī* religion, he appears to have regarded the *Aṣnām* as a sort of commentary on the poetry it contains, i.e., that the poetry is the starting-point for the prose material on the idols, sanctuaries and other topics, and not that the poetry is adduced merely to illustrate and enliven the prose.

It has already been pointed out that most of the idols and sanctuaries mentioned in the text do not appear in the Koran, and that koranic citations are relatively few. The *Aṣnām* is not, therefore, a commentary on the Koran in any conventional sense. Furthermore, as was argued in chapter 2, it is certainly not correct to say that the Koran provides 'concrete' information about the religion of the pre-Islamic Arabs. Perhaps Nyberg merely meant that the religious ideas of the opponents are such a constant object of attack in the Koran, while at the same time they are only vaguely and allusively referred to, that it would be natural for readers and hearers to want to know more about them.

As for the poetry, it may be that some details provided in the reports of the *Aṣnām* have been inspired by a verse of poetry, but it is not really possible to see the work in general as a commentary on the poetry. If Ibn al-Kalbī or anyone else had set out to compile a work that would elucidate all the verses he knew containing allusions to the old Arab paganism, the work would surely have been arranged differently. As argued above, the focus of the work is really on such things as how idolatry came to exist, the central importance of Mecca

[14] The interest in things Arab (grammar, dialects, poetry, tribal information, etc.) was a real feature of early Islamic times, part of the creation of the Islamic–Arabic culture, and it remained a strong element in that culture in its later stages. An interest in Arab paganism was undoubtedly part of it. The 'research' that such interest inspired, however, is unlikely to have been purely academic, but motivated by and used in the service of religious belief. We have the example of the creation of the 'Scottish Homer', Ossian, in the eighteenth century to remind us how a romantic impulse can use genuine materials (in this case Irish ballads) in the fabrication of a false image of the past.

and the Kaʿba, and on such things as the interpretation of the Koran, the *ḥadīth*s, and the biography of the Prophet – the concerns of Islam not of connoisseurs of poetry. Some idols are mentioned for which there are no verses, and in other sources there are verses referring to idols we do not find in the *Aṣnām*. In general one has the impression that the poetry is brought in for illustration and to enliven the prose text. One cannot rule out that some of the poetry at least has been inspired by the details reported in the prose, rather than vice versa.

Nyberg's first suggestion – that the work is an attempt to respond to a desire to know more about the religion of the opponents attacked in the Koran – seems closer to the mark. However, that does not mean that the *Aṣnām* is the result of dispassionate research and a pure desire to know more. In my opinion although, like the tradition in general, it may contain some fragments of real information, it presents them in the context of stories and an overall organisation that reflect the Muslim image of the idolatrous *mushrikūn*. It is a repository of reports resulting from the conviction that the *shirk* and *kufr* attacked in the Koran are to be identified as the pagan religion of the pre-Islamic inhabitants of inner Arabia. One effect of this is to substantiate the Arabian origins of Islam and the validity of understanding the Koran against the background of the *jāhiliyya* in Arabia.

Modern scholarship has generally been willing to accept the value of the reports about pre-Islamic *jāhilī* religion in Muslim traditional works such as the *Aṣnām* of Ibn al-Kalbī as a reflection of historical conditions in pre-Islamic Arabia. Complaints usually centre on the fragmentary and haphazard nature of the material, not on its authenticity, even though it is sometimes acknowledged that the presentation of the information has been adversely affected by Muslim rejection of the idolatry of the *jāhiliyya* and much that went with it. Discussions of the religion(s) of the *jāhiliyya* continue to draw heavily on the traditional material, and many of them begin by stressing the value of the best-known compilation of traditional material on Arab religion, the work of Ibn al-Kalbī.[15]

[15] Ryckmans, *RAP*, 7, acknowledges that by the time the Muslim scholars began their 'recherche historique' most of the details about Arab paganism had already been irredeemably lost and what remained was often falsified and deformed by legends of recent origin. Nevertheless, he then assembles a series of what are presented as facts about the religion of the *jāhiliyya*, based on the material transmitted in the tradition, noting that 'Le plus précieux de ces receuils est le *Livre des idoles* d'Ibn al-Kalbî'. Rosa Klinke-Rosenberger, in *Aṣnām K-R*, 27, says, 'Das Götzenbuch des Ibn al-Kalbî ist religionsgeschichtlich von hohem Werte'. Henninger, 'Pre-Islamic bedouin Religion', 4, criticises D. Nielsen's work as 'much too speculative' but says that 'more reliable studies' followed the discovery and publication of the *Aṣnām*. More recently, Susanne Krone, *Die altarabische Gottheit al-Lāt*, Frankfurt am Main 1992, says of the *Aṣnām*, 'somit ist es religionsgeschichtlich von hohem Wert und eine wichtige Quelle für jede Studie über eine altarabische Gottheit'. The limitations she sees in it are simply that its information is circumscribed geographically and chronologically. For Nyberg's more ambivalent position, see below, and for a more pessimistic assessment of the value of the Muslim literary material, emphasising the way in which it has been coloured by 'false dogmatic theories and apocryphal biblical legends', see D. Nielsen, 'Zur altarabischen Religion', in Nielsen et al. (eds.), *Handbuch der altarabischen Altertumskunde*, esp. 178–80.

One aspect of the traditional material on Arab idolatry which has received rather perfunctory attention is its relationship with other monotheistic literature pertaining to 'idolatry'. Although scholars such as Nielsen and G. Ryckmans have recognised the role of legends and biblical stories in Ibn al-Kalbī's *Aṣnām*, there has been little attempt to compare the Muslim traditional material about the idolatry of the Arabs of the *jāhiliyya* with other monotheist literature about idols and their worshippers. The only partial exception appears to be the article of Friedrich Stummer, 'Bemerkungen zum Götzenbuch des Ibn al-Kalbî',[16] which shows an awareness of themes and ideas common to the Muslim reports and to other literature, seeking to explain such common material by the theory of the seepage of Hellenistic culture and ideas into Arabia and the Ḥijāz.

Literary material about (i.e., denigrating and attacking) idols and their cults was produced not only by the monotheistic religious tradition (Judaism, Christianity and Islam) but also by various individuals and schools, especially the Stoics, belonging to the Graeco-Roman religious and philosophical tradition. 'Monotheism' in the world of Late Antiquity was not confined to the three representatives of monotheistic religion and it has been recognised that the ideas, motifs and language of the Graeco-Roman critics of popular religion deeply influenced Jewish and Christian writings about idolatry.[17] Apart from the Bible and various types of apocryphal and pseudepigraphical material written by Jews and Christians, it is probably early Christian polemics and apologies against contemporary paganism that provide the most substantial body of such writings.

Of course, various ideas and themes are represented in such works but modern studies would not lead one to suppose that they are particularly valuable as sources of real information about the religious ideas and practices against which they argue. While they may mention some deities or sanctuaries by name, their hostility means that the information they provide is selective and presented in ways that make it difficult to distinguish between fact and presentation. The facts alluded to are secondary to the religious or moral point the monotheist critic of 'idolatry' wishes to make, and the primacy of the religious or moral point leads to a selective and distorted approach to the reality under attack.

In general, it has been argued that Jewish literature, with the exception of that produced in Hellenistic Alexandria, was less interested in attacking paganism than was early Christian. Yehezkel Kaufmann underlined the

[16] *ZDMG*, 98 (1944), 377–94. Michael Lecker, 'Idol Worship in Pre-Islamic Medina (Yathrib)', *Le Muséon*, 106 (1993), 331–46, draws attention to the stereotypical nature of many of the stories with which he is concerned, but does not cast his net wider than the Muslim tradition.

[17] Edwyn Bevan, *Holy Images. An Inquiry into Idolatry and Image-Worship in Ancient Paganism and in Christianity*, London 1940 (Gifford Lectures for 1933), provides some idea of the influence of the Hellenistic critiques of polytheism and idolatry.

stereotyped attitude in the Hebrew Bible to the religions of the neighbouring peoples, the way in which it portrays them as a one-dimensional fetishism, and concluded that the religion of the people of Israel had long been secure against the temptations of idolatry and polytheism. The same conclusion, together with a lack of interest in proselytisation, seems to follow from Saul Lieberman's illustration of the paucity of interest in Graeco-Roman religion in rabbinic writings. The well-attested influence of Hellenistic culture on Jewish thought and art in Late Antiquity, the willingness of Jews to express their monotheism in the language and symbols of the wider culture in which they lived, presumably confirms this religious self-confidence.[18]

Early Christianity was concerned to proselytise but its literature too seems a relatively poor guide to the reality of the other religions with which it was in contact. In the Acts of the Apostles (17:22 ff.) we are told that Paul visited Athens and addressed the council of the Areopagus (at the foot of the Acropolis there), but all we learn is that the Athenians were reputed to be very religious/superstitious (*deisidaimones*) and that Paul chose to criticise them for their worship of the 'unknown god' whose inscribed altar he had seen. We might at least have expected some reference to Athena, the patroness of the city. Acts (19:23–40) does tell us of the importance of the cult of Diana in Ephesus and even that Paul converted many there by arguing that 'gods made by hand are no gods at all', but the Letter to the Ephesians, i.e., the Christians among them (the ascription of which to Paul is debated), seems more typical when it attacks sexual immorality, impurity and greed as 'worshipping a false god'.[19]

H. J. W. Drijvers has argued that Syriac texts such as the *Homily on the Fall of the Idols* of Jacob of Seruj or the *Doctrina Addai* preserve genuine information about pagan deities worshipped in Edessa in the early Christian centuries, but J. Teixidor is more sceptical and it may be noted that although Syriac texts present Nebo and Bel as the two main deities of the Edessans, Julian the Apostate's speech on King Helios (AD 362) refers only to the two deities Azizos and Monimos.[20]

There is, then, reason to question the value of Jewish and Christian writings as a source of knowledge regarding the religions of the societies in which these two monotheistic religions were developing. Generally, one would not expect

[18] Y. Kaufmann, *The Religion of Israel*, English trans. London 1961, 7 ff. (Kaufmann's analysis of the biblical material pertaining to idolatry remains valid whether or not his general thesis about the pre-exilic monotheism of the Israelites is persuasive); Lieberman, 'Rabbinic polemics against Idolatry', 'Heathen Idolatrous Rites in Rabbinic Literature', both repr. in his *Hellenism in Jewish Palestine*, 115–27, 128–38.

[19] Eph., 5:5. Michael Cook drew my attention to the story involving Diana in Acts. R. M. Grant, *Gods and the One God*, London 1986, 26, 64, seems to attribute the silence about Athena to Paul's discretion, which must be a possibility.

[20] H. J. W. Drijvers, *Cults and Beliefs at Edessa*, Leiden 1980; Teixidor, *Pagan God;* Jacob of Seruj, 'Discours de Jacques de Saroug sur la chute des idoles', ed. and trans P. Martin, *ZDMG*, 29 (1895), 107–47; *Doctrina Addai*, ed. and trans. G. Phillips, London 1876. There is a new translation by Alain Desreumaux, *Histoire du roi Abgar et de Jésus*, Brepols 1993 (information owed to Andrew Palmer).

monotheist writers to be interested in the details of pagan religion for its own sake, but only as the background for stories important for the history of monotheism. One would also expect references to pagan religion to be conventional and reflexions of monotheist preconceptions. The account of Paul winning converts from Diana by convincing them of the futility of idolatry is unusual in that references to Graeco-Roman religion in the New Testament and indications that the Christians were concerned to debate with the pagans are few. Its mockery of 'gods made by human hand' is, however, conventional and it is doubtful whether it would be very persuasive in winning converts from the cult of Diana. If it were not for its apparent concern to document its claimed pagan background, something in which Jewish and Christian literature seems uninterested to the same extent, we might not expect Muslim information about Arab idolatry to be any more substantial.

Before assessing the value of the Muslim literature about idols as a source for historical reconstruction, it is necessary to relate it to the tradition to which it belongs. I suggest that a work such as the *Kitāb al-Aṣnām* of Ibn al-Kalbī should not be understood primarily as a collection of Arabian traditions about Arab religion but as a collection of characteristic monotheistic traditions and ideas adapted to reflect Muslim concepts and concerns. If Muslim tradition contains real historical information about the religion of the Arabs of the *jāhiliyya* (and that needs to be demonstrated), that information is embedded in a literary approach that has its roots in the pre-Islamic Middle East outside Arabia.

In general, for its monotheist opponents idolatry is a result of human stupidity, gullibility or wickedness, often all combined. It originates as a corruption of a previously pure monotheism. It is often associated with general corruption, especially sexual immorality and murder, and sometimes Satan and his servants have a hand in leading men into it. Idolaters are worshippers of things made of wood, stone or other cheap or expensive materials, made by human hands – sculpted, carved or moulded. The idols have no reality, they are unable to eat, speak or defend themselves, they can do neither good nor harm, although often their priests and guardians use tricks to make it seem as if they can. The idols are vain and false. This last view, however, is in tension with the idea that they are in fact inhabited by demons or spirits and that those who attack them or seek to destroy them are in great danger. Muslim reports about the idols of the Arabs of the *jāhiliyya* display all of these common features.[21]

In spite of its apparent diversity, reports in Islamic traditional literature about the idols and sanctuaries of the Arabs in the *jāhiliyya* concentrate on a limited number of general topics. The most prominent are the origins of idolatry and of individual idols, in the world generally and in Arabia; the destruc-

[21] See, e.g., the summary, based on Jewish and Christian sources, given in Grant, *Gods and the One God*, 45–6.

tion of Arabian idols and sanctuaries with the rise of Islam; and details about the tribes and families with which the Arabian idols were associated. Many of the details about the religious ideas and practices of the *jāhiliyya*, and the names of the gods and sanctuaries, are given to us in the context of reports that focus on these themes. These topics themselves are a good indication of the fact that the Muslim literature belongs to a tradition of discourse about idolatry older and wider than Islam itself. This is obvious and will be clear from some of the comparative material below.

The persistence of a general image of the state of idolatry which associates it with corruption and immorality may be illustrated by two texts separated by a period of perhaps 800 years. The Hellenistic Jewish work The Wisdom of Solomon, probably stemming from Alexandria in the first century BC, in its denigration of paganism and its apologia for the religion of Israel, summarizes the condition of the world consequent on its adoption of idolatry:

> It was not enough, however, for them to have such misconceptions about God; for, living in the fierce warfare of ignorance (*agnoia*), they call these terrible evils peace. With their child-murdering rites, their occult mysteries, or their furious orgies with outlandish customs, they no longer retain any purity in their lives or their marriages, one treacherously murdering another or wronging him by adultery. Everywhere a welter of blood and murder, theft and fraud, corruption, treachery, riot, perjury, disturbance of decent people, forgetfulness of favours, pollution of souls, sins against nature, disorder in marriage, adultery and debauchery. For the worship of idols with no name (*anonymon*) is the beginning, cause and end of every evil.

With this may be compared summaries of the base condition of the Arabs, sunk in their idolatry, before God in His mercy sent the Prophet to them. This version is taken from a Muslim polemic against Christianity probably dating from the ninth century AD. According to it, the Arabs of the *jāhiliyya* were

> a nation (*umma*) which had not previously been given a scripture or a prophet; sunk in an ignorance (*jāhiliyyīn fī jahāla*) in which it was unaware that there is a Lord and reckoning after death; on the wrong path and given to creating falsehoods; its people were enemies one to another and in mutual hatred; disobedient to God and lacking in fear of Him; worshipping idols and eating carrion and blood; allowing what should be prohibited, rejecting the right path and complacent in error; its people killing one another and shedding their own blood; disregarding the prohibited degrees in matters of sexual relations; heedless of ties of kinship; causing harm to its own children and . . . in the worst of evil. Thus it remained until God sent them this Prophet.[22]

The latter passage seems to allude to several of the features that have often been accepted as fundamental features of life in the *jāhiliyya* and upon which traditional texts such as the *Muḥabbar* of Ibn Ḥabīb elaborate: feuds,

[22] Wisd. 14:22–7 (the translation is that of the Jerusalem Bible; this book is not part of Protestant or Jewish Bibles); see also H. A. Wolfson, *Philo*, 2 vols., Cambridge, Mass. 1948, I, 16–17; Sourdel (ed.) , 'Un pamphlet musulman', 32 (text) = 25 (trans.); the text seems difficult and perhaps corrupt in places but the general sense is clear enough. Similar (but lacking the harming of children) is Ibn Hishām, *Sīra*, I, 336 – Ja'far b. Abī Ṭālib before the Najāshī.

lawlessness, sexual immorality and lax marriage practices that led to the violation of women, the burial of unwanted female children, lack of food taboos and rules of purity, and gross idolatry. It was the achievement of Islam, we are told, to rescue the Arabs from this depravity. Modern discussions of Muslim laws on marriage and divorce usually assume that they were intended to ameliorate the evils of the *jāhiliyya*, especially as they affected the position of women.[23] The broad similarity between the two texts suggests, however, that we may be dealing with literary and conceptual stereotypes as much as any historical reality.

The maltreatment of children is particularly interesting since it is a frequent theme in monotheist attacks on 'idolaters', starting with the child sacrifices to Molech (Leviticus 18:21) and continuing to refer to the more widespread practices of the exposure and abandonment of unwanted children.[24] Muslim tradition and modern scholarship generally relate koranic allusions to the opponents' infanticide (e.g., 6:137, 140, 151) to the alleged pre-Islamic Arab practice of burial at birth of unwanted female babies, a custom known generically as *wa'd al-banāt*. The widespread occurrence of the motif in literary contexts associated with idolatry, however, at least raises the question whether the Koran does refer to a particular practice specific to the Arabs of the *jāhiliyya*. Lammens suspected that much of the Muslim traditional material about female infanticide in Arabia was the product of free elaboration of the koranic verses.[25]

It is in the themes and details contained in the reports about the origins of idolatry, in the world generally and in Arabia, and about the origins of particular idols, that the relationship between Muslim tradition and the wider monotheist discourse is most obvious.

[23] See, e.g., *EI* s.v. 'Nikāḥ' and 'Ṭalāḳ' (by Schacht).

[24] E.g., Clement of Alexandria, *Paedagogus*, 3:4: 'They will not take up an abandoned child but they support parrots and curlews'; Tertullian, *Apologeticus*, VIII, 2–3: 'In Africa infants used to be sacrificed to Saturn. . . . Yes, and to this day that holy crime persists in secret. . . . Surely your way is more cruel, to choke out the breath in water, or to expose to cold, starvation and the dogs.' Abandonment and exposure of children is attested widely enough for us to know that it is not only a polemical motif: a papyrus letter of AD1 in which a man tells his wife to 'put out' their expected baby if it turned out to be a girl is widely quoted. The charge of infanticide was also made against the early Christians by their pagan opponents. For a full treatment of the theme from Late Antiquity to the Renaissance, see John Boswell, *The Kindness of Strangers*, New York 1988, with a consideration of the Muslim data at 184–9, and the papyrus letter at 101.

[25] H. Lammens, *Etudes sur le règne du calife omaiyade Mo'âwia Ier*, Paris 1908, 77 and n. 3; Lammens, 'Qoran et tradition', 13. Only one koranic passage (16:57–9) specifically mentions 'burying' (*yadussuhu fī 'l-turāb*; note the masculine suffix pronoun) and only one (81:88–9) uses the root *w-'-d* (in the form *al-maw'ūda*). The prominence of the motif in traditional characterisations of the *jāhiliyya* is evident, e.g., in the account of Zayd b. ʿAmr's break with the religion of Quraysh (Ibn Hishām, *Sīra*, I, 224 f.): it is specified that one of the features of the *jāhilī* religion that he rejected was *qatl al-maw'ūda*. Ṭabarī, in *Tafsīr* (Cairo), XII, 155, no. 13953, cites ʿAbd al-ʿAzīz: if you want to know about the *jahl* of the Arabs, then recite what comes after verse 100 of Sūrat al-Anʿām, God's words, 'They are lost who have foolishly killed their children without knowledge' (i.e., 6:140).

So obvious that it might go unnoticed is the shared monotheist assumption that monotheism is historically prior to polytheism, that the latter is a corruption which arises for a number of reasons. Muslim accounts of the origins of idolatry and the worship of stones, both in the world generally and in Arabia specifically, follow this general monotheist pattern – which may compared with the *Urmonotheismus* theory referred to in chapter 1 above, and it presumably derives primarily from the monotheist belief that God revealed Himself at the time of the creation and that, therefore, polytheism and idolatry must have originated later. In the case of Islam, it also relates to the fundamental concept of the religion of Abraham – the claim that Islam was the inheritor of the pure monotheism of Abraham. In its reworking of the common theme of Abraham as the ancestor and exemplar of monotheism (see above, p. 23f.), Islam linked the theme with an account of its own origins in Arabia in a milieu dominated by Arab pagans. It elaborated accounts of how Abraham's monotheism had been brought to Arabia where it was subsequently corrupted by the Arab descendants of Abraham.

The introduction of idolatry – according to both Muslim and other monotheist accounts – is explained in various ways. Probably the most prominent is the view that idolatry began as the result of a human weakness which in itself is not reprehensible – the desire to commemorate and remember: an image is made, usually to remember the dead, especially a pious ancestor or a beloved relative, but it might also be of a living ruler. The Muslim account of the corruption of the religion of Abraham by his descendants displays this theme slightly differently, focusing on the wish of the Arabs to remember the sanctuary Abraham had founded and the rituals he had introduced, and their gradual slide into worshipping stones that at first had been merely symbolic and commemorative.

Perhaps the best-known statement of this theme outside Muslim tradition is again to be found in the Wisdom of Solomon:

> They [idols] did not exist at the beginning and they will not exist for ever; human vanity brought them into the world. . . . A father afflicted by untimely mourning, has an image made of his child so soon carried off, and now pays divine honours to what yesterday was only a corpse, handing on mysteries and ceremonies to his people; time passes, the custom hardens and becomes law. Rulers were the ones who ordered that statues should be worshipped: people who could not know them in person, because they lived too far away, would have a portrait made of that distant countenance, to have an image they could see of the king whom they honoured; meaning, by such zeal, to flatter the absent as if he were present . . . and the crowds, attracted by the beauty of the work, mistook for a god someone whom recently they had honoured as a man.[26]

Stummer called the idea that an image made of a dead beloved inevitably leads to idolatry a topos of Jewish, Christian and Hellenistic polemic and, drawing on the commentary on the Wisdom of Solomon by P. Heinisch, referred to a

[26] Wisd.14:12 ff.

number of early Christian texts that make use of the theme.[27] One example is Minucius Felix:

So with our ancestors' attitude to the gods: blind and credulous they yielded simple minded credence. Devoutly reverencing their kings, while, after death, desiring to see their likenesses portrayed, eager to perpetuate their memories in statues, they formed objects of worship from things designed for consolation . . . each individual group revered its founder, or some famous chief, or virtuous queen strong beyond her sex, or the inventor of some social boon or art, as a citizen worthy of remembrance. It was at once a tribute to the dead and an example to posterity.[28]

This explanation of idolatry is related to the theory of euhemerism. It is a salient feature of Muslim traditions about individual idols as well as of the accounts of the introduction of idolatry into the world by the descendants of Adam and of the corruption of the religion of Abraham in Arabia. For example, some of the reports about the origins of the idol Allāt at Ṭā'if tell us that it was originally a stone upon which a Jew used to crush or grind meal which he then made into a broth for the pilgrims; after his death the stone, or in some versions he in the form of the stone, came to be venerated and called *al-lātt*, 'the grinder'.[29]

In a slightly different way, the story of the origins of the idols Isāf and Nā'ila echoes the same theme. Turned to stone following their sexual misconduct inside the Kaʿba, the man and woman who had borne these names were set up in different parts of Mecca as a warning to others to avoid their sin, but the original intention was perverted and they became idols and objects of worship in themselves (*lam yazal amruhumā yadrusu wa-yataqādamū ḥattā ṣārā ṣanamayn*). In some versions it is reported that originally these two idols wore the same clothes they had as human beings and that these clothes were continuously replaced with new ones as they became worn out.[30]

The idea of the dangers arising from the clothing of the idol, intensifying the dangers inherent in the creation of a human form in stone, occurs also in the Muslim story of a statue that Solomon allowed to one of his wives to commemorate her dead father. In response to her request to have such a memorial, Solomon had commanded one of the *shayṭān*s to make an image for her, although, of course, it was lifeless (*lā rūḥa fīhi*). But then the woman began to put onto the statue the clothes her late father had worn, and when Solomon went off to work in the morning she and her children would prostrate themselves before the statue just as she had done when her father was alive (he had been a king). This went on for forty days before Solomon was told, 'For forty days to please a woman something other than God has been worshipped in

27 Stummer, 'Bemerkungen', 383–7.

28 *Octavius*, ed. and trans. G. H. Rendall, Loeb, London 1931, XX, 5–6.

29 Ṭab., *Tafsīr*, (Bulaq), on Koran 53:19; for a good selection of variants see Krone, *Altarabische Gottheit,* 45, n. 3.

30 *Aṣnām K-R*, 6 = 34 (trans.); Ibn Hishām, *Sīra*, I, 82–3; Azraqī, *Akhbār Makka*, I, 88, 119–22.

your house.' Thereupon he went and smashed the idol and punished the woman and her children.[31]

This last tradition perhaps also echoes the biblical theme of the corruption of Solomon's monotheism and his attraction to idolatry as a result of the influence of his foreign wives, although in the Muslim version, as one would expect, the prophet Sulaymān is immune to the temptations of idolatry.[32] In Muslim tradition the idea that idolatry occurs as the result of foreign influence nevertheless appears, evident especially in the story of the visit of ʿAmr b. Luḥayy to Syria. ʿAmr, who is closely associated in the tradition with the introduction of idols into Arabia, is reported to have visited Syria for reasons of health and to have been impressed when he saw that the people there prayed to idols to obtain rain or victory over their enemies. He, therefore, asked for some from them and brought them back with him to Mecca. The story is sometimes connected with the introduction of Hubal, the idol reported to have been inside the Kaʿba in the *jāhiliyya*, sometimes of Allāt, al-ʿUzzā and Manāt.[33] Rosa Klinke-Rosenberger noted a general similarity between the account of ʿAmr's visit to Syria and that of Naaman and Elisha in 2 Kings 5, although there is no reason to suspect a direct link.[34] At any rate, the idea that corruption comes from foreign sources is an obvious one.

It may be significant too that in the tradition Solomon had a *shayṭān* make the idol that his wife and children came to adore, even though in this story there is no suggestion that the *shayṭān* had responsibility for what ensued. The idea that demonic or satanic influence is involved in the introduction of idolatry is another element in the monotheistic explanations of it. In one Jewish account Enosh, son of Seth and grandson of Noah, made a figure out of dust and clay in order to show his people how God had created Adam, and, when he tried to show them how God had breathed life into him, Satan took advantage and animated the figure himself.[35] In another story, the corruption of the world occurred when the fallen angels came down to earth and married human women (an allusion to Genesis 6:1–8; the biblical *benē elōhīm* being

[31] Ṭabarī, *Taʾrīkh*, I, 587–89. See further J. Lassner, *Demonizing the Queen of Sheba*, Chicago and London 1993, 101 ff.

[32] 1 Kgs. 11:1–10.

[33] In the *Aṣnām K-R*, 5–6, 6–8 and 33–7 (text) = 33–4, 34–6 and 57–61 (trans.) the material about ʿAmr's introduction of the idols seems disorganised and illogical, confusing what ought to be distinct stories. Logically, as will become clear later, ʿAmr's introduction of the five 'gods of the people of Noah' to the Arabs should follow the story of his discovery of them on the seashore. The story of his journey to Syria should concern different idols. But at the beginning of the *Aṣnām* we find the story of the excursion to Syria as a prelude to ʿAmr's distribution of the gods of the people of Noah among the Arabs, and only much later in the work, when these five gods are treated again (in a part Nyberg identified as an addition to the core text) do we have the story of the find on the seashore. In the *Sīra* and Azraqī's *Akhbār Makka* the traditions are even more fragmented and dispersed. Azraqī links ʿAmr with the introduction of Allāt, Manāt and al-ʿUzzā, although he also has ʿAmr's visit to Syria as the occasion when he brought Hubal and set him up inside the Kaʿba.

[34] *Aṣnām K-R*, 79, n. 52.

[35] Ginzberg, *Legends of the Jews*, I, 122.

interpreted as the fallen angels).[36] It is notable that in some versions of the story of ʿAmr's discovery of the five idols on the seashore, ʿAmr, referred to as a *kāhin* ('soothsayer', but related to Hebrew *kōhēn*, 'priest'), is led to them by a *jinni* (*kāna lahu raʾī min al-jinn*).[37] As already reported, when the Prophet destroyed the idols of Mecca at the time of his conquest of the town, Iblīs cried out in woe for only the third time in his existence and called on his followers to abandon hope that Muḥammad's community would ever return to idolatry (*shirk*).[38]

But it is not only in general ideas of how idolatry and idols are originated that the relationship of Muslim tradition to the more general monotheistic literature about idolatry is evident; specific details are also illuminating. In the case of the accounts of how idolatry entered the world generally (as distinct from how it entered Arabia) this may not be surprising but it is nevertheless worth illustrating how the Muslim accounts reflect details to be found in non-Muslim accounts.

The rivalry of the descendants of Seth (Shīth) and those of Cain (Qābil), and the culpability of the Cainites, is a theme in Ibn al-Kalbī's traditions of how idolatry originated among the generations after Adam and how the five gods of the people of Noah in particular came to exist.[39] The theme figures too in several of the Jewish stories summarised by Louis Ginzberg. Some of the accounts given by Ginzberg associate the beginnings of idolatry with Enosh, son of Seth, but he notes that there are differences of opinion about the culpability of Enosh himself and about that of the sons of Seth in general. According to one version at least, they became corrupt only under the influence of the Cainites. This ambivalence towards the descendants of Seth seems to be reflected in the Muslim reports.[40]

In Ibn al-Kalbī's account, the five idols representing the gods of the people of Noah are said to have been made in the time of Jared.[41] Not all versions of the passage from 1 Enoch that ascribes the introduction of idolatry to the fallen angels who descended and married human women say when that event occurred, but the citation of 1 Enoch 6:6 in Greek by George Syncellus (c. AD 800), which probably reflects the Aramaic text, puts it in the time of Jared, evidently playing on the Hebrew verb in the name of Jared (*yārad*, 'to descend'). This seems to be the origin of the naming of Jared in the account of Ibn al-Kalbī.[42]

The report that ʿAmr b. Luḥayy found the five idols on the seashore whither they had been swept by Noah's flood echoes the report of Berosus that the

[36] Enoch 6–8. [37] *Aṣnām K-R*, 33 (text) = 59 (trans.); Jāḥiẓ, *Ḥayawān*, VI, 203.
[38] See above, p. 69. [39] *Aṣnām K-R*, 31–2, 32–3 (text) = 56–7, 57–8 (trans.).
[40] Ginzberg, *Legends of the Jews*, index, s.v. 'idols, idolatry'; see esp. the note at v, 150–1.
[41] *Aṣnām K-R*, 32–3 (text) = 57–8 (trans.). In the MS the name of Jared appears variantly (Yardī, Yārad) but the genealogy of Jared back to Seth is set out as in Genesis 5. The text also specifically identifies Idrīs with Enoch (Aḥnūkh) the son of Jared.
[42] Ginzberg, *Legends of the Jews*, V, 150–1. The Syncellus text is quoted in Sparks (ed.), *Apocryphal Old Testament*, 189, n. 15.

builders of the Tower of Babel derived their knowledge and skill from books that contained the wisdom of the antediluvian generations, books which were found in the valley of Shinar after the great flood had subsided. In Jewish tradition, it should be remembered, the Tower of Babel is associated with idolatry, some of those who built it being motivated by the desire to install their idols in heaven and worship them there.[43]

The traditional connexion between idolatry and sexual misconduct is found in the story of the origins of Isāf and Nā'ila, where their punishment is one of transmogrification. This punishment occurs in Jewish material in connexion with both sins: those who had participated in building the Tower of Babel in the desire to install their idols in heaven were turned into apes and 'phantoms'; it was as a result of the idolatry that followed from Enosh's attempt to make a human figure out of dust and clay that mankind ceased to resemble God and instead came to look like apes and centaurs; the women who seduced the fallen angels, who introduced idolatry to mankind, were transformed into 'sirens'.[44] The Koran, of course, twice refers to Jews who were changed into apes for profaning the Sabbath.[45]

Ibn al-Kalbī's report that Arab travellers would, when they halted for the night, collect four stones, three of which they used as a tripod to cook on, while the fourth functioned as a 'lord' to be worshipped in imitation of the Kaʿba calls to mind passages in Isaiah and the Wisdom of Solomon which ridicule the man who, having a piece of wood, uses some of it for his cooking fire and makes an idol of the rest.[46]

The accusation that the statues and images worshipped by the opponents are no more than lifeless things formed from natural materials usually of little value and made by human hands is frequently made in polemic. Tertullian

[43] *Aṣnām, K-R*, 33–7 (text) = 57–61 (trans.). Berosus, *The Babylonaica of Berossus*, trans. S. Mayer Bernstein, Malibu 1978, 20–1. Ginzberg, *Legends of the Jews*, V, 201–4.

[44] Ginzberg, *Legends of the Jews*, I, 123, 180, V, 152.

[45] Koran 2:65, 7:166. The Arabic verb *masakha* which is used in the accounts of Isāf and Nā'ila means simply 'to change into', 'to transform', and not all versions of the story qualify it with *ḥajar* ('stone') even though the story seems to require that they were petrified. Lane's first example of the verb (*Lexicon* s.v.) refers to transforming someone into an ape. The only koranic occurrence of the verb (36:37) seems ambiguous. S. D. Goitein, *Jews and Arabs*, New York 1955, 51–2, suggested that the koranic references to the Jews who were turned into apes possibly reflected Yemeni midrashim since monkeys were common in Yemen but not in Syria. Jāḥiẓ, *Ḥayawān*, VI, 78–9, gives examples of some animals that were believed to have resulted from the *maskh* of human beings, but surprisingly says that he thinks that the *ahl al-kitāb* do not agree that God had ever changed a human into a pig or an ape, although they do agree that He had changed Lot's wife into a stone. The Arabs, he says, see such transformation into animal form as a punishment for corrupt tax collectors. For a detailed treatment of this theme, see Michael Cook, 'Ibn Qutayba and the Monkeys', *JSAI* (forthcoming).

[46] *Aṣnām K-R*, 20–1 (text) = 47 (trans.); cf. Wāqidī, *Maghāzī*, 870–1; Isa. 44:9–20; Wisd. 13:10 ff. The last marvels that someone, even though he knows that what he has made is merely an image, should nevertheless harangue it for health, life, a successful journey, and profit. This perhaps relates to Ibn al-Kalbī's report (*Aṣnām K-R*, 20–1 (text) = 47 (trans.)) about the Meccans' recourse to their household gods before setting out on a journey. For another example of the use of a wooden idol as firewood, see Lecker, 'Idol Worship', 333 and n. 11.

created an elaborate and extended comparison between the tortures suffered by the Christian martyrs and those inflicted on the pagan gods by their devotees: 'What idol is there but is first moulded in clay, hung on cross and stake? . . . On your gods, over every limb of them, fall axes and planes and rasps.'[47] Judah Halevi, as we saw, made use of the traditional theme when, alluding to several passages in Deuteronomy foretelling the worship of 'other gods, of wood and of stone', he interpreted the wood as the cross worshipped by the Christians, and the stone as that worshipped by the Muslims.[48]

In Muslim traditions about the origins of idolatry we see a conflation of idolatry and litholatry in the reports about the corruption of Abraham's monotheism by his Arab descendants who carried stones from Mecca to other places in Arabia and about the practice of indigent Arabs of setting up stones as *anṣāb* or taking a stone as a *rabb*. The emphasis on Mecca and its sanctuary, the portrayal of Arab stone worship as originating as an imitation of and attempt to commemorate the rituals at Mecca, gives the theme a specifically Muslim reference but its identification of idolatry and the worship of stones is traditional. Sometimes, as with Paul's reported attempt to win the Ephesians over from the worship of Diana, the emphasis may be on the man-made nature of the idols. For example, there is the report of the offer by the descendant of Cain to sculpt (*naḥata*) an idol.[49] On other occasions the stones appear to be naturally occurring *objets trouvés* as in the account of the practice of choosing the best stone as a *rabb* and using the others to support the cooking pot.

Since they are merely things of wood, stone, clay, etc., whether man made or natural, it follows that the idols have no power or animation. The idol made for Solomon's wife, it is underlined, contained no spirit, and the Cainite who offered to make images of the five deceased who later became the gods of the people of Noah also insisted that he had no power to infuse them with spirits. ʿUmar addressed the Black Stone of the Kaʿba saying that he knew it was merely a stone which could do neither good nor ill and, if it were not that he had seen the Prophet revere it, he would not have done so himself.[50]

Idols cannot, therefore speak or eat. Habakkuk cried, 'Woe unto him who says to the wood, 'Awake!', or to the dumb stone, 'Arise, it shall teach!', and in the apocryphal 'Letter of Jeremiah' the gods of the Babylonians are taunted

[47] *Apologeticus*, ed. and trans. T. R. Glover, Loeb, London 1931, §XII. [48] See above, pp. 85–6.

[49] *Aṣnām K-R*, 31–2, 32–3 (text) = 56–7, 57–8 (trans.); Abū Bakr is reported to have reminded the Anṣār in the Saqīfa that before God sent His Prophet his *umma* had worshipped beings other than God which they thought could intercede for them and bring them benefits – 'but they were only made of sculpted stone and carved wood (*min ḥajar manḥūt wa-khashab manjūr*)': Ṭabarī, *Taʾrīkh*, I, 1840.

[50] E.g., Bukhārī, *Ṣaḥīḥ*, *Ḥajj*, 50, 57. Cf. the words of the four *ḥanīf*s rejecting the idol worship of Quraysh: on a day when Quraysh had gathered to perform rites by one of their idols, they said, 'Do we not circumambulate a stone which can neither hear nor see, and can do neither harm nor good' (Ibn Hishām, *Sīra*, I, 223).

as counterfeit and with no power to speak.[51] In the Koran, Abraham, disputing with his idolatrous contemporaries, asks, 'Can they hear you when you cry to them, or help you, or do you harm?', and in another passage he taunts the idols themselves, 'Do you not eat? What is the matter with you that you do not speak?'[52] In the *Kitāb al-Aṣnām* Khuzāʿī b. ʿAbd Nuhm addresses the idol Nuhm with verses that refer to it as dumb and without understanding.[53]

On the other hand, the idol's lack of animation and its adherents' fundamental lack of respect for it could lead to the idol itself being eaten: the tribe of Ḥanīfa worshipped a god or idol – different reports use different words – made of *ḥays* (dates mixed with clarified butter); but when they were hit by a famine they ate it. As the poet said:

> At a time of want and need, Ḥanīfa ate their lord and master;
> Of their lord they had no heed, nor of punishments thereafter.[54]

It seems likely that the traditional description of idols as vain, futile or false (in Arabic *bāṭil*) stems from this idea of their impotence.

The impotence and inanimate nature of the idols is illustrated especially in some of the stories about their destruction. The guardian of the idol Suwāʿ told ʿAmr b. al-ʿĀṣ who had been sent to destroy it that he would be unable to do so because it would protect itself. ʿAmr responded by telling the guardian that he was attached to a vain thing (*anta fiʾl-bāṭil*) and that the idol could neither hear nor see. He destroyed it easily and his men sacked its treasury but found nothing in it.[55]

When the people of Ṭāʾif expressed their fear about destroying their idol al-Rabba (Allāt), ʿUmar insisted that it was only a stone which could not know who worshipped it and who did not. When they came out expecting to see the idol defend itself against the blows of Mughīra b. Shuʿba, the latter jokingly fell down pretending that he had been laid low, but then leapt up and told them that it was merely a contemptible thing of clay and stone.[56]

The guardian of the idol of the tribe of Sulaym at Ruhāṭ accepted Islam and destroyed the idol when he saw foxes urinating around it and eating the offerings that had been made to it. That led him to protest:

[51] Hab. 2:19 (see also 2:18); Baruch 6:7. Other examples: 1 Cor. 12:2; Ps. 115:5/113:13 = Ps.135:16/134:16. [52] Koran 26:69 ff., 37:82 ff.

[53] *Aṣnām K-R*, 25 (text) = 51 (trans.). Klinke-Rosenberger accepted the suggestion of Fleischer that the text's *ayyukum* should be read *abkam* (dumb) – see her n. 295. Atallah also follows this suggestion in his edition and translation.

[54] Abū Muḥammad ʿAbd Allāh b. Muslim b. Qutayba, *Kitāb al-Maʿārif*, ed. Tharwat ʿUkāsha, Cairo 1969, 621; cited from Andalusī, *Ṭabaqāt al-umam* by Schefer in his 'Notice sur le Kitab Beïan il Edian', 148. [55] Wāqidī, *Maghāzī*, 870.

[56] Mūsā b. ʿUqba, *Maghāzī*, coll. M. Bāqshīsh Abū Mālik, Agadir 1994, 308 ff.; cf. Ibn Hishām, *Sīra*, II, 541–2, Wāqidī, *Maghāzī*, 972. Cf. the accounts of the demolition of the Kaʿba by Quraysh in the childhood of the Prophet in Azraqī, *Akhbār Makka*, I, 158–9, 161–2, and of the fear of the Meccans when Ibn al-Zubayr wished to demolish it following the siege of Ḥuṣayn b. Numayr, ibid., I, 205.

Can that a lord and master be, upon whose head two foxes pee!
To be by foxes pissed upon is base humiliatíon.

(That he also heard a voice coming from it proclaiming the prophethood of Muḥammad rather goes against the spirit of the story.)[57]

If the idols did on occasion seem to speak or eat, it was as a result of the trickery of their priests and guardians. A member of the family of guardians of the idol Wadd at Dūmat al-Jandal told Hishām Ibn al-Kalbī's father how his own father used to send him with milk to the idol, telling him, 'Give it for your god to drink,' but, he admitted, 'I would drink it myself.'[58] The apocryphal 'Letter of Jeremiah' mocks the idols of the Babylonians, telling us that 'offerings made to them might as well be made to the dead – whatever is sacrificed to them, the priests resell and pocket the profit'.[59] Possibly the best-known story of this type occurs in the tale of Bel and the Dragon, in which the trickery of the priests of Bel, who had a secret door through which they used to come and take away the offerings left for the idol, was exposed by Daniel by the simple expedient of scattering ashes around and thus showing up the priests' footprints.[60]

The idea that the idols were impotent and inanimate, however, was in some tension with the idea that they were associated with demons or spirits who gave the idol (or its sanctuary) power and life and even made them a source of danger. In the First Letter to the Corinthians Paul in one place insists that the idols are nothing since there is only one God but then goes on to remark that sacrifices to idols are in fact sacrifices to devils.[61] While it is true that some claimed that the idols could only speak because priests hid in the statues,[62] other accounts seem to accept that idols could communicate with their worshippers. The tribe of Ḥimyar used to hear voices coming from their temple (*bayt*) called Ri'ām at Ṣanʿā' (*kānū yukallamūna minhā*), and Jāḥiẓ, citing a

[57] Muḥammad b. Saʿd, *al-Ṭabaqāt al-Kubrā*, ed. E. Sachau et al., 9 vols., Leiden 1905–28, I/2, 49; Nūr al-Dīn ʿAlī b. Aḥmad al-Samhūdī, *Wafā', al-wafā*, ed. Muḥammad Muḥyi 'l-Dīn ʿAbd al-Ḥamīd, 4 vols. Cairo 1955, IV, 1225. For discussion and other sources, see Lecker, *Banū Sulaym*, 52ff., and Lecker, 'Idol Worship', for other examples of stories illustrating the helplessness of the idols and the willingness of their devotees to abandon them once the idol has been humiliated.

[58] *Aṣnām K-R*, 34 (text) = 59 (trans.). Cf. Stummer, 'Bemerkungen', 387, who cites Tyrannius Rufinus and Theodoret as witnesses for this line of thought.

[59] Baruch 6:27. Is this the reason why ʿAmr b. al-ʿĀṣ found the treasury of Suwā' empty?

[60] Dan. 14:1–21 in the Vulgate. For another example of an idol that spoke because an old woman stood behind it and answered questions on its behalf, see Lecker, 'Idol Worship', 337.

[61] Cf. 1 Cor. 8:4 and 10:20–1.

[62] Jāḥiẓ, *Ḥayawān*, VI, 201, says that several reports claim that in the *jāhiliyya* they used to hear murmurings (*hamhama*) coming from inside the idols, but, he says, God would not have subjected the Arabs to such a test (*fitna*): he does not doubt that it was the guardians playing tricks for their own benefit. You only have to have some idea of the tricks the Indians get up to in their temples, he says, to know that God has blessed mankind with the *mutakallimūn* who have arisen among them. The passage was referred to by Rosa Klinke-Rosenberger (*Aṣnām, K-R*, 87, n. 88) from Zakī Pasha's note (12, n.1) to his edition of the *Aṣnām*, and also by Stummer, 'Bemerkungen' (388–9).

poem of Aʿshā Ibn Zurāra al-Asadī in support, remarks that the Arabs believed in such voices so strongly that they were surprised that anyone should reject them.[63]

At other places the idol spoke through divining arrows cast before it. Hubal, the idol inside the Kaʿba, is the best-known example, but they are also mentioned in connection with Dhu ʾl-Khalaṣa. At the Kaʿba the arrows were cast by a man known as the *ṣāḥib al-qidāḥ*.[64] Outside Muslim tradition Ezekiel and Habakkuk link divination by means of arrows with idolatrous worship, especially involving household gods.[65]

The power of the idols to speak was connected with the idea that the idols were the dwellingplace of demons or spirits.

These unclean spirits, or demons, as revealed to Magi and philosophers, find a lurking place under statues and consecrated images, and by their breath exercise influence as of a present god; at one while they inspire prophets, at another haunt temples, at another animate the fibres of entrails, govern the flight of birds, determine lots, and are the authors of oracles mostly wrapped in falsehood.[66]

This last idea comes out particularly in some of the accounts of the destruction of the Arab idols after the conquest of Mecca. When Khālid b. al-Walīd was sent to cut down the sacred trees at the sanctuary of al-ʿUzzā in the valley of Nakhla he was confronted by a black woman (*ḥabashiyya*) with dishevelled hair, her hands on her shoulders and gnashing her teeth. Khālid split her skull and she turned to ashes. In the texts she is referred to as a *shayṭāna* and Stummer protested at Wellhausen's demotion of her to the status of a 'witch' (*Hexe*) – she is obviously the demon who inhabited the idol.[67]

The same theme occurs in a story about the destruction of Nāʾila in Mecca: the Prophet identified the black, grey-haired, naked woman who was clawing at her face, wildly pulling her hair and proclaiming her woe, as Nāʾila herself despairing of ever being worshipped in the land again.[68]

Stummer cited some parallels from early Christian texts for the idea of demons appearing at the destruction of temples and for demons as black or Ethiopians: when the temple of Zeus at Apamea was destroyed, according to Theodoret, a black demon appeared and sought to hinder the fire that was consuming the sanctuary; in the apocryphal Acts of Peter a female demon is described as 'a very ugly woman, Ethiopian in appearance, not Egyptian but totally black'. Stummer was willing to concede the authenticity of al-ʿUzzā's

[63] *Ḥayawān*, VI, 202.

[64] Riʾām: *Aṣnām K-R*, 5 (text) = 35 (trans.); Hubal: ibid., 17–18 = 44 ; Dhu ʾl-Khalaṣa: ibid., 29 = 55. The story of the vow of ʿAbd al-Muṭṭalib is the best-known reference to the divining arrows before Hubal: Ibn Hishām, *Sīra*, I, 153 (=Azraqī, *Akhbār Makka*, I, 118) mentions the *ṣāḥib al-qidāḥ*. [65] Ezek. 21:26; Hab. 2:18–19.

[66] Minucius Felix, *Octavius*, §XXVII:1. Cf. Bevan, *Holy Images*, 93.

[67] *Aṣnām K-R*, 15–16 (text) = 41–3 (trans.); cf. Ibn Hishām, *Sīra*, II, 436–7, Wāqidī, *Maghāzī*, 873 ff., Azraqī, *Akhbār Makka*, I, 127 ff.; Jāḥiẓ, *Ḥayawān*, VI, 201, says that when Khālid demolished al-ʿUzzā she fired sparks at him and set his thigh on fire, and the Prophet visited him in his sickness (*ʿādahu al-nabī*). [68] See above, p. 69.

sacred trees but referred to the idea of the *ḥabashiyya* demon as 'aus dem hellenistisch–christlichen Kulturland eingedrungen, also sekundär'.[69]

In such stories and its approach to the phenomenon of idolatry, in general terms and in many of its details, therefore, Muslim literature about the idols of the Arabs appears as a continuation of a tradition well attested in the Middle East before Islam. In itself that does not mean that the Muslim literature on this subject is without any historical foundation: the reality of child exposure and abandonment is just one example of how literary motifs and topoi may reflect an historical reality. Nor does it mean that the Muslim material is merely a borrowing from, or rehash of, earlier non-Muslim material: it is part of the same tradition of thought and its chief innovation is obviously to use traditional materials and concepts in its account of a specifically Arab idolatry.

Works such as Ibn al-Kalbī's *Aṣnām* are Islamic in that they adapt traditional monotheistic stories about, and concepts of, idolatry to Muslim concerns. They should not be understood, as it seems they often are, as collections of authentically Arabian ideas and traditions. Any concrete information they contain about idols and sanctuaries in Arabia is presented in stories and reports which are typical of monotheist critiques of 'idolatry' more generally and presented in a stylised way. How, then, might we assess the value of the names and other information about the idols of the Arabs contained in such stories?

[69] Stummer, 'Bemerkungen', 380. Ethiopians appear in connexion with the destruction of an Egyptian temple in the Sybilline Books, and in Muslim apocalyptic at the end of time the Kaʿba will be demolished by *dhu 'l-suwayqatayn min al-ḥabasha* (e.g., ʿAbd al-Razzāq, *Muṣannaf*, V, 136–8). When Ibn al-Zubayr wished to demolish the Kaʿba during the second civil war he made some of the *ḥabashī* slaves begin the work to see if this prophesied figure was among them.

CHAPTER 5

Names, tribes and places

If the stories and themes of Islamic literature regarding the idols of the pre-Islamic Arabs can frequently be understood as variants of those found in monotheist writings more generally, it is nevetheless possible that some, even much, of the detail – the names of the gods, of the tribes associated with them, of the 'priestly' families, of geographical localities, etc. – reflects historical realities to some extent. The nature of that reality and of its reflexion in the literature would still need to be clarified, but it might be argued that at least the literature provides a point from which historical reconstruction could begin.[1]

This chapter considers how far the traditional Muslim material on the idols of the Arabs is usable as a source for the facts of pre-Islamic Arab religion. We will be concerned especially with information at the most basic level, such things as names and geographical locations. The discussion does not aim to be exhaustive and is concerned with general problems and characteristics of the material rather than with collecting all the available evidence about particular gods or idols named in the tradition. There already exist several works to which readers seeking quite comprehensive collections of the evidence pertaining to particular gods, idols or sanctuaries may refer.[2] Attention is focused here on features of the evidence, not on reaching any conclusions about the particular 'gods' or other alleged objects of worship. The three 'daughters of God' involved in the story of the 'satanic verses', although occasionally referred to here, will receive a more detailed discussion later.

To begin with, it is unreasonable to think that all of the details given in the tradition have simply been made up or imagined. In spite of some reservations, to be expressed shortly, about the value of personal names, or of inscriptions, as corroborations of the names of deities or idols discussed in works such as the *Aṣnām*, there seems enough to assure us that some at least of the names that occur in Muslim tradition reflect a historical reality. There is little reason

[1] See Lecker, 'Idol Worship', 343: 'Unsurprisingly, idols figure in the stereotypical stories of conversion to Islam. . . . These stories are of little value as a direct historical source but they are a true reflection of conditions in Yathrib.' [2] Fahd, *Panthéon;* ʿAlī, *Mufaṣṣal.*

to doubt the existence among the Arabs before Islam of the theophoric personal names reported in traditional Muslim texts, such as ʿAbd Ruḍā (servant of Ruḍā), ʿAbd Manāf (servant of Manāf), or Taym Allāt (servant of Allāt), where the second element in the name is that of a deity said in the tradition to have been worshipped among those Arabs. Nor can we really doubt that the names of some gods of Muslim tradition, such as Dhu ʾl-Sharā or Nasr, are Arabic versions of those attested in inscriptions or in pre-Islamic literature, in forms such as Dusares (Latin and Greek), Dūshārā (Nabataean), *nishrā* and *néshro* (Aramaic and Syriac).

Furthermore, although the tradition about pre-Islamic idolatry could, taken as a whole, be interpreted as an attempt to elaborate the Koran in accordance with an image of Islam emerging in an Arabian setting, it is obvious that the names of most of the deities and idols which we are told the pre-Islamic Arabs worshipped are not the product of exegesis in a strict sense. As we have said, the vast majority of the names are not to be found in the Koran where, apart from the ambiguous reference to the Lord of Sirius, only the three 'daughters of Allāh' and the five noachian idols are mentioned by name.

The chief reservations about the extent to which archaeological and inscriptional evidence, or literary evidence external to the Muslim tradition, can be said to corroborate the data of the tradition are the following.

First there is the suspicion that modern scholars concerned with the inscriptions and graffiti from southern and northern Arabia have sometimes been over-eager to refer to the Muslim tradition when seeking to establish the reading of difficult names and words in the inscriptions.[3] Having apparently solved the problem by using one of the names mentioned in the *Aṣnām* or elsewhere to elucidate an ambiguous name in, say, a Nabataean inscription, scholars then tend to use the inscription as a part of the evidence pertaining to the deity or idol of Muslim tradition and it is used in discussions in a way that substantiates the historical reality of that deity or idol.

An example is the idol called Hubal in the Muslim tradition. Hubal plays a relatively prominent role in tradition but is nowhere mentioned in the Koran.[4] In a Nabataean inscription dated to the first century BC from Qaṣr al-Bint near al-Ḥijr, *w-h-b-l-w* occurs in a curse between the names of *d-sh-r* (Dūshārā, Arabic Dhū ʾl-Sharā) and *m-n-w-t-w* (perhaps the Manāt of

[3] For a general statement about the difficulties of establishing readings in Thamudic inscriptions, see F.W. Winnett, *A Study of the Lihyanite and Thamudic Inscriptions*, Toronto 1937, 8, 18–20.

[4] Hubal is said to have been the only idol inside the Kaʿba: *Aṣnām K-R*, 17–18 = 43–4 (trans.); Azraqī, *Akhbār Makka*, I, 65, 100, 117, 118, 122, 161, 166, 192, 193; Ibn Hishām, *Sīra*, I, 77, 152, 154, 226; *EI2* s.v. 'Hubal'; Fahd, *Panthéon*, 95–103; ʿAlī, *Mufaṣṣal*, VI, 250–3. The story of Abū Sufyān's appeal to Hubal on the day of Uḥud occurs also in *ḥadīth* (Bukhārī, *Ṣaḥīḥ*, *Jihād*, no. 164; Ibn Ḥanbal, *Musnad*, I, 463). Wellhausen, *Reste*, 75 suggested that Hubal had become identified with Allāh, and that is why Muḥammad did not attack him in the Koran. Fahd, *Panthéon*, 96 explains the lack of koranic reference as due to the fact that there was nothing to distinguish Hubal from the other Arab divinities such as Dhu ʾl-Khalaṣa and Dhu ʾl-Sharā, whereas other divinities named in the Koran (Allāt, al-ʿUzzā and Manāt) were distinguished by being regarded as the daughters of Allāh.

Muslim tradition). The middle series of consonants was interpreted as 'and Hubal' and the reading has frequently been repeated and referred to, most recently by Fahd, Krone and Healey. The reservations about that reading expressed by the original editor of the inscription, Euting, are generally forgotten or ignored in modern discussions.[5]

The connexion with the Hubal of Muslim tradition must be somewhat unsure. To go further and assume or imply that the Nabataean inscriptions corroborate the totality of the Muslim traditional material on Hubal, or to count all of the 'evidence' regarding Hubal as of equal value to be used in compiling a composite account, is unwarranted. It is striking that in Muslim tradition Hubal never seems to be linked with either Dhu ʾl-Sharā or Manāt, and the gap in time between the Nabataean evidence and that of Muslim tradition is large. If the link between the Nabataean deity (?) and the Hubal of Muslim tradition was found to be persuasive, caution in treating the detailed information provided by tradition would still be necessary.

Another example concerns the koranically attested noachian idol Yaghūth.[6] Attempts to find this god in sources external to Muslim tradition are not completely persuasive. The name is said to occur in Thamudic and Ṣafaitic inscriptions, but as a personal – not a divine – name and the attestations in any case are few. The one claimed attestation in Thamudic is at best unclear. The case may be stronger for the two claimed occurrences of Yaghūth in Ṣafaitic, but it is notable that neither of them was referred to by Eno Littman in his discussion of Thamudic and Ṣafaitic deities.[7]

[5] *EI2* s.v. 'Hubal' by T. Fahd; Krone; *Altarabische Gottheit*, 527; John F. Healey, *The Nabataean tomb inscriptions of Madaʾin Ṣāliḥ*, Oxford 1993, 154 (H16). Euting's reservation is given in the note to line 8 of the text in *CIS*, II, 198 (= J. A. Cooke, *Textbook of North Semitic Inscriptions*, Oxford 1903, no. 80 = J. Cantineau, *Le Nabatéen*, 2 vols., Paris 1932, II, 27). The line has been understood to mean 'Whoever sells this grave, may the curse of Dūshārā, [of Hubal], and of Manāt be upon him' Euting pointed out that *w-h-b-l-w* lacked the initial *l* that occurs before both of the accompanying names, and he suggested it should be understood as an epithet of Dūshārā. The inscription is not referred to by Allouche in his discussion of Hubal in the article 'Arabian Religions' in Eliade's *Encyclopaedia of Religion*, nor does Ryckmans, *RAP*, 14 have any references to evidence for Hubal outside Muslim tradition. Another possible attestation of Hubal in Nabataean, again between the names of Dūshārā and Manāt in a curse attached to a grave, has recently been referred to by S. Krone, *Altarabische Gottheit*, 527, who probably cites it from *RES*, II, 1099. (She gives a cross reference to *CIS*, II, 190, but the inscription there does not correspond to the text at *RES*, II, 1099.) The editor of this volume of *RES* (J.- B. Chabot) identified *h-b-l-w* as the divine name Habel, found in Babylonia in personal names such as Kha-ab-bil-u and Ilu-kha-bil. Chabot did not refer to the Hubal of the *jāhiliyya*. It may also be noted that Milik and Cantineau read *CIS*, II, 158, line 5 as containing the personal name *b-n h-b-l* ('son of *h-b-l*') but Healey regards the reading as unclear.

[6] *Aṣnām K-R*, 6–7 (text) = 34–5 (trans.), 35 (text) = 60 (trans.); Ibn Hishām, *Sīra*, I, 79; Abū ʿUbayd Allāh Muḥammad b. Aḥmad al-Qurṭubī, *al-Jāmiʿ li-aḥkām al-Qurʾān* (*Tafsīr*), 20 vols., Cairo 1935–50, XVIII, 309; Ibn Ḥabīb, *Muḥabbar*, 317; Ibn Ḥazm, *Jamhara*, 459; ʿAlī, *Mufaṣṣal*, VI, 260–2 (note the interpretative rewording of the *Aṣnām* passage about the hill called Madhḥij).

[7] Fahd, *Panthéon*, 192–3, refers to A. van den Branden, *Les Inscriptions thamoudéennes*, Louvain-Heverlé 1950, 202 for Yaghūth in Thamudic. There we find *w-d-d-t f-(y)-(ġ)-ṯ* translated as 'saluts à Yaġûṯ', but the justification for restoring the latter word thus and for reading

A slightly different example of this apparent overconfidence in establishing mutual corroboration between the Muslim traditional material and other evidence concerns another of the Koran's 'gods of the people of Noah', Suwāʿ.[8] *S-w-ʿ* is said by Ryckmans (*Les réligions arabes préislamiques*) to occur in Thamudic inscriptions as a male personal name, and in his *Noms Propres* it is listed as a divine name too, but that probably merely reflects its occurrence as such in Muslim tradition. The number of attestations for it as a personal name is small, and there is a suggestion that readings may not be certain.[9]

An interesting point here is that it has also been claimed that the Muslim genealogical tradition has Suwāʿ as a personal name. Scholars refer to an ʿAbd Wadd (or Wudd) b. Suwāʿ among the tribe of Hudhayl, which would certainly be interesting, given the traditional association of the idol with Hudhayl, if it could be authenticated. However, all references are to only one source, the *Register*, which H. F. Wüstenfeld provided in the second volume of his *Genealogische Tabellen* of 1852–3. In that volume (p. 5) there is a reference to an (in Wüstenfeld's transliteration) ʾAbd Wodd ben Sowâ, the source for which is indicated as the *Tahdhīb al-asmāʾ waʾl-lugha* of al-Nawawī. In the published text of that work the name appears with a final *hamza*, not an *ʿayn*.[10]

These instances of possible exaggeration of the extent to which Muslim tradition and external sources may be said to corroborate one another do not, of course, mean that examples of such corroboration can never be found. The examples of Dhu ʾl-Sharā and Nasr have already been mentioned and there are certainly others where the reading of inscriptions is not in doubt and the connexion between the name of an idol or god as reported in Muslim tradition is sufficiently close to that of the inscriptions and other sources.[11] The attempt to relate the different sorts of evidence is important and necessary but

Footnote 7 (*cont.*)
it Yaghūth is not at all obvious. The copies provided by van den Branden of the original publications of this inscription by J. Euting and by C. Huber do not show any trace of a *gh (ġ)* but read *w-d-d-t-f-ṯ-y*. Van den Branden says that the reading *y-ġ-ṯ* has been made 'avec' Ryckmans, *NP*, and there, sure enough, in the list of noms propres de personnes (I, 173), under *gh-w-th*, we find Yaghūth as attested twice in Ṣafaitic (once in a Greek transcription, ʾΙαουθος) and once in Thamudic (the text cited by van den Branden). There is no explanation there of how or why the Thamudic inscription has been read as containing the name Yaghūth. We might have missed something, for Littman also says that Yaghūth belonged to the 'Thamudic pantheon' but he does not cite any evidence (E. Littman, *Thamūd und Ṣafā*, (Abhandlungen für die Kunde des Morgenlandes 25), 1940; he discusses the Thamūdic gods at 29–31 and those of the Ṣafaites at 105–8). For the suggestion, not generally accepted, that Yaghūth occurs in Hebrew as Yeʿūsh, the name of one of the sons of Esau in Gen. 36:18, see the note 69 at p. 82 of *Aṣnām K-R*, and Fahd, *Panthéon*, 192–3.

8 Wellhausen, *Reste*, 18–19; Lecker, *Banū Sulaym*, index s.v.

9 *RAP*, 16, 21; *NP*, I, 23, 147–8; in the latter reference Ryckmans indicates that Huber thought that at least one occurrence should be read *s-b-ʿ* rather than *s-w-ʿ*.

10 For references to Suwāʿ as a personal name in Arabic see, e.g., Wellhausen, *Reste*, 19, Fahd, *Panthéon*, 156, n. 3, and Lecker, *Banū Sulaym*, 53, n. 14. Cf. Abu ʾl-Zakariyyā Yaḥyā b. Sharaf al-Nawawī, *Tahdhīb al-asmāʾ waʾl-lugha*, 3 vols., Beirut n.d. (Idārat al-Ṭibāʿa al-Munīriyya), I, 288 (in the notice devoted to ʿAbd Allāh b. Masʿūd).

11 E.g., Wadd and the names of the three 'daughters of Allāh' (on which see the subsequent chapter).

the possibility of overestimating the extent to which the external sources corroborate the details given in Muslim tradition is also obvious.

Even when one is convinced that the name of a deity or idol reported in Muslim tradition does match that of one known from outside the tradition, the nature of the corroboration thus provided may be unclear. In the case of the god Nasr of the Koran and Muslim tradition, for example, we seem to have epigraphic attestation of the name as that of a divinity in south Arabia [12] as well as at Hatra (al-Ḥaḍr, in the region of Mosul) in Mesopotamia.[13] Additionally, a name related to the Nasr of Muslim tradition, and associated with Arabian idolatry, occurs in pre-Islamic literary sources from Mesopotamia. The Babylonian Talmud tractate ʿAvodāh Zārāh refers to 'Nishrā which is in Arabia' as one of five temples devoted to idol worship, the Syriac *Doctrina Addai* (late fourth–early fifth century AD in its present form) mentions the 'eagle (*nèshro*) which is worshipped by the Arabs', while the Syriac Jacob of Seruj (451–521) tells us that the *Persians* had been led by the devil to make an eagle (*n-s-r-*ʾ) which was worshipped.[14]

It may be tempting to see this relative wealth of outside reference as proof of the authenticity of the reports in Muslim tradition about the worship of an idol called Nasr by the Arabs of the *jāhiliyya*, but how exactly does the Muslim evidence relate to that of other sources? Is the material in Muslim tradition evidence of real knowledge of the idol and its worship, or is it a reflexion merely of an established tradition associating Arabs and an eagle deity? In other words, is the Muslim tradition valuable as an independent source of evidence about the cult of Nasr, to be set alongside or added to the epigraphic and non-Muslim literary evidence, or is it no more than an elaboration of an already possibly etiolated literary or oral memory? Some may find that question hair-splitting, but we are not here questioning that at some times (when?) and in some places (where?) there was a cult dedicated to a god bearing a name that could be translated as 'eagle' or 'vulture'; rather our concern is with the value of Muslim tradition as evidence for the religious cults of the pre-Islamic Arabs (specifically those of the *jāhiliyya*).

The association between the eagle god and Arabs or Arabia in Aramaic and Syriac texts does not confirm the worship of Nasr in the *jāhiliyya*. The passages in the Talmud and the *Doctrina Addai* must relate, if they reflect a reality, to local Arabs in Mesopotamia, and Jacob of Seruj calls the adherents of the

[12] Fahd, *Panthéon*, 133 cites A. Jamme, 'Le Panthéon sud-arabe préislamique d'après les sources epigraphiques', *Le Muséon*, 60 (1947), 130 as noting five relevant inscriptions (*CIS*, 189, 552; *RES*, 4048, 4084; Ry. 196). In others *n-s-r* occurs as a noun or preposition – 'territory' or 'in the direction of' (Ryckmans, *RAP*, 46 and n. 499 correcting Wellhausen, *Reste*, 23 where it is said that the inscriptions refer to an eastern and western Nasr).

[13] J. Hoftijzer, *Religio Aramaica: godsdienstige verschijnselen in aramese teksten*, Leiden: Ex Oriente Lux, 1968, 54–5.

[14] Babylonian Talmud, ʿAvodāh Zārāh, fo. 11b (Eng. tr. 59–60); *Doctrina Addai*, 23 (trans.) = text, 24; (Desreumaux trans., 84, section 50; and see Drijvers, *Cults and Beliefs*, 34); Jacob of Seruj, 'Discours', 133 (trans.) = text, 111 (and see Drijvers, *Cults and Beliefs*, 36); Wellhausen, *Reste*, 23; Ryckmans, *RAP*, 16, 39, 46 and notes 497–500; Ryckmans, *NP*, I, 22, 23.

deity 'Persians'. It could even be that the association between the eagle and the Arabs in pre-Islamic literary tradition about idolatry has influenced the development of Muslim tradition on the idolatry of the Arabs of the *jāhiliyya*. The context of the reference to Nishrā in the Talmud passage, as one of five existing temples of idolatry, could be reflected in the koranic passage that lists Nasr as one of the five gods of the people of Noah.

The fact that Muslim tradition associates Nasr with south Arabia may be more persuasive of the fact that the tradition rests on some historical basis in view of the attestation of the name in inscriptions from south Arabia, but even on this point it is difficult to be sure that the Muslim tradition is based on secure and detailed knowledge. For one thing, Nasr is only one of several idols that are associated with the Yemen by the tradition, and it might be thought that that area would be an obvious one in which early Islamic scholars seeking traces of Arab idolatry would find it, even though its relevance for the *jāhiliyya* in a strict sense (i.e., central and western Arabia) is questionable. The *Aṣnām*, in its two separate passages discussing Nasr, says that it was erected at a place in the Yemen called Balkhaʿ, a name that occurs in other sources as the site of another noachian idol, Yaʿūq.[15] Others name different Yemeni locations – Ghumdān, Ṣanʿāʾ – as the site of Nasr.[16] In the *Aṣnām* Ibn al-Kalbī says that the worship of Nasr had in fact died out before Islam as a consequence of the spread of Judaism in south Arabia and that he knew of no poetic attestation of the name. Ṭabarī and Yāqūt, however, could provide a relevant verse, which Wellhausen characterised as 'ein archaisirendes Machwerk ohne geschichtlichen Wert'.[17] The report, attributed to Wāqidī, that the idol of Nasr was in the form of a bird is no more than a deduction from the meaning of the name.[18]

Similar considerations might apply to the traditional material about Dhu ʾl-Sharā/Dusares. Here too the traditional material is characterised by variants and other features (see below) which appear to call into question the extent to which the tradition is based on secure knowledge; and here too one finds the idea of Dusares as a specifically Arabian deity attested in pre-Islamic literature from outside the tradition. Again, 'Arabia' probably does not refer to the peninsula proper but to one of the regions adjoining Palestine.[19]

The nature of the corroboration that occurs when a name occurring in Muslim tradition is attested also outside the tradition can be, therefore, rather ambiguous.

[15] *Aṣnām K-R*, 7 (text) = 35 (trans.), 36 (text) = 61 (trans.); for Balkhaʿ as the site of Yaʿūq, see Ṭab., *Tafsīr* (Bulaq), XIX, 62 , Qurṭubī, *Tafsīr*, XVIII, 309.

[16] Ibn Ḥabīb, *Muḥabbar*, 317 (Ghumdān); Ibn Ḥazm, *Jamhara*, 459 (Ṣanʿāʾ).

[17] Ṭabarī, *Taʾrīkh*, I, 761; Yāqūt b. ʿAbd Allāh al-Ḥamawī *Muʿjam al-Buldān*, ed. as *Jacut's geographisches Wörterbuch*, ed. F. Wüstenfeld, 6 vols., Leipzig 1866–73 IV, 781; Wellhausen, *Reste*, 23. [18] Qurṭubī, *Tafsīr*, XVIII, 309.

[19] E.g., Tertullian, *Apologeticus*, §XXIV, 7: 'Unicuique etiam provinciae et civitati suus deus est, ut Syriae Astartes, ut Arabiae Dusares', etc.

In this connexion attention should also be drawn to the assumption that similar names from different places and times indicate the continuous existence of the same cult. If, for example, various names that look similar to the Allāt of Muslim tradition appear (as they do) in ancient Babylonia, in Herodotus, and in inscriptions from Arabia and elsewhere over several centuries before Islam, that has sometimes been taken to show that the same deity under the same name was worshipped in all these times and places before entering the Muslim traditional literature or the Koran, even though the evidence may point to widely differing conceptions of the nature of the deity – a fertility god, a god of war, an astral god, etc. While that assumption could hold in the case of a specific name such as Dusares/Dushārā/Dhu ʾl-Sharā, attested in a relatively confined area such as the northern Arabia/southern Syria border zone, it seems more questionable where we are faced with names that only have a general similarity in languages such as Babylonian, Greek and Arabic, over a long time-span and a broad geographical area, or which – like Allāt (the Goddess) – are in themselves unspecific.

It is possible that this assumption of continuity, resting on postulations about influences or borrowings, also contributes to an overestimation of the confirmation that the inscriptions and the Muslim traditional material offer each other.

The tendency to assume mutual corroboration between the inscriptions and the traditional material is also reflected in the widespread use of the traditional Arabic form of a divine name as the standard form for reference in modern discussions. For example, names that occur in inscriptions in forms such as *r-ḍ-w*, *r-ḍ-y*, *r-ḍ-ʾ*, *r-ḍ-h*, *r-ḍ*, etc. may be discussed in a chapter or section the title of which indicates that it is all connected with the deity Ruḍā of Muslim tradition. The author may be convinced that these forms all relate to the same cult, but the effect could be to prejudge the issue and to give the impression that the Muslim tradition is the reliable reference point to which the data of the inscriptions must be related.[20]

As for reservations about the value of the theophoric names as evidence regarding pre-Islamic Arab religion(s), they are obvious and more general. Names tend to be conservative and traditional and may not necessarily indicate the strength or even the existence of the cult or religion they seem to reflect. There is too the possibility that the early Muslim scholars who were aware of apparently theophoric names among the Arabs deduced the worship of a god or idol from them and supplied details about the cult to meet the demand for concrete information about the idolatry that, it was agreed, the Koran and the Prophet had attacked. Even if a cult of the god mentioned in the name did exist in pre-Islamic Arabia, we often cannot know whether the

[20] E.g., Krone, *Altarabische Gottheit*, 441 ff. Of course, the use of the Muslim traditional form of the name as the reference form is also a result of the fact that the names in the inscriptions are unvocalised and therefore cumbersome to reproduce and difficult to remember.

Muslim traditional evidence about that cult reflects real knowledge as opposed to speculation.[21]

For example, the Muslim genealogical tradition knows of several individuals bearing the name ʿAbd Ruḍā, as well as persons called Ruḍā and Ruḍāʾ, and it is following the mention of the existence of the apparently theophoric name that the *Aṣnām* introduces the material on this 'idol'.[22] The tradition knows little about Ruḍā: we are told that it belonged to the clan of Rabīʿa b. Saʿd b. Kaʿb b. Zayd Manāt of Tamīm; verses are given attributed to a certain Mustawghir of this clan, and referring to his destruction of Ruḍāʾ (spelled thus in the verse, which requires such a form for reasons of metre); we are further told that 'some of the narrators' have reported that Ruḍā was a sanctuary or stele (*bayt*).[23] Ruḍā seems to play no part in the stories about the Prophet or the *jāhiliyya* and little can be gleaned from the verses about its nature: it is not obvious whether it refers to a deity, a sanctuary, an idol or even a human being.

Names similar to that given in Muslim tradition occur, however, in inscriptions and elsewhere. Forms such as Ru-ul-da-a-a-u, *r-ḍ-w*, *r-ḍ-y*, *r-ḍ-ʾ*, *r-ḍ-h*, *r-ḍ*, and *r-ṭ-y* have been seen to to relate to the Ruḍā of tradition and to offer support for the historicity of the information about the idol of the *jāhiliyya*.[24]

[21] It has been suggested that the traditional scholars may sometimes have changed theophoric names containing the name of a pagan deity or idol into the more innocuous ʿAbd Allāh, especially in the case of ancestors of prominent early Muslims. That may also account for the occasional occurrence of ʿAbd as a name by itself, i.e., the embarrassing element has simply been omitted, although Michael Cook reminds me that ʿAbd was used as a name in Islamic times too. On the other hand there is the case of the Prophet's grandfather whose name is universally reported as ʿAbd al-Muṭṭalib even though the tradition knows of no god called al-Muṭṭalib (a puzzling grammatical form too) but provides an aetiological story associating him with a man called al-Muṭṭalib whose slave he pretended to be.

[22] *Aṣnām K-R*, 19 (text) = 45 (trans.). For the personal names see, e.g., W. Caskel and G. Strenziok, *Ǧamharat an-nasab. Das genealogische Werk des Hišām b. Muḥammad al-Kalbī*, 2 vols., Leiden 1966, II, index s.v.v. ʿAbdruḍā and Ruḍā/Ruḍāʾ.

[23] *Asnām K-R*, 19 (text) = 45 (trans.); Ibn Hishām, *Sīra*, I, 87 (reads Ruḍāʾ); ʿAlī, *Mufaṣṣal*, VI, 268–9. The second hemistich, in which the condition in which the attacker left Ruḍā is described, is difficult to understand – see Stummer, 'Bemerkungen', 379, and cf. the translations.

[24] The earliest attestation of the name has been found in an Assyrian report of the seventh century BC referring to an expedition of Sennacherib against Adummatu in the course of which the Arab king Haza'il received back some gods which had previously been taken from him. Among them was 'Ruldayu' (Krone, *Altarabische Gottheit*, 76, 443). Another early reference to this god, it has been suggested, is the mention by Herodotus of Orotalt as one of the two gods of the Arabs, the other being Alilat. Modern scholars have frequently identified Alilat with Allāt, but have been puzzled by Oratalt. The identification with Ruḍā seems to have been suggested first by Starcky ('Petra et la Nabatène', *Supplement au Dictionnaire de la Bible*, Paris 1964, VII, col. 991) and has been accepted by Teixidor (*Pagan God*, 69) and by Krone (*Altarabische Gottheit*, 71). The identification involves supposition about the way in which the name was pronounced in the time of Herodotus and how that would have been rendered in Greek script. The name does not seem to occur in Nabataean material, but may at Palmyra if it is identical with the *r-ṣ-w*/Arṣū who is named there. (Wellhausen, *Reste*, 59, n.1, wanted to identify the Nabataean *r-ṣ-w-ʾ* with Ruḍā but Nöldeke argued against this and subsequent

In discussions of this god whose continuity from the seventh century BC to early Islam is sometimes postulated, the data of Muslim tradition has been given equal weight with that of other sources so that the material of the *Aṣnām* and the *Sīra* has been used, for example, in the debate about the deity's gender or in the argument that it was identified with Venus.[25] Furthermore, it has been suggested that the cult of the deity extended as far south as Mecca, although Muslim tradition makes no such claim itself.[26] Again one feels that the material of Muslim tradition and of the inscriptions is being interpreted beyond its legitimate limits.

The information in Muslim tradition about such things as the geographical situation of a particular idol or the tribe(s) with which it was connected is most obviously characterised by proliferation of detail which is often lightly variant and sometimes openly contradictory. This is such a widespread feature of Muslim tradition in general (not just that relating to the idolatry of the Arabs before Islam) that it might be thought unneccessary, and certainly would be tiresome, to illustrate it in great detail. However, a few examples will be given with a view to how it might influence our attitude to the historical value of the material on the idols of the Arabs.

The diversity of the traditional information about the idol called Suwāʿ, for instance, one of the 'gods of the people of Noah' mentioned in the Koran, was

scholarship seems to have agreed. See Krone, *Altarabische Gottheit*, 445–8 for a discussion of the possible relationship of Palmyran Arṣū with Ruḍā and a survey of the literature. Fahd, *Panthéon*, 144–5 accepts the identity of the two.) It is in Thamudic and Ṣafaitic that it occurs most frequently in various forms: *r-ḍ-w*, *r-ḍ-y*, *r-ḍ* (e.g., Littman, *Thamūd und Ṣafā*, s.v *r-ṣ-w* in the Namen- und Wörterverzeichnis).

25 For the suggested identification of Ruḍā with Venus, see Fahd, *Panthéon*, 146. For a survey of the discussion of the gender of *r-ḍ-w* (and variant forms), see J. Henninger, *Arabica Sacra. Aufsätze zur Religionsgeschichte Arabiens und seiner Randgebiete*, Fribourg and Göttingen 1981, 75, n. 93. (Some scholars make the deity feminine on the basis of such things as the grammatical indications of some inscriptions (an argument that naturally depends on how the inscription has been read and understood), theories about the noun form behind the Arabic Ruḍā (Lundin wanted to see it as the feminine form of the elative – *fuʿlā*, giving a parallel with names such as that of al-ʿUzzā), the fact that the name sometimes appears accompanied by a representation of a naked woman, and the use of the feminine pronoun suffix in the verse quoted in the *Aṣnām*. Some argue for a masculine identity also from the grammar of particular inscriptions, from their acceptance of the god's identity with the (masculine) Orotalt of Herodotus, and from the fact that *r-ḍ-w* often accompanies a female deity and is understood to be the male partner of the goddess. Muslim tradition also discusses the form of the name Ruḍā, which is grammatically a problem if, as the tradition assumes, it is related to the verb *raḍiya*.)

26 S. Krone, *Altarabische Gottheit*, 448–9; Krone points out that the inscriptions reflect the prominence of *r-ḍ-w* in the region of north Arabia and particularly in the area around Taymā', which she calls an important centre of the cult, but is willing to extend its territory as far as Mecca apparently merely because the name of Ruḍā occurs in Muslim tradition. Of the fourteen individuals named ʿAbd Ruḍā listed in the index of Caskel and Strenziok, *Ǧamhara*, ten belong to the various subgroups of Ṭayyi' whose territory was in the north extending into the Syrian desert. As Krone says, this would fit in with the concentration of references around Taymā'.

apparent already in Wellhausen's discussion and is even more so in the wealth of references gathered in Michael Lecker's *Banū Sulaym*.[27]

The *Aṣnām* treats that idol in two separate passages, in both of which it is associated with a place called Ruhāṭ. The difficulty lies in reconciling the additional information about Ruhāṭ supplied in each passage. The first tells us that the place was near Yanbuʿ (on the Red Sea, near Medina), the latter that it was in the *baṭn* (depression) of Nakhla. Nakhla, which other reports link with the idol al-ʿUzzā (see the next chapter), occurs in the name of two valleys (the northern Nakhla and the southern Nakhla) in the vicinity of Mecca, although scholars seem to differ regarding their precise location.[28]

Whether or not we can be precise about Nakhla, it is difficult to establish an association between it and Ruhāṭ, other than from Ibn al-Kalbī's (second) report situating Suwāʿ at *Ruhāṭ bi-baṭni Nakhla*. Muslim tradition tends to associate Suwāʿ with the tribe of Hudhayl which lived in the vicinity of Mecca, and the name Ruhāṭ is mentioned twice in poems ascribed to men of the tribe of Hudhayl, once as Baṭn Ruhāṭ, once Wādī Ruhāṭ. Neither of those poems refer to Suwāʿ and nor do any others in the extensive collection of poetry ascribed to Hudhalī poets. Sukkarī, the collector and commentator of the Hudhalī *dīwān*, says that Baṭn Ruhāṭ was three nights (*layāl*) away from Mecca, the geographer Bakrī, who cites the poems, reproduced that report as three miles (*amyāl*). Modern commentators, following the second of Ibn Kalbī's reports, generally prefer to situate Suwāʿ at the Ruhāṭ of Baṭn Nakhla but that seems an arbitrary choice, probably influenced by the wish to place Suwāʿ somewhere near Mecca. To complicate the matter further, the *Muḥabbar* locates Suwāʿ at a place called Naʿmān. Qurṭubī's reference to it as being 'by the sea shore', presumably reflects the reference to Yanbuʿ in the first of the reports in the *Aṣnām*.[29]

As for the tribes associated with Suwāʿ, the first passage in the *Aṣnām* refers

[27] Wellhausen, *Reste*, 18–19; Lecker, *Banū Sulaym*, index s.v.

[28] Lecker, *Banū Sulaym*, on the map at p. xiii, shows the two Nakhlas to the north-east of Mecca at a distance of about 25 to 50 km. George Rentz, s.v. 'Hudhayl' in *EI2*, describes the southern Nakhla as the main tributary of Baṭn Marr or Marr ẓahrān (modern Wādī Fāṭima) between Mecca and Jedda, implying that it is to the west of Mecca. The identification of geographical features named in the traditional texts and the situating of them on modern maps seems problematic and dependent on other identifications which themselves may not be secure.

[29] *Aṣnām K-R*, 6 (text) = 34 (trans.), 35 (text) = 60 (trans.); Ibn Hishām, *Sīra*, I, 78; Ibn Ḥabīb, *Muḥabbar*, 316; Qurṭubī, *Tafsīr*, XVIII, 309. For the Hudhalī poems, see ʿAbd Allāh b. ʿAbd al-ʿAzīz Abū ʿUbayd al-Bakrī, *Muʿjam ma ʾstaʿjam*, ed. Muṣṭafā al-Saqqā, 4 vols., Cairo 1947–51, II, 678–9 s.v. Ruhāṭ. The two occurrences of the name Ruhāṭ in the poems do not help us to identify or situate it. From Lecker's discussion the difficulty of situating Ruhāṭ is apparent. On the map, the name only occurs in the name Ḥarrat Ruhāṭ which seems to refer to the huge lava bed stretching southwards from Medina to the north eastern vicinities of Mecca. On p. 18, however, we are told that Ruhāṭ was 'close' to Wādī Ghurān, which the map situates north and north west of Mecca, only tenuously connected with the area of lava. The sources cited by Lecker, *Banū Sulaym*, at p. 52, however, connect Ruhāṭ with Wādī Fāṭima/Marr al-ẓahrān which seems to be well south of Wādī Ghurān.

simply to the tribe of Hudhayl as a whole as its adherents, and then mentions that the family of Liḥyān (of Hudhayl) were the guardians of the idol. The later passage in the work suggests that all of the Muḍar, of which Hudhayl were a part, worshipped the idol, and it names one individual – al-Ḥārith b. Tamīm – as responsible for taking Suwāʿ from ʿAmr b. Luḥayy.[30] The connexion with Hudhayl is common, but the *Muḥabbar* mentions in addition to them Kināna, Muzayna and ʿAmr b. Qays b. ʿAylān, and says that its guardians were Banū Saḥāla of Hudhayl. Possibly Saḥāla is an orthographic variant on Liḥyān.

In the first passage in the *Aṣnām* Ibn al-Kalbī tells us that he does not know any verse of an Hudhalī poet which mentions Suwāʿ although he does know one by 'a man of the Yaman', in the second the lack of a Hudhalī poetic attestation is not mentioned and a poem referring to Suwāʿ by 'a man of the Arabs' is given.[31]

Neither the *Aṣnām* nor Ibn Hishām's *Sīra* have any report about the destruction of Suwāʿ, but Wāqidī (followed by Azraqī and Ibn Saʿd) knows that it was destroyed by ʿAmr b. al-ʿĀṣ on the orders of the Prophet following his conquest of Mecca. The story has no geographical information, although it does refer to Suwāʿ as the idol of Hudhayl. Again Wellhausen's comment seems apt: 'diese Geschichten von der Zerstörung der Götzen im Auftrage Muhammads werden immer vollständiger, je weiter die Überlieferung sich von ihrem Ursprunge entfernt, und die Relationen widersprechen sich dabei'.[32]

In Ibn Saʿd's *Ṭabaqāt* there is a report which includes among the idols destroyed on the orders of the Prophet after the conquest of Mecca a certain Buwāna.[33] Neither the *Aṣnām* nor Yāqūt seems to know Buwāna as an idol, although the latter knows it as a place name. In other reports in the *Ṭabaqāt* Buwāna appears to be a place where there was an idol, rather than an idol

[30] Wellhausen, *Reste*, 18, citing the *Aṣnām* from Yāqūt (s.v. 'Suwāʿ'), was puzzled by the phrase *baʿīdata min Muḍar* which followed the reference to Nakhla in the second passage and which he translated as 'weit von Mudar'. The printed texts of the *Aṣnām* have here *taʿbuduhu man yalīhi min Muḍar* ('. . . Nakhla, where those of the Muḍar who were close to him worshipped him' – thus Klinke-Rosenberger, *Aṣnām K-R* 60, and Lecker, *Banū Sulaym* 53, but Atallah has 'where he was worshipped by the Hudhayl and their allies among the Muḍar').

[31] In the first hemistich of the second verse, the printed text of the *Aṣnām* reads: *taẓallu janābahu ṣarʿā ladayhi* ('[the sacrifices] continue alongside of him to be cast down before him?'). Wellhausen, however, preferred the reading in Muḥammad al-Murtaḍā al-Zabīdī's *Tāj al-ʿArūs*, ed. ʿAlī Shīrī, 20 vols., Beirut 1994 V, 390 which names Ruhāṭ: *taẓallu janābahu bi-Ruhāṭin ṣarʿā* ('[the sacrifices] continue to be cast down alongside him at Ruhāṭ').

[32] Wāqidī, *Maghāzī*, 870; Azraqī, *Akhbār Makka*, I, 131; Ibn Saʿd, *Ṭabaqāt*, II/1, 105; Wellhausen, *Reste*, 19. For an argument against the view that more information came into existence in the time between Ibn Isḥāq and Wāqidī, see M. Lecker, 'The Death of the Prophet Muḥammad's Father: Did Wāqidī Invent Some of the Evidence?', *ZDMG*, 145 (1995), 9–27.

[33] Ibn Saʿd, *Ṭabaqāt*, II/1, 99: 'The Prophet sent raiding parties to the idols which were around the Kaʿba and smashed them. Among them were al-ʿUzzā, Manāt, Suwāʿ, Buwāna and Dhu 'l-Kaffayn.' See also Dhahabī, *Taʾrīkh al-Islām*, I, 80, citing Ibn Saʿd. On this 'idol', see Fahd, *Panthéon*, 56–7.

itself.[34] In *ḥadīths*, however, it is specifically stated that there were no idols at Buwāna: a man, sometimes named as Kardam the father of Maymūna, had taken a vow before Islam that he would sacrifice a certain number of livestock at Buwāna and he came to the Prophet to ask if he should fulfil his vow (the validity of vows taken before Islam is a much-discussed topic); the Prophet asked him if any idol had been worshipped there (in the *jāhiliyya*) and, when assured that there had not been, he ordered the man to fulfil his vow.[35] Clearly the name Buwāna is associated in the tradition with the idea of idols and idolatry, but one could hardly take the traditional material as evidence of real knowledge.

Sometimes the detail that proliferates is not necessarily inconsistent, on other occasions it is. It is difficult to reconcile the information attached to the toponym Ruhāṭ, and when the *Aṣnām* tells us that the guardians of the idol Wadd were the descendants of ʿĀmir al-Ajdār of the tribe of Kalb but the *Muḥabbar* informs us that they were the descendants of Farāfiṣa b. al-Aḥwaṣ of Kalb it seems hard to decide between the two. Wellhausen denied the veracity of the *Muḥabbar* account on the grounds that Farāfiṣa, the father of the caliph ʿUthmān's wife Nāʾila, was generally reported to have been a Christian and was not a descendant of either of the sons of ʿAwf b. ʿUdhra, the man named by the *Aṣnām* as having taken Wadd from ʿAmr b. Luḥayy and having set it up at Dūmat al-Jandal. But that just makes it more difficult to explain the origin of the report saying that Farāfiṣa's descendants were the guardians of the idol.[36]

Proliferation, lack of consistency and variant detail are to be found too in the traditional material concerning Dhu ʾl-Sharā/Dusares. Since the attestation of this name outside Muslim tradition is especially strong, and since it is by no means inconceivable that the Nabataean cult had survived and spread south into central Arabia, it seems worthwhile to illustrate these features of the material here to underline again the lack of certainty and solidity in the Muslim tradition about even this god.[37]

There are two main references for the god in Muslim tradition. In the *Sīra* some detail about its sanctuary is given in the account of the acceptance of Islam by Ṭufayl b. ʿAmr of the tribe of Daws (part of Azd Sarāt). In the *Aṣnām* it is merely said that it was an idol (*ṣanam*) of Banū al-Ḥārith b.

[34] Ibn Saʿd, *Ṭabaqāt*, I/1, 105: 'we were sittting by an idol at Buwāna . . .'; ibid., III/1, 276 is perhaps ambiguous: *wa-anā ʿinda ṣanami Buwāna*.

[35] Sulaymān b. al-Ashʿath Abū Dāwūd, *Kitāb al-Sunan*, 4 vols., Cairo 1935, *Aymān* 22; Yāqūt, *Buldān*, I, 754.

[36] *Aṣnām K-R*, 34–5 (text) = 59–60 (trans.); Ibn Habīb, *Muḥabbar*, 316; so too Ibn Ḥazm, *Jamhara*, 458; Wellhausen, *Reste*, 17. For Farāfiṣa as a Christian see, e.g., Aḥmad b. Yaḥyā al-Balādhurī, *Ansāb al-ashrāf*, V, ed. S. D. Goitein, Jerusalem 1936, 12.

[37] The Nabataean cult seems to be attested epigraphically from Boṣrā in the north to as far south as al-Ḥijr/Madāʾ in Ṣāliḥ, and there was a major centre at Petra, see *EI2* s.v. 'Dhu ʾl-Sharā, by G. Ryckmans.

Yashkur b. Mubashshir of Azd. The Banū Yashkur b. Mubashshir of Azd do not appear closely related to Banū Daws b. ʿUdthān of Azd .[38]

The reference in the *Sīra* is relatively brief, part of the longer story of the conversion of Ṭufayl. Having returned to his people after accepting Islam, Ṭufayl told his wife that they could no longer remain together since Islam had separated them. Thereupon she protested that she was willing to follow the same religion as her husband and Ṭufayl responded by telling her to go the *ḥinā* (sic) of Dhu ʾl-Sharā and to purify herself from it/him (*taṭṭahharī minhu*). There then follows a comment by the redactor of the *Sīra*, Ibn Hishām, explaining that *ḥinā* means *ḥimā* (an area reserved for the grazing of animals dedicated to the gods), that Dhu ʾl-Sharā was an idol of the Daws and that in the *ḥimā* was a small stream (*washal*) of water coming down from the mountain. The text in the edition is then slightly confusing and ambiguous but it seems that the woman expressed some fear that the god would harm either herself or their child.[39] Ṭufayl, however, assured her that he would take responsibility that nothing untoward should happen, she went off and washed herself, and then, after her husband had explained Islam to her, she too accepted Islam.

There are some obviously puzzling questions here. What was the woman supposed to purify herself from? Presumably the answer is idolatry and paganism. Would an obvious way of doing that to be to go to the god's temenos (if that is what *ḥinā* in fact means) and take a ritual bath in the (presumably sacred to the god) stream there? Also notable is the fact that in the immediately preceding passage in the *Sīra* a similar conversation and procedure had occurred involving Ṭufayl and his father. There too Ṭufayl had insisted that the father wash and purify his robes but in that story there was no reference to the idol or the *ḥinā*. Wansbrough has drawn attention to washing and purification of clothes as a stylised ingredient in conversion accounts.[40]

One possibility for the reference to Dhu ʾl-Sharā in this story is a mental association between the name of the tribe Daws and the first part of that of the idol. G. Ryckmans refers to the suggestion that there was some confusion

[38] Ibn Hishām, *Sīra*, I, 382 ff.; *Aṣnām K-R*, 24 (text) = 50 (trans.); ʿAlī, *Mufaṣṣal*, VI, 275 for subsequent repetitions of these two. For Banū Yashkur b. Mubashshir of Azd, see Caskel and Strenziok, *Ǧamhara*, I, table 217, and for Banū Daws b. ʿUdthān of Azd tables 210, 215. Ṭufayl b. ʿAmr appears in *ḥadīth* asking the Prophet to invoke God against his tribe of Daws, but the Prophet instead asked God to guide them and bring them to Islam (see Wensinck et al., *Concordance*, VIII, s.v. 'Ṭufayl b. ʿAmr' for references). Dhu ʾl-Sharā is not mentioned in those *ḥadīth*s.

[39] Cf. the story reported by Lecker, 'Idol Worship', 338 where an old man excuses himself for continuing to worship 'wood which you made with your own hand' by saying that he was worried about his young children.

[40] *Sectarian Milieu*, 101; and cf. Koran 74:4. It may be that the detail about the stream may have been suggested by the order that Ṭufayl's wife wash herself. In the secondary literature this possibly incidental detail, provided by Ibn Hishām not Ibn Isḥāq, becomes integrated into discussion of the nature of Dhu ʾl-Sharā as a vegetation god (e.g., Fahd, *Panthéon*, 73).

between the tribal name Daws and the name Duserani, 'the worshippers of Dusares', as a designation of the Nabataeans. The name of the god may have suggested to the elaborators of Muslim tradition an association with the tribe of Daws. [41]

Another problem is that there seems some overlap between Dhu 'l-Sharā and another idol, known in the tradition as Dhu 'l-Khalaṣa.[42] This latter is not attested outside the tradition.[43] In *ḥadīth*, but not so much in the traditional literature about the idolatry of the *jāhiliyya*, Dhu 'l-Khalaṣa is strongly associated with the Daws, the tribal group of Ṭufayl b. ʿAmr who figures in the *Sīra* story that refers to Dhu 'l-Sharā. One of the signs of the end of time, the Prophet is reported to have said, will be the commotion of the 'backsides' of the women of Daws around or upon Dhu 'l-Khalaṣa.[44]

In addition there is apparently some overlap of ideas between *shary* and *khalaṣa*: both are said to refer to types of creeping plants, among other meanings, and both Dhu 'l-Sharā and Dhu 'l-Khalaṣa are associated with the idea of *kaʿba*. The Christian heresiologist Epiphanius (d. AD 403) said that the Nabataeans regarded Dusares as the son of 'a virgin (*kaabon*)' and it has been suggested that that arose from the fact that Dusares was worshipped as a stone referred to as a *kaʿba* (cube, stele, bethel) but that Epiphanius had (for apologetic purposes) confused the word *kaʿba* with a form such as *kaʿiba* or *kuʿba*

[41] See s.v. 'Dhu 'l-Sharā' in *EI2* , citing R. Dussaud and F. Macler, *Mission dans les régions désertiques de la Syrie moyenne*, Paris 1903, 67, n.3.

[42] Azraqī (*Akhbār Makka*, I, 124, from Ibn Isḥāq, but not in Ibn Hishām's recension of the *Sīra*) refers to an idol at Mecca which he calls simply al-Khalaṣa. Most other accounts talk of a Dhu 'l-Khalaṣa (some read Dhu 'l-Khuluṣa, others Dhu 'l-Khulṣa), and do not associate it with Mecca. Some say that it was an idol, some that it was a sanctuary (*bayt*) which contained an idol, implying that the idol was called al-Khalaṣa and that Dhu 'l-Khalaṣa refers to the building that 'possesses' or contains it. An opposite interpretation is that the idol was called Dhu 'l-Khalaṣa because it was the 'master' or 'owner' of the sanctuary (presumably called al-Khalaṣa) within which it was situated. Yet another view is that al-Khalaṣa is a collective designation of those who worshipped and made circumambulation of the idol, which was called Dhu 'l-Khalaṣa (apparently) since it was the 'master' of its servants (*Aṣnām K-R*, 22; Aḥmad b. ʿAlī, b. Ḥajar, al-ʿAsqalānī *Fatḥ al-bārī bi-sharḥ Ṣaḥīḥ al-Bukhārī*, 14 vols., Cairo 1988, VIII, 62, XIII, 64; Yūsuf b. ʿAbd as-Raḥmān al-Mizzī, *Tahdhīb al-kamāl*, ed. Bashshar, 35 vols., Beirut 1984–92, IV, 537).

[43] But see Francis Brown, S. R. Driver and Charles A. Briggs, *A Hebrew and English Lexicon of the Old Testament*, Oxford 1906; repr. 1979, s.v. '*ḥ-l-ṣ*' for the expression *ḥ-l-ṣ b-ʿ-l* in Phoenician, understood as 'Baal has rescued'; Fahd, *Panthéon*, 63, n.3 cites Littmann, *Thamūd und Ṣafā*, 50, 85 and van den Branden, *Inscriptions thamoudéennes*, 205, 419, 530, index s.v. '*ḫlṣt*', for examples of the root in personal names; for Khalaṣa as the name of a plant, Yāqūt, *Buldān* II, 461.

[44] For the apocalyptic *ḥadīth* , see Nuʿaym b. Ḥammād al-Marwazī, *Kitāb al-Fitan*, ed. Suhayl Zakkar, Mecca 1991, 365; ʿAbd al-Razzāq, *Muṣannaf*, XI, 379; Bukhārī, *Ṣaḥīḥ*, *Fitan*, no. 23; Muslim, *Ṣaḥīḥ Fitan*, no. 51; Ibn Ḥanbal, *Musnad*, II, 271. The common wording is *lā taqūmu 'l-sāʿa ḥattā taḍṭariba alayātu nisāʾi Daws ʿalā/ḥawla Dhi 'l-Khalaṣa*. *Aṣnām K-R*, 23 (trans. 49), however, has: *lā tadhhabu al-dunyā ḥattā taṣṭakka alayātu nisāʾi Daws ʿalā* . . . Note the completely unspecific version in Abū Bakr ʿAbd Allāh b. Muḥammad b. Abī Shayba, *al-Muṣannaf*, ed. ʿAbd al-Khāliq al-Afghanī 15 vols., Karachi 1986–7, XV, 53: *lā taqūmu 'l-sāʿa ḥattā taḍṭariba alayātu al-nisāʾi ḥawla 'l-aṣnām*. This is not transmitted from Abū Hurayra like the other versions.

which refer to young females and female breasts. According to the tenth-century Byzantine encyclopaedia *Suidas*, the bethel of Dusares was a black rectangular stone (similar to the Kaʿba at Mecca). Mordtmann referred to 'diese nabatäische Kaʿbah' and linked it with reports by Maximus of Tyre and Clement of Alexandria that the Arabs worshipped a stone.[45] Dhu ʾl-Khalaṣa, on the other hand, is sometimes referred to as the southern Kaʿba (*al-kaʿba al-yamaniyya*) in contrast with the Kaʿba of Mecca (*al-kaʿba al-shāmiyya*).[46]

It has even been suggested that yet another idol of the traditional literature, whose name also begins with the particle Dhū ('lord' or 'possessor'), may be the result of proliferation and confusion in this material: Dhu ʾl-Kaffayn (or Kafayn). References to this 'idol' in tradition are sparse and uninformative,[47] and the name is not attested externally, but reports linking it with the Daws and with Ṭufayl b. ʿAmr al-Dawsī (whom we have met above in connexion with Dhu ʾl-Sharā and who is named as the destroyer of Dhu ʾl-Kaffayn)) led first L. Krehl in 1863 and subsequently T. Fahd to suggest that it may be another name for Dhu ʾl-Sharā.[48]

Faced with such proliferation and variation of detail, some of it could be explained as the result of orthographic variants. When the *Aṣnām* names the site of the idol Dhu ʾl-Khalaṣa as Tabāla at seven stages distance from Mecca en route to the Yemen and the *Muḥabbar* gives it as al-ʿAblāʾ four stages from Mecca towards the Yemen, it could be that orthographic confusion between the Arabic words for seven/four and Tabāla/ʿAblāʾ has something to do with it, even though both toponyms are said to refer to real places.[49]

45 J. H. Mordtmann, 'Dusares bei Epiphanius', *ZDMG*, 29 (1876), 99–106; *EI2* s.v. 'Dhu l-Sharā' by G. Ryckmans; D. Sourdel, *Les Cultes du Hauran*, Paris 1952, 59. In the text of Epiphanius some read χααμον, but χααβον seems to have been generally preferred.

46 Yāqūt, *Buldān*, II, 461.

47 At *Sīra*, I, 81 Ibn Isḥāq apparently refers to it but does not mention it by name: he merely says that Daws had an idol which belonged to ʿAmr b. Ḥumama al-Dawsī. Subsequently, at I, 385 he reports how Ṭufayl b. ʿAmr al-Dawsī , the man whose conversion story involves reference to Dhu ʾl-Sharā, after the conquest of Mecca, asked the Prophet for permission to go to destroy Dhu ʾl-Kaffayn (vocalised thus in the edition), 'the idol of ʿAmr b. Ḥumama'. Then verses recited by Ṭufayl on the occasion of his destruction of the idol are given; in them the name is vocalised (for reasons of metre) Dhu ʾl-Kafayn. The short section on Dhu ʾl-Kaffayn in *Aṣnām K-R*, 24 (text) = 50 (trans.) also gives the verses of Ṭufayl, and specifies that it belonged to the clan of Munhib of Daws (*wa-kāna li-Daws thumma li-banī Munhibi ʾbni Daws*); see also Azraqī, *Akhbār Makka*, I, 131, Ibn Saʿd, *Ṭabaqāt*, II/1, 113–14. Ibn Ḥazm, *Jamhara*, 460 attributes the destruction of Dhu ʾl-Kaffayn to ʿAmr b. Ḥumama himself, but that is probably a slip of a copyist's pen. ʿAmr b. Ḥumama is listed as a descendant of Munhib b. Daws in Caskel and Strenziok, *Ǧamhara*, I, table 215. The additional detail given by Ḥusayn b. Muḥammad al-Diyārbakrī, *Taʾrīkh al-Khamīs*, 2 vols., ʿUthmān ʿAbd al-Razzāq Press 1302 AH, II, 121, that it was an idol made of wood, probably arises (as well as from the traditional topos of the idol as a wooden thing) from the report that Ṭufayl burned it (see Jawād ʿAlī's reasoning along these lines in *Mufaṣṣal*, VI, 275).

48 L. Krehl, *Über die Religion der vorislamischen Araber*, Leipzig 1863, 50 cited in Fahd, *Panthéon*, 69–70. See also on Dhu ʾl-Kaffayn, n. 275 of *Aṣnām K-R*.

49 *Aṣnām K-R*, 22 (text) = 48 (trans.); Ibn Ḥabīb, *Muḥabbar*, 317; for al-ʿAblāʾ see Yāqūt, *Buldān*, III, 607; for Tabāla, which is more certainly attested, see Yāqūt, *Buldān*, I, 816–17 and *EI1* s.v. 'Tabāla', by J. Tkatsch.

That sort of a solution is, however, possible only rarely and even if one could somehow account for the proliferation and inconsistency of detail in ways that would make it possible to isolate primary forms of the tradition, that would still not necessarily guarantee the accuracy of any facts it claims to convey. If the material visibly diversifies and proliferates in the written texts available to us, it may be suspected that it did so too in its transmission before the textual tradition became established. When one tradition tells us that 'today' Dhu 'l-Khalaṣa is the threshold (*ʿatabat al-bāb*) of the mosque at Tabāla, another that its site is that of the congregational mosque of a district called al-ʿAblāt in the territory of Khathʿam, and another that it is a *bayt qaṣṣār* (house of a washerman), it is possible that we do not have evidence of the fate of Dhu 'l-Khalaṣa in Islamic times so much as evidence that the local or the written tradition sometimes felt the need to enliven the details in this way.[50]

Naturally, there are many ways in which apparently inconsistent information can be presented in a way that seems to remove the inconsistencies. When one report about the idol al-ʿUzzā tells us that its guardians (*sadana*) were the clan of Ṣirma b. Murra of the Ghaṭafān, another that when Khālid b. al-Walīd went to destroy it its guardians were the clan of Shaybān of the Sulaym, and another perhaps suggests that the Meccan Abū Uḥayḥa was its guardian, it is possible to envisage, as does Michael Lecker, that the reports relate to different times, the guardianship having changed hands.[51] Confronted by one tradition that says that al-ʿUzzā was destroyed by Zuhayr b. Janāb al-Kalbī and another that says it was destroyed by Khālid b. al-Walīd, Wellhausen sought to reconcile them by positing two distinct sanctuaries of this deity, while Lecker again prefers to see one sanctuary but two events at different times.[52] A similar problem regarding the destruction of the idol Suwāʿ is solved by Lecker in much the same way.[53]

Strategies such as these were used too by the traditional scholars. Yāqūt, knowing a proverb, 'of less importance than was Tabāla to al-Ḥajjāj', and knowing also that the place name occurred in connexion with the site of Dhu 'l-Khalaṣa in Muslim's *Ṣaḥīḥ*, suggested that there must be two different places with that name: that alluded to in the proverb was the well-known place in the Tihāma on the Yemen road, while that mentioned by Muslim was simply 'in the land of the Yemen'. Yāqūt's sources, however, speak only of one Tabāla. Nawawī, faced with the same problem, reasoned that since there was no reason

50 *Aṣnām K-R*, 23 (text) =49 (trans.); al-Mubarrad (in Yāqūt, *Buldān*, II, 462); Ibn Ḥabīb, *Muḥabbar*, 317; Wellhausen, *Reste*, 46 has 'tanner' (Gerber) for the Arabic *qaṣṣār*. Note that nineteenth-century travellers to Ṭā'if were shown stones which were identified as idols of the *jāhiliyya*.

51 See Lecker, *Banū Sulaym*, 38, n.198 and 42 for argumentation and references. Lecker is concerned only with the Ṣirma/Shaybān variant. For the suggestion that the story about the dying Abū Uḥayḥa envisages him as the *sādin* of al-ʿUzzā, see above, p. 27, n. 14.

52 Cf. Wellhausen, *Reste*, 37–8 and Lecker, *Banū Sulaym*, 37–8.

53 Lecker, *Banū Sulaym*, 52.

to connect the famous Umayyad governor Ḥajjāj with the Yemeni Tabāla, the Tabāla associated with Ḥajjāj was at Ṭā'if.[54]

Given the difficulty of tracing lines of development in the tradition it is theoretically possible that such harmonising readings of it are valid. If one presumes that the tradition fundamentally reflects a historical reality, then they are necessary. It is also possible, however, to emphasise the tradition as a continuously developing whole which supplies answers to questions that it itself has thrown up, provides names for people and places who were once anonymous, makes links between and produces variants around similar themes and details, and thus generates many variants in the course of its transmission. Traditional and modern scholars will then sometimes give preference to one version over another but at other times try to reduce inconsistencies and contradictions by strategies such as those already referred to.

When Ibn Saʿd knew a report about a Ẓālim of the tribe of Sulaym who was associated with a place called Ruhāṭ where there was an anonymous idol it was natural, given the association of the idol Suwāʿ with a place called Ruhāṭ, that later tradition would identify Ẓālim's idol as Suwāʿ. The ensuing problem – that the story about Ẓālim tells us that he destroyed his idol (having become disillusioned when he saw foxes urinating on it) and thus conflicts with the tradition that Suwāʿ was destroyed by ʿAmr b. al-ʿĀṣ following the Prophet's conquest of Mecca – could be solved by having the idol reinstituted following its 'first' destruction.[55]

It may be that the wealth of variant detail is essential to the nature of Muslim tradition in which the individual details, although the subject of considerable research and debate, are ultimately of less importance than the broad picture. Individual scholars may ponder the facts about about, say, Nasr or Dhu 'l-Khalaṣa, but the ultimate effect of the tradition as a whole is to convince us that pre-Islamic Arabia was full of idols and idolaters.[56] Anyone who has worked with traditional reports such as those about Dhu 'l-Sharā or Suwāʿ will be aware of the difficulty, or impossibility, of keeping the details of the

[54] Yāqūt, *Buldān*, I, 816–17; Abu 'l-Zakariyyā' Yaḥyā b. Sharaf al-Nawawī, *Sharḥ Ṣaḥīḥ Muslim*, 10 vols., ed. Khalīl al-Mays, Beirut 1987, part 18, 245. J. Tkatsch, s.v. 'Tabāla' in *EI2*, relates the proverb and the report about Dhu 'l-Khalaṣa to the same Tabāla. Although Yāqūt himself knew that Muslim's *ḥadīth* situated Dhu 'l-Khalaṣa at Tabāla, none of the material that he reports about Tabāla refers to the idol. For the proverb (*ahwanu ʿalā al-Ḥajjāj min Tabāla*) the story is that Tabāla was the first governorship offered Ḥajjāj by ʿAbd al-Malik, but he refused to take it up when he found it was such a paltry place.

[55] Cf. the story of Ẓālim's destruction of the anonymous idol in Ibn Saʿd, *Ṭabaqāt*, I/2, 49 with that naming Suwā' in Samhūdī, *Wafā'*, IV, 1225; and see pp. 107–8 above.

[56] After his discussion of the reports given by Maqrīzī (d. 845/1441–2) about the idols worshipped in pre-Islamic Medina, one of Michael Lecker's conclusions is: 'One thing is certain: the Arabs of Medina on the eve of the Hijra were immersed in idol worship' ('Idol Worship', 343). He then perceptively points out that this is surprising since many modern scholars (following Muslim tradition, see, e.g., Ibn Hishām, *Sīra*, I, 428, which says that the Medinese pagans were prepared to accept Islam because they had learned from the Jews that a prophet was to arise) have argued that Medina was prepared for acceptance of the Prophet's message by the fact that large numbers of Jews lived there and had made monotheism familiar.

stories in one's head: they are constantly blurring and dissolving into each other. One suspects that the situation was not too different for the traditional scholars in spite of their more retentive memories and that that may have something to do with the inconsistencies and contradictions within the tradition. In the end what endures is the general picture.

It would be wrong to conclude from the above, however, that the traditional material is no more than a mass of variant, sometimes conflicting, material without organisation or message. One clear principle governing the presentation and organisation of the *Aṣnām*, and frequently but not always to be seen in the traditional material more generally, is the wish to link the various gods and idols in some way with Mecca and thus convey the message that they are the background of the Koran and of Islam. This is done most obviously by presenting the details and the stories about the gods, idols and sanctuaries within the context of the account of the corruption of monotheism among the descendants of Ishmael in Arabia. By listing the idols within the framework story of the dispersion of the descendants of Ishmael from Mecca and emphasising that their idolatry began as an attempt to commemorate and symbolise the Meccan sanctuary and its rituals, even idols that the tradition situates at some distance from Mecca are made relevant to the *jāhiliyya* in its narrow sense.

Another, more specific, way in which this is achieved is to have the Meccan ʿAmr b. Luḥayy responsible for bringing the idols to Mecca and there distribute them among the tribes. In this way Wadd, situated by the tradition in Dūmat al-Jandal, or Yaʿūq, located in variant localities in the Yemen, become not merely 'gods of the people of Noah' but also a part of a tradition that focuses on Mecca.

In some cases it was not enough to make the link in this way only: it was also necessary to have idols that the tradition overwhelmingly links with places other than Mecca more intimately linked with that town. We will see an example of that in the discussion of the idols known as the 'daughters of Allāh' in the next chapter, but even more obvious is the way in which Dhu 'l-Khalaṣa, which as we have seen is most widely sited at Tabāla some distance from Mecca towards the Yemen, is brought to Mecca in the account of the 'local historian' of Mecca, Azraqī. In fact he calls the idol simply al-Khalaṣa, without the particle *dhū*, but it seems clear that we are concerned with the same thing. He tells us that al-Khalaṣa was erected by ʿAmr b. Luḥayy in the lower part of Mecca (*bi-asfali Makkata*) and leads us to think that milk was poured over it and garlands and ostrich eggs hung from it (the *Aṣnām* says that Dhu 'l-Khalaṣa at Tabāla was a white rock (*marwa*) with something like a crown upon it).

Unsurprisingly, we then find Azraqī's account used (together with the *ḥadīth* about the behaviour of the women of Daws at Dhu 'l-Khalaṣa) by modern scholars who wish to argue that we have here a fertility god, while others use the *Aṣnām*'s description together with stories about the use of divining arrows before this idol to support their interpretation of it as a warrior god.[57] In this connexion it is salutary to recall the words of Javier Teixidor: 'Our meager information about the North Arabian cults does not permit more than hypothetical conclusions, and the pretentious lists of Arabian gods compiled by some scholars from the inscriptions so far uncovered are far from presenting a well-defined pantheon.'[58]

The way in which the traditional material on the idols of Arabia before Islam is made to relate to Mecca and thus to Islam emphasises even more the questionable nature of the argument that the inscriptions and other evidence from outside the tradition somehow confirm the facts of the tradition. The non-traditional material comes from north and south Arabia, from Syria and from Mesopotamia, and not from Mecca, Medina and the surrounding regions which are traditionally seen as the birthplace of Islam.To use the evidence of, say, the Nabataean inscriptions to illuminate conditions in Mecca at the beginning of the seventh century is to take a step in space and time of which we at least ought to be aware. As we have seen, much of the traditional material too relates to the regions of north and south Arabia and not to the inner Arabian areas of the Ḥijāz, Najd and Yamāma. The tradition's use of reports about Fals the idol of the Ṭayyi', or about Yaghūth the idol of the Madhḥij in the Yemen, to substantiate accounts of Quraysh as worshippers of Hubal, al-ʿUzzā and others, and of the Kaʿba at Mecca as the home of 360 idols, is matched by the willingness of some scholars to use the evidence of north and south Arabian epigraphy to corroborate the traditional accounts.

[57] Azraqī, *Akhbār Makka*, I, 124 (cited from Ibn Isḥāq, but not found in Ibn Hishām's recension of the *Sīra*); *Aṣnām K-R*, 22 (text) = 48 (trans.): the sense is slightly ambiguous – does it mean that Dhu 'l-Khalaṣa was a sculpted rock upon which there was the shape of a crown, or that it was a (natural) rock upon which the likeness of a crown was sculpted? For use of this evidence in discussions about Dhu 'l-Khalaṣa as a fertility or warrior god, see, e.g., Fahd, *Panthéon*, 65–8. [58] Teixidor, *Pagan God*, 75.

CHAPTER 6

The daughters of God

Central to the traditional image of the idolatry of the *jāhiliyya* are the three deities or idols Allāt, al-ʿUzzā and Manāt, said to have been viewed by the Meccan opponents of the Prophet as daughters of Allāh.[1] Apart from the five gods of the people of Noah, and the more marginal Sirius, these are really the only names appearing in the Koran (53:19–20) which the tradition is able to identify as objects of worship by the *mushrikūn*. None of the many other names of *jāhilī* gods, idols or objects of worship that the tradition provides appears in the Koran.

The traditional material has references to these three entities in many reports about pre- and early Islam, and the *Kitāb al-Aṣnām* and other works give details about them, their locations, the tribes associated with their worship, and their destruction. In addition the names are attested outside Muslim tradition, in inscriptions and literature from north Arabia and places around the Mediterranean. It remains to be considered how far the relative prolixity of traditional material may result from speculative elaboration of the koranic reference, how far it reflects the prominence of the names in the ideas about pagan religion in the circles from which Islam emerged, and how far it indicates real knowledge about cults involving the three.[2]

We begin with what is probably the most notorious traditional story relating to Allāt, al-ʿUzzā and Manāt, that which modern scholarship has come to refer to as the incident of the 'satanic verses':

[1] E.g., in the story in which Abū Bakr's relative Ṭalḥa b. ʿUbayd Allāh is sent to win him back to paganism after he had accepted Islam, Ṭalḥa calls the future caliph to the worship of Allāt and al-ʿUzzā (as often in tradition, these two are referred to jointly and there is no reference to Manāt). Abū Bakr asks what Allāt and al-ʿUzzā are, and receives the answer, 'The daughters of God (*banāt Allāh*).' 'In that case,' Abū Bakr demands, 'Who is their mother?' When neither Ṭalḥa nor others present can answer, Ṭalḥa himself recognises the truth and accepts Islam (Aḥmad b. Yaḥyā al-Balādhurī, *Ansāb al-ashrāf*, Teil 5, ed. Iḥsān ʿAbbās, Beirut 1996, 185).

[2] That Allāt and al-ʿUzzā sometimes occur in the traditional material without Manāt and that we also find reference to the 'two ʿUzzas' (*al-ʿuzzatān*) suggests that the traditional material is to some extent independent of the koranic verse; see Fahd, *Panthéon*, 118–19 for references. Other aspects of the traditional material which are not easily explained as mere koranic midrash will be taken up below.

The Prophet was eager for the welfare of his people, desiring to win them to him by any means he could. It has been reported that he longed for a way to win them, and part of what he did to that end is what Ibn Ḥumayd told me, from Salama, from Muḥammad ibn Isḥāq, from Yazīd ibn Ziyād al-Madanī, from Muḥammad ibn Kaʿb al-Quraẓī:

When the Prophet saw his people turning away from him, and was tormented by their distancing themselves from what he had brought to them from God, he longed in himself for something to come to him from God which would draw him closer to them. With his love for his people and his eagerness for them, it would gladden him if some of the hard things he had found in dealing with them could be alleviated. He pondered this in himself, longed for it, and desired it.

Then God sent down the revelation, 'By the star when it sets! Your companion has not erred or gone astray, and does not speak from mere fancy . . .' [Koran, 53:1 and following]. When he reached God's words, 'Have you seen Allāt and al-ʿUzzā, and Manāt, the third, the other?' [53:19–20], Satan cast upon his tongue, because of what he had pondered in himself and longed to bring to his people, 'These are the high-flying cranes (*al-gharānīq al-ʿulā*) and their intercession is to be hoped for'.[3]

When Quraysh [the people of Mecca] heard that, they rejoiced. What he had said about their gods pleased and delighted them, and they gave ear to him. The Believers trusted in their prophet with respect to what he brought them from their Lord; they did not suspect any slip, delusion or error. When he came to the prostration [which is commanded in the last verse of chap. 53] and finished the chapter, he prostrated and the Muslims followed their prophet in it, having faith in what he brought them and obeying his command. Those *mushrikūn* of Quraysh and others who were in the mosque also prostrated on account of what they had heard him say about their gods. In the whole mosque (*masjid*) there was no believer or *kāfir* who did not prostrate. Only al-Walīd b. al-Mughīra [one of the leaders of the pagans of Quraysh], who was an aged shaykh and could not make prostration, scooped up in his hand some of the soil from the valley of Mecca [and pressed it it to his forehead]. Then everybody dispersed from the mosque.[4]

Quraysh went out and were delighted by what they had heard of the way in which he spoke of their gods. They were saying, 'Muḥammad has referred to our gods most favourably. In what he has recited he said that they are "high-flying cranes whose intercession is to be hoped for".'

Those followers of the Prophet who had emigrated to the land of Abyssinia heard about the affair of the prostration, and it was reported to them that Quraysh had accepted Islam. Some men among them decided to return while others remained behind.

Gabriel came to the Prophet and said, 'O Muḥammad, what have you done! You have recited to the people something which I have not brought you from God, and you have spoken what He did not say to you.'

[3] *Al-gharānīq al-ʿulā*, literally 'the high cranes' ('cranes' in the ornithological sense) is problematic and will be discussed in more detail later. 'High-flying' is a frequent translation of *al-ʿulā* in this context.

[4] Whatever the factual basis of this story, the image of believers and unbelievers worshipping together in the same *masjid* in the early stages of the development of the new form of monotheism is remarkable and suggestive.

At that the Prophet was mightily saddened and greatly feared God. But God, of His mercy, sent him a revelation, comforting him and diminishing the magnitude of what had happened. God told him that there had never been a previous prophet or apostle who had longed just as Muḥammad had longed, and desired just as Muḥammad had desired, but that Satan had cast into his longing just as he had cast onto the tongue of Muḥammad. But God abrogates (*yansakhu*) what Satan has cast, and puts His verses in proper order. That is, [God was saying to him] 'You are just like other prophets and apostles'.

And God revealed: 'We never sent any apostle or prophet before you but that, when he longed, Satan cast into his longing. But God abrogates what Satan casts in, and then God puts His verses in proper order, for God is all-knowing and wise' [Koran, 22:52].

So God drove out the sadness from His prophet and gave him security against what he feared. He abrogated what Satan had cast upon his tongue in referring to their gods: 'They are the high-flying cranes whose intercession is accepted',[5] [replacing those words with] the words of God when Allāt, al-ʿUzzā and Manāt the third, the other are mentioned: 'Should you have males [as offspring] and He females! That, indeed, would be an unfair [*ḍīzā*, which Ibn Isḥāq glosses as *ʿawjāʾ*, 'odd', 'crooked'] division. They are only names which you and your fathers have given them' . . . as far as 'As many as are the angels in heaven, their intercession shall be of no avail unless after God has permitted it to whom He pleases and accepts' [53:21–6] – meaning, how can the intercession of their gods be of any avail with Him?

When there had come from God the words which abrogated what Satan had cast on to the tongue of His prophet, Quraysh said, 'Muḥammad has gone back on what he said about the status of our gods relative to God, changed it and brought something else', for the two phrases ['these are the high-flying cranes', 'whose intercession is to be hoped for'] which Satan had cast on to the tongue of the Prophet had found a place in the mouth of every polytheist. They, therefore, increased in their evil and in their oppression of everyone among them who had accepted Islam and followed the Prophet.

That band of the Prophet's followers who had left the land of Abyssinia on account of the report that the people of Mecca had accepted Islam when they prostrated together with the Prophet, drew near. But when they approached Mecca they heard that the talk about the acceptance of Islam by the people of Mecca was wrong. Therefore, they only entered Mecca in secret or after having obtained a promise of protection.

Among those of them who came to Mecca at that time and remained there until emigrating to Medina and taking part in the battle of Badr alongside Muḥammad there was, from the family of ʿAbd Shams b. ʿAbd Manāf b. Quṣayy, ʿUthmān b. ʿAffān together with his wife Ruqayya the daughter of the Prophet, Abū Ḥudhayfa b. ʿUtba with his wife Sahla bint Suhayl, and another group with them, numbering together 33 men.'[6]

[5] Sic – *turtaḍā*, previously it has been *turtajā*.

[6] Ṭabarī, *Taʾrīkh*, I, 1192 ff. This account of the 'satanic verses' incident which Ṭabarī quotes from Ibn Isḥāq does not occur in the version of the latter's *Sīra* made by Ibn Hishām. Muḥammad b. Kaʿb al-Quraẓī, the claimed source of the report, was the son of a Companion of the Prophet.

This is probably the best-known report of the incident. In it we are told that the Prophet was misled into giving out as divine revelation certain phrases which had not in fact come from God. The false verses concerned Allāt, al-ʿUzzā and Manāt who are presented in the story as three gods (or rather goddesses) worshipped by the Meccan fellow townsmen of the Prophet. The Prophet is reported to have given the three – for a short time – some recognition alongside God, as being able to intercede with Him, and thus to have won their devotees over to Islam. This situation lasted until the falsity of the verses was made clear to the Prophet by Gabriel and the true verses, the text of the Koran as we know it, revealed. In the true revelation the three beings are attacked as 'mere names which you and your fathers have called them', and the idea that God should have female offspring is ridiculed.

The story is reported only to a limited extent in Muslim tradition and has been rejected by many Muslim scholars as an invention.[7] Nevertheless, it is part of the material of the tradition, widely known if not so often explicitly reported.[8]

First, it may be asked whether the reports about the 'satanic verses' reflect a real historical event or situation, a question which has received a variety of answers in modern scholarship. If they do, if there was indeed an event or episode resembling that reported in accounts such as that cited above, the importance of polytheism and idolatry in the society addressed by the Prophet would seem to be established and the traditional view of the koranic *mushrikūn* confirmed. If it could be shown that the story is not historical, that would not call into doubt the whole traditional image of the paganism of the *jāhiliyya* (it might still be true that the three goddesses were worshipped by the pre-Islamic Arabs), but at least one apparently compelling piece of evidence for Meccan idolatry could be put on one side.

It seems unlikely that the question can be resolved in a way that is completely decisive. Those who accept that the traditional reports about the life of the Prophet have a factual basis and should be accepted as historical unless proven to be false are unlikely to be persuaded otherwise by suggestions about why the 'satanic verses' story might have come to exist. Here, as in so much of the discussion of the origins of Islam, much depends on theoretical presuppositions and outlook.

The main arguments in support of the historical basis of the reports have been two. First, that there is a sufficiently large number of versions of the story, preceded by different statements about the authorities and transmitters

[7] See editor's note 64 in Mūsā b. ʿUqba, *Maghāzī*, 68, where different views among the Muslim scholars are summarised following the presentation of Nāṣir al-Dīn al-Albānī, *Naṣb al-majānīq li-nasfi qiṣṣat al-gharānīq* ('The Erection of Catapults for the Destruction of the Story of the *Gharānīq*'), Damascus 1952. Note the title inserted, presumably by the editor, before Mūsā b. ʿUqba's account of the incident: ' The Return of the Emigrants to Abyssinia and the Invention (*ikhtirāʾ*) of the Story of the *Gharānīq*'.

[8] For the different versions see al-Albānī, *Naṣb*; Rubin, *Eye of the Beholder*, 156–66.

of the reports, to make one believe that there must be some basis in fact for them. Second, that since the story shows the Prophet giving in to temptation and compromising with idolatry, albeit temporarily, and that since the embarrassment felt by many Muslims has led them to deny the truth of it, we may presume that there is no reason for the story to have been invented by Muslims and it must, therefore, reflect a real event. A slightly more sophisticated argument holds that the story may not be literally true, but it at least reflects the fact that Muḥammad's monotheism took some time to develop and that there must have been a period when his attitude to the local polytheists and idolaters was less uncompromising than it became. According to that approach, the story of the 'satanic verses' merely condenses into a short time-span a development of perhaps several years.[9]

Both those arguments can be countered. The diversity of the reports, together with the inconsistencies and contradictions they contain, could be an argument against them rather than one in their favour, and, to those who see the tradition as constantly evolving and supplying answers to questions that it itself has raised, the argument that there would be no reason to develop and transmit material which seems derogatory of the Prophet or of Islam is too simple. For one thing, ideas about what is derogatory may change over time. We know that the doctrine of the Prophet's infallibility and impeccability (the doctrine regarding his *ʿiṣma*) emerged only slowly.[10] For another, material which we now find in the biography of the Prophet originated in various circumstances to meet various needs and one has to understand why material exists before one can make a judgement about its basis in fact. Just because the reasons are not always readily apparent does not mean that the historical reality of the reports is to be taken for granted.

Recently two scholarly discussions of the reports about the 'satanic verses' have argued, in different ways, that they may be accounted for other than as reflexions of historical fact.

John Burton sought to link the stories with theories about 'abrogation' (*naskh*) in Muslim law – the theory that certain verses of the Koran or certain *ḥadīth*s do not have any status as sources of law because their legal rulings or implications have been made obsolete by the revelation of other (later) verses or by reports about another (later) view or practice of the Prophet. As Burton showed, the theories can be very complex and cover a variety of different phenomena, and it is in fact difficult to subsume them all under the term *naskh*.

However, Burton noted that the story of the 'satanic verses' is usually adduced by the exegetes in their commentaries on Koran 22:52, which uses the Arabic verb *nasakha* ('God "abrogates" – *yansakhu* – what Satan casts in'), and not, as might have been expected, in commentary on 53:19 ff., the place in which the 'satanic verses' are said to have been interpolated. He suggested,

[9] E.g., Watt, *Muhammad at Mecca*, 101–9; Welch, 'Allāh and Other Supernatural Beings', throughout. [10] See *EI2* s.v. "ʿiṣma' by W. Madelung.

therefore, that the story may have arisen in the course of exegesis of the former verse. The purpose of the story, he proposed, was to provide a justificatory example of one of the forms of *naskh*. The story concerns a verse which was at one time accepted as part of the revelation but was then removed from it.

I think it is true to say that, in spite of Burton's recognition that the purpose of a report needs to be understood before a judgement about its historicity can be made, his solution to the problem has not been widely accepted. That is partly due to the extreme complexity of some of his argument. Mainly, though, it is because a story in which Satan casts things on to the tongue of the Prophet, and God then intervenes to restore the true relevation, does not really serve to justify or exemplify a theory that God reveals something and later replaces it Himself with another true revelation.[11]

Uri Rubin's approach is more concerned with the way in which biographical material on the Prophet originated and was developed as it found its way into various sorts of Muslim texts. He notices that the reports of the 'satanic verses' affair share a certain amount of material with other narratives that focus on the way in which the Prophet was isolated by his community but do not refer to temptation by Satan as such. He suggests a development whereby stories came to exist which applied to Muḥammad themes and elements common in the lives of prophets or holy men – in this case the theme of rejection and isolation of the prophet by his community – and that these themes were further developed under the influence of the Koran.

Koran 17:73–4 talks of the opponents as trying to *tempt* the Prophet away from what God had revealed and to get him falsely to attribute something else to God, while 22:52, as we have seen, says that all prophets have been subject to satanic interference but that God removes or 'abrogates' what Satan has cast in. Rubin suggests that such verses, which themselves reflect the common themes of rejection and temptation in the lives of prophets or holy men, have helped to develop the stories about the Prophet's isolation from his community and that the accounts of the 'satanic verses' have developed from a combination of such ideas. Because of the conflict between the stories and the strong reverence for the Prophet which grew in early Islam, the reports about the 'satanic verses' could be transmitted only in certain types of Muslim literature and they did not penetrate as a whole into the major collections of *ḥadīth*s. There they became truncated and inoffensive.[12]

Rubin makes no direct comment on the historicity of the event reported in the accounts of the 'satanic verses' but the introduction to his book makes it clear that he thinks that such material should be treated as literature and that any attempt to go beyond that to discuss the 'facts' is likely to be futile. Whether or not one agrees with all the details of his discussion of the accounts of the 'satanic verses', his argument that they, like many other stories about

[11] J. Burton, 'Those are the High-Flying Cranes', *JSS*, 15 (1970), 246–65.
[12] Rubin, *Eye of the Beholder*, 156–66.

the Prophet, can be understood as reflexions of common monotheist ideas about prophets and holy men are persuasive. The Muslim image of the Prophet was developed in conformity with models shared with other monotheists at the time of its formation. Rubin suggests how and why stories that later Muslim piety found uncomfortable could have arisen without being accounts of real events.

It is also a possibility that the core of the story of the 'satanic verses' reflects arguments with opponents about the authenticity of the revelation. The story could be understood as a guarantee that the totality of the revelation is of divine origin, directed at opponents who asked how that could be known. It shows the futility of possible satanic attempts to subvert the word of God since God would always intervene to remove any corruptions and restore the true revelation. The implications of the story for the figure of the Prophet would only become evident as the doctrine of his infallibility evolved.

Neither Burton nor Rubin were concerned with the three idols as such or with the question of whether the *jāhiliyya* as traditionally conceived was the background for the Koran and the origins of Islam. Their arguments concern the status of the 'satanic verses' story as historical fact, but not the generally accepted view that Allāt, al-ʿUzzā and Manāt were three goddesses worshipped in Mecca. Their approaches and conclusions may affect a part of the evidence supporting the traditional view of the Meccans as polytheists whose divinities included the three 'daughters of God' but the question remains of the historical reality behind the names.

We may remind ourselves of what we may deduce from the Koran about the three entities named in Sūra 53:19–20 and of what is dependent on extra-koranic sources. Negatively, the Koran does not tell us that the names refer to goddesses or idols, and it does not specifically associate them with Quraysh or Mecca. It is the tradition – mainly commentary on scripture and lives of the Prophet – that makes those identifications and associations.

Positively, in Sūra 53:19 and the following verses the opponents are charged with giving the names Allāt, al-ʿUzzā and Manāt to beings they regarded as female offspring of God (53:21–2: 'Are there males for you and females for Him? That would be an unfair division'), and it is suggested that they regarded them as angels who could intercede for them (53:26–7: 'How many are the angels in the heavens whose intercession is useless unless after God has given permission for he whom He wishes and accepts. They who do not believe in the world to come name the angels with female names'). The opponents are accused of attaching the three names to beings whom they regard as angels and, as such, offspring of God with power to intercede with Him.

It looks as if it is both the propriety of the names and the role attributed to the beings to whom they are given that the koranic passage is concerned to attack, not necessarily the existence of the entities themselves: 'They are only names which you and your fathers have given to them. God has not sent down any authority regarding them. They[13] follow mere supposition and their own desires. Yet the guidance has come to them from their Lord' (53:23). 'Those who do not believe in the world to come have named the angels with female names' (53:27).

Naturally, one should not necessarily conclude that the opponents really did or believed what they are accused of. It can be said, however, that the polemic of Koran 53:19–28 is consistent with other koranic passages which associate *shirk* with the belief in or veneration of angels, accuse the opponents of regarding the angels and *jinn* as the offspring of God, and charge them with making the angels female and granting them the power to intercede with God. Some of these passages were discussed in chapter 2 above. The distinctive element in 53:19–28 is the names that, it is here charged, the opponents give to the angels.

Of course, it is possible, as has sometimes been suggested, that the koranic passage as we know it is the result of interpolation and combination of materials that were at one time distinct. Read by itself it may be judged to have an element of inconsequentiality (the transition from the three names to the talk of angels and intercession at first seems odd), it switches from addressing the opponents directly to referring to them in the third person, and the story of the 'satanic verses' seems at least to envisage a text that has been disrupted at some point. It is preferable, however, to resort to such explanations only when a text cannot be made sense of as it stands, and it is not only possible to comprehend Koran 53:19–28 without recourse to the possibility of interpolation but the passage is of a piece with others that polemicise against the *mushrikūn*: more than that, it helps to make sense of a feature of those other passages that is otherwise puzzling. We will come back to this shortly. I do recognise, however, that I may be laying myself open to the charge of attempting to harmonise conflicting materials, a criticism I have made against some others above.

At this point, however, the main thing is that the only koranic reference to the names Allāt, al-ʿUzzā and Manāt establishes a rather different image from the one we would have of them if we relied on the traditional information about these three 'goddesses' or 'idols'. In the traditional material relating to them, the koranic polemic against the idea of intercession is visible only in the reports about the 'satanic verses', where, naturally, it could be a consequence of the fact that the story concerns the revelation of Koran 53:19 ff. which ridicules the opponents' hopes for intercession. On the other hand, the 'high-flying cranes' tag suggests that there might more to it than that – that the reference to intercession in connexion with the three beings may not be entirely explicable by the theory that it reflects the words of the koranic passage. But none of the other traditional reports about the three idols refer

[13] I.e., presumably, the opponents, now referred to in the third, rather than addressed in the second, person.

to the idea of intercession, and outside the Koran the three beings appear fundamentally as idols.

Before taking further this apparent tension between the koranic passage and the traditional material identifying the three as goddesses or idols, and before taking up some features of the 'satanic verses' story, we should return – in connexion with Allāt, al-ʿUzzā and Manāt – to some of the issues examined in the previous chapter. How far is the traditional material consistent in what it tells us about the geographical locations, tribal associations, etc. of the three 'idols', and how far might material from outside the tradition be said to corroborate the traditional material?

Like the material discussed in the previous chapter, the reports about Allāt, al-ʿUzzā and Manāt too are variant and sometimes inconsistent although, again, it is hardly possible to isolate completely distinct and independent traditions.

The traditional Muslim sources tend to associate Allāt with Ṭā'if, although there are also reports associating her with Nakhla (a site connected in tradition also with al-ʿUzzā and Suwāʿ), ʿUkāẓ and Mecca.[14] The *Aṣnām* gives its precise location in Ṭā'if: 'where the left minaret of the mosque is today'.[15]

It is sometimes described as a cube-shaped rock (*ṣakhra murabbaʿa*) although there is reference to a building (*binā'*) having been constructed over it and sometimes Allāt is described as a sanctuary or stele (*bayt*) rather than as an idol or rock.[16] Wāqidī's reference to the 'head' (*ra's*) of Allāt (here called al-Rabba, 'the Lady') might indicate that there was a view of her as an idol in human or animal form, although Wellhausen resisted that implication.[17] Sometimes the rock is said to have been white.[18]

She is said to have been the object of veneration (*taʿẓīm*) by Quraysh and 'all the Arabs', and her guardians (*sadana*) came from the Banū Thaqīf, the dominant tribe of Ṭā'if. The name of the clan within Thaqīf that controlled the *sidāna* is variantly given.[19] The destruction of Allāt in Ṭā'if is said to have

[14] Ṭab., *Tafsīr* (Bulaq), XXVII, 35 l.2 on Koran 53:19–22: it was a *bayt* at Nakhla that Quraysh worshipped but some say that it was at Ṭā'if. See too Krone, *Altarabische Gottheit*, 201 and n.76. Ṭabarī cites Qatāda as thinking it was in Ṭā'if, Ibn Zayd as thinking it was in Nakhla. The associations with ʿUkāẓ and Mecca arise in the accounts of the etymology of the name Allāt (for the story of the 'grinder', al-Lātt, see above, chap. 4, p. 102, n. 29). Wellhausen, *Reste*, 31 notes what he identifies as a tendency by later generations to conflate Allāt and al-ʿUzzā. Wellhausen's insistence that early tradition knew of Allāt only in connexion with Ṭā'if and al-ʿUzzā only in connexion with Nakhla seems contradicted, however, by Ṭabarī's citation of Ibn Zayd as placing Allāt at Nakhla. (W. Robertson Smith, *The Religion of the Semites*, 2nd ed., 1894, repr. New York 1972, 211–12 situated Allāt at Tabāla; that is probably a confusion with Dhu 'l-Khalaṣa – an example of how easy it is to generate variant material.)

[15] *Aṣnām K-R*, 10 (text) = 37 (trans.).

[16] Ṭabarī, *Tafsīr*, XXVII, 35 l.2 (*bayt*); *Aṣnām K-R*, 10 (text) = 37 (trans.) (a squared rock at Ṭā'if . . . its *sādin*s had erected a building [*binā'*] over it).

[17] Wāqidī, *Maghāzī*, 971; Wellhausen, *Reste*, 32. [18] Yāqūt cited in Wellhausen, *Reste*, 30.

[19] *Aṣnām K-R*, 10 (text) = 32 (trans.); Ibn Ḥabīb, *Muḥabbar*, 312; Wellhausen, *Reste*, 31, citing also Wāqidī and *Sīra*; in spite of the variants they all seem to agree that the *sādin*s belonged to the tribe of Thaqīf.

occurred at the hands of the Thaqafī Mughīra b. Shuʿba (usually, but not always, accompanied by Abū Sufyān).[20]

As for al-ʿUzzā, the main difficulty regarding the traditional reports is the relationship, if any, between the following blocks of material.

1 Material in which al-ʿUzzā is associated with the tribe of Ghaṭafān. The man named as responsible for adopting the idol from ʿAmr b. Luḥayy is a certain Ẓālim b. Asʿad whom the tradition ascribes to the clan of Murra of Ghaṭafān. The guardians of the idol are named as the clan of Ṣirma b. Murra (of Ghaṭafān). Ẓālim is reported to have built a *buss* over al-ʿUzzā. The site of the idol is connected with the toponym Nakhla.[21]
2 A tradition that a *buss* associated with Ghaṭafān was destroyed by Zuhayr b. Janāb al-Kalbī. The reports emphasise that this *buss* was related in some way to the Meccan sanctuary (e.g. that it contained stones from al-Ṣafā and al-Marwa). It is suggested that it was built to rival the sanctuary at Mecca and that the people of Ẓālim b. Asʿad used to worship it (rather than the Meccan sanctuary?). One version says that when Zuhayr destroyed it he also killed Ẓālim. These reports do not seem to refer to al-ʿUzzā and do not have the toponym Nakhla.[22]
3 The standard tradition about the destruction of al-ʿUzzā says that the Prophet sent Khālid b. al-Walīd to Nakhla to destroy it. The guardian clan was that of Shaybān of the tribe of Sulaym, and the last guardian was a man called Dubayya of Shaybān. Khālid killed him. We do not need to repeat here the well known story about the cutting down of the trees and the appearance of the naked black old woman.[23]

As will be apparent, the information about the family of guardians in 1 is difficult to square with that in 3, and the report about the destruction of the *buss* in 2 seems to conflict with the story of Khālid's attack on the idol in 3.

[20] *Aṣnām K-R*, 10 (text) =32 (trans.); Ibn Ḥabīb, *Muḥabbar*, 315; Ibn Hishām, *Sīra*, II, 541; Wāqidī, *Maghāzī*, 971–2; Mūsā b. ʿUqba, *Maghāzī*, 312–13; Wellhausen, *Reste*, 30–1; Fahd, *Panthéon*, 120; ʿAlī, *Mufaṣṣal*, VI, 234; Krone, *Altarabische Gottheit*,, 198–200.

[21] *Aṣnām K-R*, 11–12 (text) = 38–9 (trans.); Ibn Ḥabīb, *Muḥabbar*, 315. The *Aṣnām* does not specifically mention Ghaṭafān by name, but tells us about Ẓālim. The *Muḥabbar* does not refer to Ẓālim but mentions Ghaṭafān by name and the name of the clan of guardians. The *Aṣnām* glosses *buss* as *bayt* , 'house, sanctuary, stele' (*fa-banā ʿalayhā bussan yurīdu baytan*). While the *Muḥabbar* says that al-ʿUzzā was a tree at Nakhla by which there was an idol (*wathan*), the *Aṣnām* talks of the *buss*/*bayt* as a place in which a voice could be heard and gives a relatively detailed topographical account of the site of the idol which begins with the specification that it was in a *wādī* of Nakhlat al-Shāmiyya called Ḥurāḍ.

[22] M. J. Kister, 'Mecca and the Tribes of Arabia', in M. Sharon (ed.), *Studies in Islamic History and Civilization in Honour of Prof. David Ayalon*, Jerusalem and Leiden 1986, 43. The main sources cited by Kister are Abu ʾl-Faraj ʿAlī b. Ḥusayn al-Iṣfahānī, *Kitāb al-Aghānī*, 24 vols., Cairo 1927–74, XII, 126 (commenting on a verse), Muḥammad b. Yaʿqūb al-Fayrūzābādī, *al-Qāmūs al-muḥīt*, 4 vols., Bulaq 1301–2 AH, s.v. '*bss*', Balādhurī, *Ansāb* (in MS), and Ibn al-Kalbī, *Jamharat al-nasab, Riwāyat al-Sukkarī ʿan Ibn Ḥabīb* (in MS (ed. Nājī Ḥasan, Beirut 1986, 476)). Both Kister and Lecker prefer to interpret Buss as a toponym, and there is some support for this in the traditional material (Lecker, *Banū Sulaym*, 39).

[23] *Aṣnām K-R*, 15–16 (text) = 41 (trans.); Ibn Ḥabīb, *Muḥabbar*, 124, 315.

Other features of the tradition are also confusing. For example, in spite of the reports associating al-ʿUzzā with Ghaṭafān, others specify that it was worshipped by Quraysh and Kināna.[24] In spite of those reports that understand *buss* as a *bayt* or building of some sort, others have it as a place name whether connected with Nakhla or not.[25]

Faced with these difficulties, Wellhausen sought to resolve the inconsistencies by postulating a confusion between two different sanctuaries of al-ʿUzzā, one at Nakhla and one at a place called Buss nearby, a confusion caused in part by the traditional assumption that ʿAmr b.Luḥayy had only one version of each idol to distribute to the Arabs. Lecker, on the other hand, was persuaded that the topographical details are consistent enough to indicate one sanctuary only and sought to resolve the difficulties in the traditional material by postulating a change in circumstances over time, Sulaym taking over the guardianship from Ghaṭafān, and Quraysh coming into the picture following Zuhayr's destruction of the so-called Kaʿba of Ghaṭafān. Iḥsān ʿAbbās, who published a text of Abū Ṭālib al-Marrakushī containing an account specific to Ghaṭafān of the corruption of Abrahamic monotheism among the descendants of Ishmael, also postulated a development over time. Similar views were put forward by Fahd and followed by Krone.

In theory both solutions are possible, as is the view that it is not possible to put the material into an orderly pattern since we do not know enough about its sources or the reasons why it has generated so many variants. The material summarised here, and characterised by Krone as 'somewhat contradictory', is only a small part of the total traditional material relating to, or made to relate to, al-ʿUzzā.[26]

The diversity of the information about Manāt and the difficulty of deducing sure information about this 'goddess' is well brought out in Jawād ʿAlī's collection of material.[27] While there is general agreement on her site, said in the *Aṣnām* to be 'on the seashore in the district of al-Mushallal at Qudayd between Medina and Mecca',[28] a wide variety of tribal or clan names are given with reference to those associated with her cult and guardianship. There is a tendency to link her especially with the Anṣār (Aws and Khazraj) but Azd (especially the Ghaṭārīf), the Khuzāʿa, Quraysh and 'all of the Arabs' are mentioned in different sources.

Some say that she was worshipped in the form of a rock (the name is sometimes explained from the fact that the blood of sacrificial offerings was poured

[24] Ibn Hishām, *Sīra*, I, 84; Azraqī, *Akhbār Makka*, I, 126 mentions Khuzāʿa as well as Quraysh and Kināna. [25] Wellhausen, *Reste*, 37–8; Lecker, *Banū Sulaym*, 39.

[26] Wellhausen, *Reste*, 34–40; Lecker, *Banū Sulaym*, 37–42; Iḥsān ʿAbbās, 'Two Hitherto Unpublished Texts on Pre-Islamic Religion', in *La Signification du bas moyen âge dans l'histoire et la culture du monde musulman (Actes du 8e congrès de l'union européenne des arabisants et islamisants)*, Aix-en-Provence 1976, 7–16; Fahd, *Panthéon*, 165; S. Krone, *Altarabische Gottheit*, 516 draws attention to the fact that the hypothesis of two sanctuaries might help to explain the dual al-ʿUzzatān which occurs in poetry, but nevertheless favours a single sanctuary solution. [27] *Mufaṣṣal*, VI, 246–50.

[28] Note, however, the references to Wadān (Yāqūt) and Fadak (Yaʿqūbī): ʿAlī, *Mufaṣṣal*, VI, 246, notes 4 and 5.

– *tumnā* – over the rock), others as an idol (*ṣanam*) sculpted in a particular shape from a rock, others that Manāt was a *bayt* (stele, sanctuary).

Reports about the destruction of Manāt sometimes name ʿAlī as the one responsible, sometimes Abū Sufyān, and sometimes Saʿd b. Zayd al-Ashhalī. These stories sometimes include reference to the appearance of a naked black old woman, just as in the stories about al-ʿUzzā.

It can be seen, therefore, that much of the traditional material pertaining to the three 'daughters of God' displays the stereotypical features and the variants and inconsistencies that characterise the reports about *jāhilī* idolatry in general. It is difficult to establish from this material the basic facts about these 'idols' of the *jāhiliyya*, let alone to deduce anything about their character or to use them to illuminate religious conditions in Arabia before Islam.

How far do the attestations of the names outside the tradition affect our attitude to the traditional material? There is no reason to doubt that *names* related to those the Koran says were given by the opponents to beings whom they regarded as 'daughters of God', and which Muslim tradition identifies as those of goddesses, idols or sanctuaries, were in common use with reference to deities or other supernatural entities in the Near East, including Arabia, before Islam.

There are certainly difficulties in connecting the Allāt of the Koran and Muslim tradition with the Alilat that Herodotus (fifth century BC) identifies with Ourania and pairs with Oratalt as the sole deities of the Arabs (of Sinai and the adjoining regions).[29] Nevertheless, forms similar to the Arabic are widely attested epigraphically and in theophoric names from before Islam. Zenobia's son and co-ruler was, for example, called Ouaballathos (i.e., probably Wahb Allāt, 'The Gift of Allāt'), and that he was also known as Athēnodōros implies that Athene might have been assimilated with Allāt. Since the Semitic form merely means 'the Goddess', it is not surprising to find it frequently recurring in the Middle East and around the Mediterranean among Semitic-speaking non-monotheist peoples.

Names that seem to be connected with the al-ʿUzzā and Manāt of Muslim tradition are less frequently attested but occur often enough to show that the koranic names are not mere inventions. Forms related to the former are attested, for example, in Liḥyanite (*h-n* ʿ*-z-y*), in Nabataean (ʿ*-z-y*), and in south Arabian (ʿ*-z-y-n*), and the toponym Elusa (modern Ḥalaṣa, south-west of Beersheba) has been suggested as a Latin form of the name. An apparently plural form of Manāt (*m-n-w-t-w*) occurs in Nabataean inscriptions (see above on Dhu ʾl-Sharā) and, famously, in Latin as Manavat in an inscription made by a Roman soldier of Palmyrene origin in Hungary.[30]

It is apparent, therefore, that the names given in the Koran and in Muslim

[29] Krone, *Altarabische Gottheit*, 55 f., 70 ff.

[30] See Wellhausen, *Reste*, 28, 32–4, 40–5, *ERE*, s.v. 'Arabs (Ancient)' by Nöldeke; Fahd, *Panthéon*, 111–20, 123–6, and 163–82; the articles in *EI* s.vv. 'Lāt', 'Manāt' and ''Uzzā'; and Krone, *Altarabische Gottheit*, for fuller references to occurrences of the three names outside Muslim tradition.

tradition relate to forms relatively well attested over a broad chronological span before Islam and, notably, especially in the north Arabian and Syrian desert region. It is also the case, however, that Muslim tradition is either not aware of this or chooses to ignore it. It explains and describes Allāt, al-ʿUzzā and Manāt entirely in the context of the *jāhiliyya*, linking them with the story of ʿAmr b. Luḥayy's introduction of idolatry and attempting to account for the names by etymologies and legends such as that of *al-lātt*, 'the grinder'.[31]

Drawing on evidence external to the Muslim tradition, evidence relating to Syria, Mesopotamia and the Sinai, modern scholars have frequently associated the names, especially that of al-ʿUzzā, with cults devoted to astral bodies, particularly Venus. Her worship was ascribed to the Arabs of the northern border regions by several writers of Late Antiquity. The name of Manāt has also been associated with the worship of Fate, which might be implied by the Arabic root *m-n-y/w* with which it seems to be associated, although the Nabataean and Latin attestations seem to offer a plural form (in classical antiquity Fate was often conceived of as a trio of goddesses). It is notable, however, that there is little if anything in the Muslim traditional material that explicitly supports such identifications and links. Discussing al-ʿUzzā, Nöldeke could find no evidence in the Muslim traditional literature of a realisation of her astral character – he argued that that was to be explained by the fact that worshippers of a deity tend to personify it and do not ask what was its original significance – and Fahd, once he moves away from the non-Muslim to the Muslim material, becomes very speculative and tenuous in attempting to support the argument that the cult of al-ʿUzzā and the others was derived from the cult of Venus.[32] I am not arguing that these identifications and associations are wrong – indeed the argument identifying al-ʿUzzā with Venus is strong – but underlining the remoteness of the Muslim traditional from the other evidence.

One notable feature of the traditional material, again, is the way in which it is made to relate to Mecca. In much of the traditional material the three 'idols' are associated with places other than Mecca (with Ṭāʾif, Nakhla and Qudayd, for example) and with tribes and families other than Quraysh (with Thaqīf, Ghaṭafān, and others). In other reports, however, the tradition seems concerned to establish Meccan connexions.

This is done in various ways. The most obvious is to present the three beings in the context of the Meccan ʿAmr b. Luḥayy's distribution of idols among the Arabs. Another is to link up both al-ʿUzzā and Manāt with the Meccan sanctuary and its ceremonies by telling us that the devotees of the idol con-

[31] See above, (chap. 4, n. 29). Michael Cook draws attention to the oddity that the story of the 'grinder' would make Allāt masculine.

[32] For the suggestion that Allāt represented the sun (feminine in Arabic and most Semitic languages), see Wellhausen, *Reste*, 33 – a suggestion that *is* supported by reference to Muslim tradition. Fahd, *Panthéon*, 118–19 proposes that all three were associated in Arabia with the worship of Venus. For the suggested link between Manāt and the Canaanite Menī (Fate?) in Isaiah 65:11, see *ERE*, s.v. 'Arabs (Ancient)' by Nöldeke, 661.

cerned included a visit to the idol in their *ḥajj* rituals. Quraysh, we are told, did not consider their *ḥajj* complete until they had made a visit to the idol of al-ʿUzzā where they desacralised themselves by shaving their heads (cf. the report alluding to Isāf and Nāʾila, p. 68 above); on the other hand we are sometimes told that the adherents of Manāt did not regard their participation in the Meccan *ḥajj* as complete until they had visited the idol (or *bayt* or rock) where they would shave their heads and 'stand', sometimes that they began their pilgrimage to Mecca there (*yuhillūna minhā li'l-ḥajj ilā 'l-Kaʿba*).[33]

The different versions of the etymological story linking the name of Allāt with the person who ground cereal (*al-lātt*, 'the grinder') to make a broth for the pilgrims in particular seem to show an almost subconscious urge to bring Allāt into a connexion with Mecca. While many of the stories place the man who ground up the cereal in Ṭāʾif (the most common view in the tradition is that the sanctuary of Allāt was there) and make him a man of Thaqīf, the tribe of that town,[34] others seem to imagine that he was active in Mecca. One version talks of him providing broth for the 'pilgrims' (*al-ḥājj*) and says that he was deified after Khuzāʿa had driven out Jurhum, which is a part of the traditions relating to Mecca. In one version it was ʿAmr b. Luḥayy himself who was responsible for deifying the grinder. In another he is said to have made a *kiswa* (covering) for the sanctuary (*al-bayt*), again making a link with Mecca. Yet another version situates his activity at ʿUkāẓ, the fair associated with Mecca in tradition.[35]

In the story of the 'satanic verses' the three goddesses appear as the major deities of Mecca. When the Prophet wishes to win the support of his fellow townsmen, his first thought – under Satan's influence – is to give Allāt, al-ʿUzzā and Manāt a place in Islam, and that is sufficient to bring about the conversion of Quraysh. According to the *Aṣnām*, 'Quraysh in Mecca and those of the Arabs who abode there with them did not revere anything of the idols more than al-ʿUzzā, then Allāt and then Manāt'.[36] It could be that these reports connecting the three idols with Mecca reflect the ideas and preconceptions of the creators and collectors of Muslim tradition, influenced by the fact that they are named in the Koran and the general 'Meccocentricity' of tradition, rather than arising from whatever original material was available to them.

It is, nevertheless, unlikely that all of the material in Muslim tradition relating to the three beings is the result of mere speculation generated by the fact

[33] *Aṣnām K-R*, 8–9 (text) = 36–7 (trans.); 'When ʿAmr b. Luḥayy had done that [i.e., distributed the idols], the Arabs yielded to the idols, worshipped them and adopted them. The oldest of them all was Manāt.' It was the people of Yathrib, and others who followed them, who, having fulfilled the duties of the *ḥajj*, remained in a sacral state until they had visited Manāt. Cf. the report of Ibn Isḥāq in Azraqī, *Akhbār Makka*, I, 124–5; for a similar report referring to al-ʿUzzā and Quraysh, see 126.

[34] Remarkably, one version says that the man came from Nakhla, a site sometimes associated with Allāt but more often with al-ʿUzzā.

[35] For a conspectus, see Krone *Altarabische Gottheit*, 44 ff.

[36] *Aṣnām K-R*, 16 (text) = 43 (trans.).

that the three names occur in the Koran. As well as the solidity of the names themselves, we have just noted that many of the reports about Allāt, al-ʿUzzā and Manāt do not obviously relate to Mecca and that the traditional scholars often seem concerned to make such a connexion. In addition we have features such as the fact that some oaths and verses mention Allāt and al-ʿUzzā in tandem without mentioning Manāt, and that sometimes we meet the problematic 'two ʿUzzās' (*al-ʿuzzatān*). On top of that there is the the *al-gharānīq al-ʿulā* tag. None of this is easily explicable as arising merely out of exegesis of Koran 53:19 ff. and some of it seems to create difficulties for the tradition – it would have been simpler if the material consistently portrayed idols, unambiguously connected them with Mecca and Quraysh, and always referred to them together as a trinity.

There is a tension between the koranic passage relating to the three beings and the traditional material treating them as typical idols, but the traditional material cannot be written off completely as the product of speculative exegesis or of mere invention. Although its general tenor is to assimilate Allāt, al-ʿUzzā and Manāt to the image of pre-Islamic Arab idolatry as a corruption of Abrahamic monotheism with Mecca as the focus of the whole development, the tradition seems to preserve fragments of material which might be valuable if they could be disentangled from the framework within which they are presented. However, the inconsistencies and confusions in the basic information the tradition conveys make one pessimistic about establishing what the facts were and warn against building far-reaching theories on them. It is also doubtful how far the facts, if they can be isolated,will help us to understand the background to the Koran and to Islam.

We now revert to the significance of the koranic passage (53:19–28) and the *al-gharānīq al-ʿulā* tag in the story of the 'satanic verses'.

The lack of consistency between the traditional material which portrays the three beings as idols or goddesses and the koranic verses which associate the names, in the opponents' usage, with angels has sometimes been noticed by scholars. The dominant influence of the tradition has generally meant that in such cases it has been the koranic image that has been taken to be distorted: the three beings were really gods or idols of the pagans, especially the Meccans, but for particular reasons it is alleged in the Koran that the opponents regarded them as angels and as daughters of God. Thus Paul Eichler suggested that the pagans chose to represent their gods as angels and daughters of Allāh in the hope that Muḥammad would allow them to continue to venerate them. The concept emerged under the pressure the Prophet was exerting on the Meccans but, of course, Muḥammad would have nothing to do with it.[37] Alford Welch, on the other hand, understands the koranic passage 53:19 ff. as an attack upon three goddesses worshipped by the Meccans who did indeed identify them as 'daughters of Allāh'. The identification of them as

[37] Eichler, *Dschinn, Teufel und Engel*, 101–2.

angels is a part of the koranic polemic and was not accepted by the Meccans themselves. It was a stage in the process whereby the Prophet gradually redefined and thus diminished the gods of his opponents, a process that culminated in the denial of their existence. The issue of intercession, according to Welch, 'although an important statement on this subject is made here' (i.e., 53:26–8), is not of central importance.[38]

Such approaches give priority to the traditional data over the words of the Koran itself,[39] and Welch's playing down of the issue of intercession seems unjustified. Can we make sense of the koranic passage without assuming with the tradition that the opponents were polytheists and idolaters, and in a way that does not involve supposition about a fragmented and interpolated text?

The koranic passage beginning 'Have you not seen [or 'considered'] Allāt, al-ʿUzzā and Manāt' goes on to criticise the opponents for attributing female offspring to God while having males for themselves, to insist that the names are simply names which the opponents have traditionally given the three entities, to deny that the intercession of the angels can be of any use, except for those to whom God grants it and finds it acceptable, and finally to accuse those who give female names to the angels of not believing in the world to come.[40]

Other passages in the Koran, as we have seen, attack the opponents for viewing the angels as female offspring of God and seem to accuse them of angel worship. 'On the day when [God] gathers them all together, He will ask the angels, "Was it these who worshipped you?" They will reply, "Glory be to You! You are our patron, not these. Rather they worshipped the jinn and most of them had faith in them."' (34:40–1) '[God] does not command you that you take the angels and the prophets as lords' (3:80). Of the various passages accusing the opponents of regarding the angels as female, we may confine ourselves to 17:40: 'Has your Lord granted sons to you and taken [for Himself] females from among the angels? You say a grave thing.' Even allowing for polemical distortion, there is a consistency here which it seems arbitrary to reject in favour of the traditional image of the opponents' one-dimensional idolatry.

[38] Welch, 'Allah and Other Supernatural Beings', 739.

[39] Although it should be noted that Welch does not necessarily accept the historicity of the 'satanic verses' story; see Welch, 'Allah and Other Supernatural Beings', n.12.

[40] For convenience a translation of the relevant passage from Sūra 53 may be given here: 'And have you seen Allāt and al-ʿUzzā/19/ and Manāt the third the other?/20/ Is it that there are males for you and females for Him?/21/ That would be an unfair division./22/ They are only names which you and your fathers have given them. God has not revealed any authority regarding them. They follow only supposition and personal impulses, but the Guidance has come to them from their Lord./23/ Does man have whatever he desires?/24/ To God belongs the world to come and this one./25/ How many are the angels in the heavens but their intercession is good for nothing unless after God has given permission to whomever He desires and finds acceptable./26/ Those who do not believe in the world to come call the angels with female names./27/ They have no certain knowledge about it but follow only supposition. Supposition is good for nothing regarding the truth./28/'

The idea of angels as female and as daughters of God has puzzled modern scholars. The identification of angels as *sons* of God or as some kind of emanation of God is quite easy to document, the most obvious example being the traditional Jewish and Christian interpretation of the 'sons of God' in Genesis chapter 6 as fallen angels. Other references to 'sons of God' in the Hebrew Bible were also traditionally often interpreted as angels (Job 1:6 ff., Psalm 29:1, etc.).[41] Angels as female and daughters, however, have been difficult to document. Paul Eichler argued that koranic attacks on the veneration of angels could make sense in a Jewish or Christian context, but could find no evidence of identification of the angels as female among Jewish or Christian groups. He concluded that the idea of the angels as daughters of God must be a product of Arab pagan syncretism: 'Wherever there is talk of the daughters of Allāh we find ourselves in contact with Arab paganism. . . . The pagans must, therefore, have invented this heresy (diese Ketzerei).'[42]

Ilse Lichtenstadter sought to break the link between 'the daughters of Allāh' and angels completely, arguing instead that we should associate the 'daughters' with folk stories about water birds, and attributing the willingness of both Muslim and western scholars to accept their identification with angels as a reflexion of 'Western medieval ideas of the character of angels'.[43] Her treatment of the koranic material is unconvincing, however, and again one sees the dominance of the traditional material – in this case the 'satanic verses' story – over the koranic text itself.

Without Koran 53:19 ff. the attack on the opponents for regarding the angels as female offspring of God would indeed be puzzling. But at least that koranic passage goes some way towards helping us understand the charge: the *mushrikūn* regard the angels as female because they give (some of) them female names – Allāt, al-ʿUzzā and Manāt. One might speculate that the opponents themselves would not have admitted that they regarded the angels as female but that they had left themselves open to the accusation because they identified as angels entities that were traditionally given female names, whether or not they really went so far as to use the three names the Koran provides. Other koranic passages that deplore the opponents' idea that the angels are female offspring of God could be explained as reflexions of the charge made in Koran 53:19–20.

That suggestion must be speculative, but at least it does not go beyond the koranic evidence.The identification as angels of entities bearing female names could make sense in relation to a group that saw stars, planets and other astral bodies as angels, ideas which seem to have flourished in some early Jewish and Christian sects.[44] The book of Enoch 6–8 gives the names of several angels,

[41] Of course, the connotations of 'son(s) of God', 'children of God', etc. in the monotheistic tradition extended beyond simply the angels by early Islamic times: Wansbrough, *Sectarian Milieu*, 20, 43. [42] Eichler, *Dschinn, Teufel und Engel*, 98–9.

[43] I. Lichtenstadter, 'A Note on the *gharānīq* and Related Qur'ānic Problems', *IOS*, 5 (1975), 54–61. [44] See above, p. 53 note 20.

among them Kōkābiel (Star of God) and Satarel, which L. Ginzberg suggested contains the name of Ishtar/Astarte, the Semitic mother goddess with affinities to the western Aphrodite/Venus.[45]

As has been mentioned, the non-Muslim evidence, especially that relating to al-ʿUzzā but to some extent also that relating to the other two, has led modern scholars frequently to associate the cults of the three 'goddesses' with the worship of astral bodies, particularly Venus. It is conceivable that this idea underlies the koranic accusation that the opponents gave the angels female names and regarded them as the daughters of God. If the three names given in Koran 53:19–20 had been used to refer to Venus or any other of the heavenly bodies, and if the opponents did associate the heavenly bodies with angels, the koranic polemic against them would be understandable.[46]

The *al-gharānīq al-ʿulā* tag also relates to angels. That tag has a distinctive quality and is not obviously explicable as an elaboration of anything koranic. In the *Aṣnām* 'these are *al-gharānīq al-ʿulā* whose intercession is to be hoped for' is not associated with the 'satanic verses' affair (which is not alluded to in that work) but rather is said to have been part of a ritual verbal formula which Quraysh recited in the *jāhiliyya* when they circumambulated the Kaʿba. That ritual formula began, according to the report in the *Aṣnām*, with a slight variant upon Koran 53:19–20 and then finished with the 'high-flying cranes' tag. The tag, therefore, may have an existence independent of the 'satanic verses' story, and perhaps of Ibn Kalbī's report too.[47]

Although the exact significance of the phrase must remain uncertain, *al-ʿulā*, often understood as 'high-flying', could also punningly reflect designations of the angels as the 'exalted ones' or 'high beings'. In Koran 37:8 and 38:69 there is a reference to the 'high assembly' (*al-malaʾ al-aʿlā*), referring to the heavenly court of God and the angels. The former verse is part of a passage in which it is said that the stars are set in the lower heaven (*al-samāʾ al-dunyā*) so that the rebellious satans may not overhear what passes in the high assembly.[48]

Although *gharānīq* is understood in a variety of ways in the Muslim

[45] For the passage from Enoch see R. H. Charles (ed.), *The Apocrypha and Pseudepigraphia of the Old Testament*, 2 vols., Oxford 1913, II, *The Pseudepigraphia*, 191–2; for Satarel's possible link with Ishtar, see Ginzberg, *Legends of the Jews*, V, 152, and for references to Ishtar in Aramaic incantation texts, apparently as an angel or demon, see J. A. Montgomery, *Aramaic Incantation Texts from Nippur*, Philadelphia 1913, Glossary A: Personal names and epithets of deities, s.v. 'str'.

[46] Allāt ('the Goddess') and al-ʿUzzā ('the Mighty Lady') are in themselves so unspecific that they could refer to any of the stars or planets or something else. The name of Manāt is most obviously associated with Fate but it has been suggested that, in the form Menūtum, it was one of the names of Ishtar in ancient Mesopotamia (see the literature cited by Fahd at the beginning of his article s.v. 'Manāt' in *EI2*).

[47] *Aṣnām K-R*, 12 (text) = 39 (trans.). Eichler, *Dschinn, Teufel und Engel* 100, and Rubin, *Eye of the Beholder*, 159, appear to accept that the Qurashī ritual formula was the real *Sitz im Leben* for the 'high-flying cranes' tag and that it found its way from there into the 'satanic verses' story.

[48] See further Montgomery, *Samaritans*, 216 for designations of angels in Aramaic including 'celestial folk' (*ʿ-m ʿ-l-ʾ-y*) and 'powers of heaven' (*ḥ-y-l sh-m-y-ʾ*: in Daniel 4:32).

lexicographical tradition,[49] the most obvious sense is that of 'cranes' or some other sort of long-necked water fowl such as storks, herons or even swans. There is a possible conceptual link with angels: apart from traditional angelic imagery, such birds may have a role in popular belief as messengers of God or the gods just as an angel is a messenger of God. In European folklore the stork is the deliverer of new babies. Some association of the ideas of angel and stork is perhaps shown in the book of the prophet Zechariah 5:9, where the angel shows him a vision of two women with wings 'like those of a stork' (*ke-kanfē ha-ḥasīdāh*) who carry away the barrel of wickedness to the land of Shinar.[50]

These can only be tentative suggestions and I am less concerned to argue for a 'real' meaning of Koran 53:19 ff. or of the *al-gharānīq al-ʿulā* tag than to stress the lack of fit between the koranic passage referring to the three 'daughters of God' in the context of an attack on the opponents' ideas about angels on the one hand and the traditional identification of them as three chief idols of the Meccans on the other. It also seems that the designation of Allāt, al-ʿUzzā and Manāt as *al-gharānīq al-ʿulā* in the story of the 'satanic verses' is sufficiently distinctive to indicate that here, at least, the traditional material shows some understanding of the context in which the names occur in the Koran. It may even be a remnant in the traditional material of polemic against the beliefs of the koranic *mushrikūn*. Although the 'satanic verses' story (and Ibn al-Kalbī's explanation of the phrase too) implies that the Meccans saw *al-gharānīq al-ʿulā* as a favourable way of referring to their goddesses, it is more likely to have been a term of mockery used against people accused of the worship of angels. In any case, the remainder of the 'satanic verses' story, like the rest of the traditional material, portrays the three 'daughters of God' as mere idols or goddesses in keeping with the image of pre-Islamic pagan idolatry in general.

We may attempt to summarise the general conclusions that emerge from the discussion of the material on the daughters of God in this chapter and that of the idolatry of the Arabs more generally in the previous one. First, the traditional Muslim material cannot all be explained as the result of mere speculation or elaboration of the koranic material. It seems to contain details that cannot be explained in that way and some of which are inconvenient for the tradition. Those details, however, are fragmentary, lack a real context, and are reported with variants and inconsistencies that make it difficult, perhaps impossible, to see their significance for any general discussion of Arabian or Middle Eastern religion before Islam. Attempts by traditional and modern scholars to harmonise the sometimes contradictory material are generally not persuasive. Whatever historical details the traditional material has preserved,

[49] Summarised in Fahd, *Panthéon*, 88–90.

[50] Another meaning of *gharānīq* according to the tradition is with reference to 'gentle youths' or 'elegant and refined people'. Possibly that is derived from the gracefulness of the birds in question (Eichler, *Dschinn, Teufel und Engel*, 100, n.1; Lichtenstadter, 'A Note on the *gharānīq*', 54).

it tends to be formulaic in its interests (places, tribes, origins and destruction), and we now find the details embedded in a framework account of Arab idolatry which is schematic and centred on Mecca.

Second, the image of Arab idolatry and polytheism offered by the tradition bears little relation to the koranic material attacking the *mushrikūn* for their attachment to intermediaries between themselves and God, their hope for the intercession of angels, and their half-hearted and imperfect monotheism. The traditional material in general portrays a world of primitive idols and a multiplicity of gods. One exception, it has been suggested, is the *al-gharānīq al-ʿulā* formula.

Finally, the corroboration offered the traditional material by inscriptions and non-Muslim literature cannot be said to consist of much more than names. The distance in time and place between the external evidence and that provided by Muslim tradition tends to be ignored or not given much importance by many modern scholars, and in general there seems to have been an overestimation of the extent to which the non-Muslim and Muslim evidence coheres and offers mutual support.

Conclusion

It has been argued here that the Muslim accounts of pre-Islamic Arabian idolatrous religion are of questionable value as a source of information about the religion of the *jāhiliyya*, informed mainly by the traditional understanding that the *mushrikūn* of the Koran were idolatrous Arabs in and around Mecca and developing, in a way that reflected Muslim concerns, stories and ideas about idolatry that were common to monotheism in the Middle East. Once this image had become established, the tradition perpetuated it and interest in Arab idolatry became a standard ingredient in the tradition's concern with the Arabian background of Islam. An obvious question is: why would that traditional understanding of the *mushrikūn* and of the milieu in which the Koran was revealed come about? That question can probably only be answered speculatively.

It has already been suggested that one possibility is to explain it as a misreading of the koranic polemic. Perhaps the Muslim scholars, removed from the world in which the attacks against the *mushrikūn* had originated, were misled into understanding the polemic in a literal sense. Since the Koran insinuated that the *mushrikūn* were polytheists and idolators, it may have been deduced that the opponents thus attacked were in fact real polytheists and idolaters. That understanding of the koranic material would then have led to explanations of individual verses and passages in ways reflecting that idea and to the elaboration of the descriptions of pre-Islamic Arab idolatry to document the fact – no doubt using whatever fragments of information about cults among the Arabs was available.

That explanation involves the supposition that the early scholars did not really understand the koranic polemic, a supposition that is difficult, if not impossible, to square with the continuing prominence of idolatry as a motif in arguments between monotheists including Muslims. Nevertheless, it may not require much for polemic to take on a life of its own and to be transformed into fact.

An alternative would be to envisage a development in which the early Muslims elaborated an understanding of the milieu in which the revelation was made, aware to some extent of their involvement in a creative process.

Modern awareness of the way in which traditions form[1] is certainly relevant here, although terms such as 'invention' and 'fabrication' overstress the participants' awareness of their role. There must be a level at which because something is believed to be self-evident and of supreme importance, it is natural to produce evidence in support of it. All societies create their own myths, and the idea of scholarly objectivity is unlikely to be the dominant one in the formation of a religious community. In modern academic circles too, where scientific detachment and according priority to evidence over the preconceptions of the researcher are key values, research papers based on evidence subsequently found to have been falsified are not unknown. It is too simple in all cases to think of their authors as merely liars or cheats.

If one is prepared to think of a more active process of myth formation in this way, one possible reason for the emphasis on the *jāhiliyya*, as it was conceived in Muslim tradition, as the background to the Koran would be to associate the revelation with the career of Muḥammad who was remembered as having been active in Arabia (even though it could be argued that much of the traditional life of Muḥammad in fact depends on a prior understanding of the Koran).

An origin for the Koran in pagan inner Arabia also could be seen to underline its status as revelation. The singularity, if one accepts the tradition, of Islam's origins on the very periphery of the monotheistic world in a debate with people who were literally polytheistic and idolatrous has already been pointed out. If the Koran and Islam, with their monotheistic faith and detailed knowledge of monotheist tradition, originated in a pagan Mecca devoid of a Jewish or Christian presence, then it is difficult to account for it other than by divine revelation.

It is likely that if there was a conscious level of myth creation involved it must have been at the very beginning of the formation of the tradition and have lasted only for a short time. By the time of the appearance of the texts in the forms in which we have them the myth, if that is what it was, of the emergence of a new form of monotheism amidst idolatrous and polytheistic Meccans and other Arabs would have been so well established that it had taken on a life of its own. Myths and idols have much in common.

[1] Eric Hobsbawm and Terence Ranger (eds.), *The Invention of Tradition*, Cambridge 1983.

Bibliography

ʿAbbās, Iḥsān: 'Two Hitherto Unpublished Texts on Pre-Islamic Religion', in *La Signification du bas moyen âge dans l'histoire et la culture du monde musulman* (*Actes du 8e congrès de l'union européenne des arabisants et islamisants*), Aix-en-Provence, 1976, 7–16

Abbott, Nabia: *Studies in Arabic Literary Papyri*, 3 vols., Chicago 1957–72

ʿAbd al-Razzāq al-Ṣanʿānī: *Al-Muṣannaf*, ed. Habīb al-Rahmān al-Aʿẓamī, 12 vols., Beirut 1983–7

Abel, Armand: 'Le chapitre CI du Livre des Héresies de Jean Damascène: son inauthenticité', *SI*, 19 (1963), 5–25

Abū Dāwūd, Sulaymān b. al-Ashʿath: *Kitāb al-Sunan*, 4 vols., Cairo 1935 (cited by name of *Kitāb* and number of *bāb*)

Abu ʾl-Maʿālī: *Kitāb bayān al-adyān* (text in C. Schefer, *Chrestomathie persane*, Paris 1883, I, 131–203; French trans. by H. Massé in *RHR*, 94 (1926), 17–75)

Abū Nuʿaym al-Iṣfahānī, *Dalāʾil al-nubuwwa*, Beirut 1988

Albānī, Nāṣir al-Dīn, al-: *Naṣb al-majānīq li-nasfi qiṣṣat al-gharānīq*, Damascus 1952

ʿAlī, Jawād: *Taʾrīkh al-ʿArab qabla ʾl-islām*, 8 vols., Baghdad 1951–60

al-Mufaṣṣal fī Taʾrīkh al-ʿArab qabla ʾl-islām, 10 vols., Beirut 1968–73

Andalusī, Saʿīd b. Aḥmad, al-: *Kitāb Ṭabaqāt al-umam*, Fr. trans. by R. Blachère, Paris 1935

Andrae, Tor Julius Efraim: *Mohammed, the Man and his Faith*, Eng. trans. London 1936

Les origines de l'Islam et le Christianisme, Paris 1955 (originally 'Der Ursprung des Islams und das Christentum', *Kyrkhistorisk Arsskrift*, 1923–5, republished as *Der Ursprung des Islams und das Christentum*, Uppsala 1926)

Anon.: *Lamʿ al-shihāb fī sīrat Muḥammad ibn ʿAbd al-Wahhāb*, ed. A. M. Abū Ḥākima, Beirut n.d. (1967?)

Aʿshā, Maymūn b. Qays, al-: *Gedichte von ʾAbû Basîr Maimûn ibn Qais al-ʾAʿšâ*, ed. Rudolf Geyer, London 1928

Azraqī, Abu ʾl-Walīd Muḥammad, al-: *Akhbār Makka*, ed. Rushdī Malḥas, 2 vols., Beirut 1969

Babylonian Talmud, cited according to tractate title and standard folio number (Eng. trans., I. Epstein (ed.), *The Babylonian Talmud*, 35 vols., London, 1935–52, cited by tractate and page)

Bakrī, ʿAbd Allāh b. ʿAbd al-ʿAzīz Abū ʿUbayd, al-: *Muʿjam ma ʾstaʿjam*, ed. Muṣṭafā al-Saqqā, 4 vols., Cairo 1947–51

Balādhurī, Aḥmad b. Yaḥyā, al-: *Ansāb al-ashrāf*, vol. V, ed. S. D. Goitein, Jerusalem 1936

Ansāb al-aṣrāf, Teil 5, ed. Iḥsān ʿAbbās, Beirut 1996

Barker, Eileen (ed.): *New Religious Movements: A Perspective for Understanding Society*, New York 1982

Becker, C. H.: 'Der Islam als Problem', *Isl.*, 1 (1910), 1–21; reprinted in C. H. Becker, *Islamstudien: vom Werden und Wesen der islamischen Welt*, vol. I, Leipzig 1924, 1–23

'The Expansion of the Saracens', in H. M. Gwatkin (ed.), *The Cambridge Mediaeval History*, 1st edn, vol. II, Cambridge 1913, 329–90

Bell, Richard: *The Origin of Islam in its Christian Environment*, Edinburgh 1926; repr. London 1968

Berg, Herbert (ed.): *MTSR*, 9/1 (1997), special issue, *Islamic Origins Reconsidered: John Wansbrough and the Study of Early Islam*

Berger, David: *The Jewish–Christian Debate in the High Middle Ages. A Critical Edition of the Nizzaḥon Vetus*, Philadelphia 1979

Berosus: *The Babylonaica of Berossus*, trans. S. Mayer Bernstein, Malibu 1978

Bevan, Edwyn: *Holy Images. An Inquiry into Idolatry and Image-Worship in Ancient Paganism and in Christianity*, London 1940 (Gifford Lectures for 1933)

Blau, Joshua: 'Arabic Lexicographical Miscellanies', *JSS*, 17 (1972), 175–7

Boswell, John: *The Kindness of Strangers*, New York 1988

Brigden, Susan: *London and the Reformation*, Oxford 1989

Brock, Sebastian: 'Syriac Sources for Seventh-Century History', in *BMGS*, 2 (1976), §1, no. 13

Brockelmann, Carl: 'Allah und die Götzen: der Ursprung des islamischen Monotheismus', *AR*, 21 (1922), 99–121

Brown, Francis, Driver, S. R. and Briggs, Charles A.: *A Hebrew and English Lexicon of the Old Testament*, Oxford 1906; repr. 1979

Brown, Peter: *The Cult of the Saints*, London 1981

Bukhārī, Muḥammad b. Ismāʿīl, al-: *Ṣaḥīḥ*, ed L. Krehl and T. W. Juynboll, 4 vols., Leiden 1862–1908 (cited by title of *Kitāb* and number of *bāb*)

Burton, John: 'Those are the High-Flying Cranes', *JSS*, 15 (1970), 246–65

Calder, Norman: *Studies in Early Muslim Jurisprudence*, Oxford 1993

Cameron, Averil: 'The Eastern Provinces in the Seventh Century AD. Hellenism and the Emergence of Islam', in S. Saïd (ed.), *Hellenismos. Quelques jalons pour une histoire de l'identité grecque*, Leiden 1991

The Mediterranean World in Late Antiquity, AD 395–600, London 1993

Cantineau, J.: *Le Nabatéen*, 2 vols., Paris 1932

Caskel, W. and Strenziok, G.: *Ǧamharat an-nasab. Das genealogische Werk des Hišām b. Muḥammad al-Kalbī*, 2 vols., Leiden 1966

Chadwick, Henry: *The Early Church*, Harmondsworth 1967

Charles, R. H. (ed.): *The Apocrypha and Pseudepigraphia of the Old Testament*, 2 vols., Oxford 1913

Conti Rossini, C.: *Chrestomathia Arabica Meridionalis Epigraphica*, Rome 1931

Cook, Michael A.: *Early Muslim Dogma*, Cambridge 1981

Muhammad, Oxford 1983

"Anan and Islam: The Origins of Karaite Scripturalism', *JSAI*, 9 (1987), 161–82

'Ibn Qutayba and the Monkeys', *JSAI* (forthcoming)

Cooke, J. A.: *Textbook of North Semitic Inscriptions*, Oxford 1903
Crone, Patricia: *Meccan Trade and the Rise of Islam*, Princeton 1987
'Two Legal Problems Bearing on the Early History of the Qur'ān', *JSAI*, 18 (1994), 1–37
Crone, Patricia and Cook, Michael A.: *Hagarism. The Making of the Islamic World*, Cambridge 1977
Crone, Patricia and Hinds, Martin: *God's Caliph*, Cambridge 1986
Cumont, Franz: 'L'Origine de la formule grecque d'abjuration imposée aux musulmans', *RHR*, 64 (1911), 143–50
Daniel, Norman: *Islam and the West*, Edinburgh 1960
Islam, Europe and Empire, Edinburgh 1966
Dhahabī, Muḥammad b. Aḥmad (d.748/1347), al-: *Ta'rīkh al-Islām*, ed. Tadmurī, 38 vols., Beirut 1987–
Diyārbakrī, Ḥusayn b. Muḥammad, al-: *Ta'rīkh al-Khamīs*, 2 vols., ʿUthman ʿAbd al-Razzāq Press 1302 AH
Doctrina Addae: *The Doctrine of Addai, the Apostle*, ed. and trans. G. Phillips, London 1876; new Fr. trans. Alain Desreumaux as *Histoire du roi Abgar et de Jésus*, Brepols 1993
Dostal, Walter: 'Mecca before the Time of the Prophet – Attempt of an Anthropological Interpretation', *Isl.*, 68 (1991), 193–231
Dozy, Reinhart: *Die Israeliten zu Mekka*, Leiden 1864
Drijvers, H. J. W.: *Cults and Beliefs at Edessa*, Leiden 1980
Drory, Rina: 'The Abbasid Construction of the Jahiliyya: Cultural Authority in the Making', *SI*, 83 (1996), 33–49
Duffy, Eamon: *The Stripping of the Altars. Traditional Religion in England 1400–1580*, New Haven and London 1992
Dussaud, R. and Macler, F.: *Mission dans les régions désertiques de la Syrie moyenne*, Paris 1903
Eichler, Paul Arno: *Die Dschinn, Teufel und Engel im Koran*, Leipzig 1928
Eire, Carlos M. N.: *War against the Idols*, Cambridge 1986
Elad, Amikam: *Medieval Jerusalem and Islamic Worship*, Leiden 1995
Encyclopaedia Judaica, 16 vols., Jerusalem 1971–2
Encyclopaedia of Islam, 1st edition, 4 vols. and *Supplement*, Leiden 1913–42; 2nd edn, in course of publication, Leiden 1954–
Encyclopaedia of Religion, ed. Mircea Eliade, 16 vols., New York 1987
Encyclopaedia of Religion and Ethics, ed. James Hastings, 13 vols., Edinburgh 1908–26
Ephʿal, I.: ' "Ishmael" and "Arab(s)": A Transformation of Ethnological Terms', *JNES*, 35 (1976), 225–35
Fabietti, U.: 'The Role Played by the Organization of the "Ḥums" in the Evolution of Political Ideas in Pre-Islamic Mecca', *Proceedings of the Seminar for Arabian Studies*, 18 (1988), 25–33
Fahd, Tewfic: *Le panthéon de l'Arabie centrale à la veille de l'Hégire*, Paris 1968
Farazdaq, al-: *Divan de Férazdak*, ed. and trans. R. Boucher, Paris 1876
Fayrūzābādī, Muḥammad b. Yaʿqūb, al-: *al-Qāmūs al-muḥīṭ*, 4 vols., Bulaq 1301–2 AH
Finkel, Joshua: 'Jewish, Christian and Samaritan Influences on Arabia', *The Macdonald Presentation Volume*, Princeton 1933, 145–66
Fossum, J.: 'Samaritan Demiurgical Traditions and the Alleged Dove Cult of the

Samaritans', in R. van den Broek and M. J. Vermaseren (eds.), *Studies in Gnosticism and Hellenistic Religions*, Leiden 1981, 143–60

Fowden, Garth: *Empire to Commonwealth. Consequences of Monotheism in Late Antiquity*, Princeton 1993

Gellner, Ernest: 'Flux and Reflux in the Faith of Men', in Ernest Gellner, *Muslim Society*, Cambridge 1981, 1–85

Gibb, H. A. R.: 'The Structure of Religious Thought in Islam', *MW*, 38 (1948), 17–28, 113–23, 185–97, 280–91 (repr. in Stanford J. Shaw and William R. Polk (eds.), *Studies on the Civilization of Islam*, London 1962, 176–218)

'Pre-Islamic Monotheism in Arabia', *Harvard Theological Review*, 55 (1962), 269–80

Gil, Moshe: 'The Origin of the Jews of Yathrib', *JSAI*, 4 (1984), 203–24

Ginzberg, Louis: *The Legends of the Jews*, 7 vols., Philadelphia 1911–38

Goitein, S. D.: *Jews and Arabs*, New York 1955

Goldfeld, Isaiah: "Umyānis the Idol of Khawlān', *IOS*, 3 (1977), 108–19

Goldziher, Ignaz: 'Le culte des saints chez les musulmans', *RHR*, 2 (1880), 257–351 (= *GS*, VI, 62–156)

'Le monothéisme dans la vie religieuse des musulmans', *RHR*, 16 (1887), 157–65 (= *GS*, II, 173–81)

'Materialen zur Kenntniss der Almohadenbewegung in Nordafrika', *ZDMG*, 41 (1887), 30–140 (= *GS*, II, 191–301)

'Usages juifs d'après la littérateur religieuse des musulmans', *REJ*, 28 (1894), 75–94 (= *GS*, III, 322–41)

'Mélanges Judéo-Arabes', *REJ*, 47 (1902), 41–6, 179–86 (= *GS*, IV, 410–23)

'Mohammed Ibn Toumert et la théologie de l'Islam dans le maghreb au XIe siècle', introduction to J. D. Luciani (ed.), *Le Livre de Mohammed Ibn Toumert*, Algiers 1903

Muslim Studies, 2 vols., Eng. trans. London 1967, 1971 (= *Muhammedanische Studien*, 2 vols., Halle 1889–90)

Introduction to Islamic Theology and Law (updated English trans. of his *Vorlesungen über den Islam*, 1910), Princeton 1981

Gesammelte Schriften, ed. Joseph Desomogyi, 6 vols., Hildesheim 1967–73

Grabar, Oleg: 'The Umayyad Dome of the Rock in Jerusalem', *Ars Orientalis*, 3 (1959), 33–62

Grant, R. M.: *Gods and the One God*, London 1986

Grégoire, Henri: 'Des dieux Cahu, Baraton, Tervagant . . . et de maints autres dieux non moins extravagants', *AIPHOS*, 7 (1939–44), 451–72

Grohmann, Adolf: *From the World of Arabic Papyri*, Cairo 1952

Arabic Papyri from Ḫirbet al-Mird, Louvain 1963

Guillaume, Alfred: *The Life of Muhammad. A Translation of Ibn Ishaq's Sirat Rasul Allah*, Oxford 1955

'Stroking an Idol', *BSOAS*, 27 (1964), 430

Halbertal, Moshe and Margalit, Avishai: *Idolatry*, Eng. trans., Cambridge, Mass. and London 1992

Halevi, Judah: *Kitāb al-Radd wa'l-dalīl fi'l-dīn al-dhalīl (Kitāb al-Khazarī)*, ed. D. H. Baneth and prepared for the press by H. Ben Shammai, Jerusalem 1977; partial Eng. trans. by Isaak Heinemann, Oxford 1947

Hawting, Gerald R.: 'The Significance of the Slogan *lā ḥukma illā lillāh . . .*', *BSOAS*, 41 (1978), 453–63

'Two Citations of the Qur'ān in 'historical' sources for early Islam', in G. R. Hawting and A. Shereef (eds.), *Approaches to the Qur'ān*, London 1993, 260–8

Hayman, Peter: 'Monotheism – a Misused Word in Jewish Studies?', *JJS*, 42 (1991), 1–15

Healey, John F.: *The Nabataean Tomb Inscriptions of Madā'in Ṣāliḥ*, Oxford 1993

Henninger, Josef: 'Pre-Islamic Bedouin Religion', Eng. trans. in Merlin L. Swartz (ed. and trans.), *Studies on Islam*, New York and Oxford 1981, 3–22

Arabica Sacra. Aufsätze zur Religionsgeschichte Arabiens und seiner Randgebiete, Fribourg and Göttingen 1981

Hirschberg, J. W.: *Jüdische und christliche Lehren im vor- und frühislamischen Arabien*, Cracow 1939

Hitti, Philip K.: *History of the Arabs*, 7th edn, London 1961

Hobsbawm, Eric and Ranger, Terence (eds.): *The Invention of Tradition*, Cambridge 1983

Hodgson, Marshall G. S.: *The Venture of Islam*, 3 vols., 2nd edn, Chicago and London 1974

Hoftijzer, J.: *Religio Aramaica: godsdienstige Verschijnselen in aramese Teksten*, Leiden 1968

Hoyland, Robert: *Seeing Islam as Others Saw It*, Princeton 1997

Ibn ʿAbd al-Wahhāb, Muḥammad: *Fī arbaʿ qawāʿid al-dīn – tamīzu bayna 'l-mu'minīna wa'l-mushrikīn*, in *Majmūʿat al-tawḥīd al-najdiyya*, Mecca 1319 AH, 110–12

Masā'il al-jāhiliyya , *Majmūʿat al-tawḥīd*, 89–97

Fī maʿnā al-ṭāghūt wa-ru'ūs anwāʿihi, *Majmūʿat al-tawḥīd*, 117–18

Fī tafsīr kalimat al-tawḥīd, *Majmūʿat al-tawḥīd*, 105–9

Ibn Abī Shayba, Abū Bakr ʿAbd Allāh b. Muḥammad: *al-Muṣannaf*, ed. ʿAbd al-Khāliq al-Afghānī, 15 vols., Karachi 1986–7

Ibn Ḥabīb, Abū Jaʿfar Muḥammad: *Kitāb al-Muḥabbar*, ed. Ilse Lichtenstadter, Hyderabad Deccan 1942

Ibn Ḥajar, Aḥmad b. ʿAlī, al-ʿAsqalānī: *Fatḥ al-bārī bi-sharḥ Ṣaḥīḥ al-Bukhārī*, 14 vols., Cairo 1988

Ibn Ḥanbal, Aḥmad: *Musnad*, 6 vols., Cairo 1313

Ibn Ḥazm, Abū Muḥammad ʿAlī b. Aḥmad: *Jamharat ansāb al-ʿarab*, ed. E. Lévi-Provençal, Cairo 1948

Ibn Hishām, ʿAbd al-Malik: *al-Sīra al-nabawiyya*, ed. Muṣṭafā al-Saqqā et al., 4 parts in 2 vols., 2nd printing Cairo 1955

Ibn al-Kalbī, Hishām b. Muḥammad: *Kitāb al-Aṣnām* (text and Ger. trans. in Rosa Klinke-Rosenberger, *Das Götzenbuch: Kitâb al-Aṣnām des Ibn al-Kalbī*, Leipzig 1941; text and Fr. trans. in Wahib Atallah, *Les idoles de Hicham ibn al-Kalbī*, Paris 1969; Eng. trans. by N. A. Faris, *The Book of Idols*, Princeton 1952)

Jamharat al-nasab, Riwāyat al-Sukkarī ʿan Ibn Ḥabīb, ed. Nājī Ḥasan, Beirut 1986

Ibn Kathīr, Abu 'l-Fidā' Ismāʿīl: *Tafsīr al-Qur'ān al-ʿaẓīm*, 7 vols., Beirut 1966

Ibn Khallikān, Shams al-Dīn Abu 'l-ʿAbbās: *Wafayāt al-aʿyān*, ed. Iḥsān ʿAbbās, 8 vols., Beirut n.d.

Ibn al-Muʿtazz, ʿAbd Allāh: *Ṭabaqāt al-shuʿarā'*, ed. ʿAbd al-Sattār Aḥmad Farrāj, Cairo 1956

Ibn Qayyim al-Jawziyya, Shams al-Dīn Muḥammad b. Abī Bakr: *Hidāyat al-ḥayārā fī ajwibat al-yahūd wa'l-naṣārā*, Beirut 1987
Ibn Qutayba, Abū Muḥammad ʿAbd Allāh b. Muslim: *Kitāb al-Maʿārif*, ed. Tharwat ʿUkāsha, Cairo 1969
Ibn Saʿd, Muḥammad: *al-Ṭabaqāt al-kubrā*, 9 vols., ed. E. Sachau et al., Leiden 1905–28
Iṣfahānī, Abu 'l-Faraj ʿAlī b. Ḥusayn, al-: *Kitāb al-Aghānī*, 24 vols., Cairo 1927–74
Jacob of Seruj: 'Discours de Jacques de Saroug sur la chute des idoles', ed. and trans. P. Martin, *ZDMG*, 29 (1895), 107–47
Jāḥiẓ, ʿAmr b. Baḥr, al-: *Kitāb al-Ḥayawān*, ed. ʿAbd al-Salām Muḥammad Hārūn, 7 vols., Cairo 1938–45
Jamme, A.: 'Le panthéon sud-arabe préislamique d'après les sources epigraphiques', *Le Muséon*, 60 (1947), 54–147
Jeffery, Arthur: *The Foreign Vocabulary of the Qur'ān*, Baroda 1938
Jerusalem Talmud (Eng. trans. J. Neusner et al., *The Talmud of the Land of Israel*, 35 vols., Chicago 1982–94)
Kaufmann, Yehezkel: *The Religion of Israel*, Eng. trans. London 1961
Kedar, Benjamin Z.: *Crusade and Mission*, Princeton 1984
Kessler, C: "Abd al-Malik's Inscription in the Dome of the Rock, a reconsideration', *JRAS* (1970), 2–14
Khoury, A. T.: *Polémique byzantine contre l'Islam*, Leiden 1972
Khoury, P.: *Paul d'Antioche évêque melkite de Sidon (XIIe s.)*, Beirut 1964
Khuzistanī Chronicle: I. Guidi (ed. and trans.), *Chronica Minora* (*Corpus Scriptorum Christianorum Orientalium*, vol. I, *Scriptores Syri*, Tom. I), I, Louvain 1903, 15–39 (text) = 13–32 (trans.); see also below – Nöldeke, 'Die von Guidi herausgegebene. . . .'
Kindī, al- (attrib.): *Risālat ʿAbd al-Masīḥ Ibn Isḥāq al-Kindī*, London 1870
Kister, Meir J.: 'Al-Ḥīra. Some Notes on its Relations with Arabia', *Arabica*, 15 (1968), 143–69
'Labbayka, Allāhumma, Labbayka . . .', *JSAI*, 2 (1980), 33–57
'Mecca and the Tribes of Arabia', in M. Sharon (ed.), *Studies in Islamic History and Civilization in Honour of Prof. David Ayalon*, Jerusalem and Leiden 1986, 33–57
Köbert, R.: 'Das koranische 'ṭāġūt'', *Orientalia*, n.s. 30 (1961), 415–16
Koren, Judith and Nevo, Yehuda. 'Methodological Approaches to Islamic Studies', *Isl.*, 68 (1991), 87–107
Kotter, B. (ed.): *Die Schriften des Johannes von Damaskos. IV Liber De Haeresibus*, Berlin and New York 1981
Krehl, L.: *Über die Religion der vorislamischen Araber*, Leipzig 1863
Krone, Susanne: *Die altarabische Gottheit al-Lāt*, Frankfurt-am-Main 1992
Lammens, Henri: *Études sur le règne du calife omaiyade Moʿâwia Ier*, Paris 1908
'Qoran et tradition: comment fut composée la vie de Mahomet', *RSR*, 1 (1910), 5–20
'Les Chrétiens à la Mecque à la veille de l'hégire', *BIFAO*, 14 (1918), 191–230
Lampe, G. W. H.: *A Patristic Greek Lexicon*, Oxford 1961
Lane, Edward W.: *An Arabic–English Lexicon*, 8 vols., London 1863–93
Laoust, Henri: *Essai sur les doctrines sociales et politiques de Taḳī-d-Dīn Aḥmad b. Taimīya*, Cairo 1939
Lassner, Jacob: *Demonizing the Queen of Sheba*, Chicago and London 1993

Lecker, Michael: *The Banū Sulaym. A Contribution to the Study of Early Islam*, Jerusalem 1989

'Idol Worship in Pre-Islamic Medina (Yathrib)', *Le Muséon*, 106 (1993), 331–46

Muslims, Jews and Pagans: Studies on Early Islamic Medina, Leiden 1995

'The Death of the Prophet Muḥammad's Father: Did Wāqidī Invent Some of the Evidence?', *ZDMG*, 145 (1995), 9–27

Leibowitz, Yeshayahu: *Judaism, Human Values and the Jewish State*, Cambridge, Mass. 1992

Levy, J.: *Wörterbuch über die Talmudim und Midraschim*, 4 vols., 2nd edn, Berlin 1924; repr. Darmstadt 1963

Lichtenstadter, Ilse: 'A Note on the *gharānīq* and Related Qur'ānic Problems', *IOS*, 5 (1975), 54–61

Lieberman, Saul: 'Rabbinic Polemics against Idolatry', in Saul Lieberman, *Hellenism and Jewish Palestine*, (1950), 2nd edn New York 1962, 115–27

Littman, Enno: *Thamūd und Ṣafā*, Abhandlungen für die Kunde des Morgenlandes, 25, Leipzig 1940

Lüling, Günter: *Die Wiederentdeckung des Propheten Muhammad*, Erlangen 1981

Macuch, Rudolf: 'Zur Vorgeschichte der Bekenntnisformel *lā ilāha illā llāhu*', *ZDMG*, 128 (1978), 20–38

Madigan, D. A.: 'Reflections on Some Current Directions in Qur'anic Studies', *MW*, 85 (1995), 345–62

Masʿūdī, Abu'l-Ḥasan, al-: *Murūj al-dhahab*, ed. and French trans. Barbier de Meynard and Pavet de Courteille, 9 vols., Paris 1861–77; Arabic text revised by Charles Pellat, 3 vols., Beirut 1966

Milik, J.- T.: 'Un lettre de Siméon Bar Kokheba', *RB*, 60 (1953), 276–94

Dédicaces faites par des dieux, Paris 1972

Millar, Fergus: 'Hagar, Ishmael, Josephus and the Origins of Islam', *JJS*, 44 (1993), 23–45

Minucius Felix, *Octavius*, ed. and trans. G. H. Rendall, Loeb Classical Library, London 1931

Mizzī, Yūsuf b. ʿAbd al-Raḥmān, al-: *Tahdhīb al-kamāl*, ed. Bashshar ʿAwad Maʿrūf, 35 vols., Beirut 1984–92

Monnot, Guy: 'L'Histoire des religions en Islam: Ibn al-Kalbī et Rāzī', *RHR*, 188 (1975), 23–34

Montet, E.: 'Un rituel d'abjuration des musulmans dans l'église grecque', *RHR*, 53 (1906), 145–63

Montgomery, James A.: *The Samaritans*, Philadelphia 1907

Aramaic Incantation Texts from Nippur, Philadelphia 1913

Mordtmann, J. H.: 'Dusares bei Epiphanius', *ZDMG*, 29 (1876), 99–106

Mordtmann, J. H. and Müller, D. H.: 'Eine monotheistische sabäische Inschrift', *VOJ*, 10 (1896), 265–92

Motzki, Harald: *Die Anfänge der islamischen Jurisprudenz*, Stuttgart 1991

'The *Muṣannaf* of ʿAbd al-Razzāq aṣ-Ṣanʿānī as a Source of Authentic *aḥādīth* of the First Century AH', *JNES*, 50 (1991), 1–21

'Der Prophet und die Katze: zur Datierung eines *ḥadīth*', paper read at the 7th Colloquium 'From Jāhiliyya to Islam', Jerusalem, 28 July–1 August, 1996, trans. as 'The Prophet and the Cat. On Dating Mālik's *Muwaṭṭaʾ* and Legal Traditions', *JSAI*, 22 (1998), 18–83

Mūsā b. ʿUqba, *Maghāzī*, collected by M. Bāqshīsh Abū Mālik, Agadir 1994

Muslim b. al-Ḥajjāj al-Qushayrī, *Ṣaḥīḥ*, ed. Muḥammad Fu'ād ʿAbd al-Baqī, 5 vols., Cairo 1955–6 (cited by name of *Kitāb* and number of *bāb*)

Nadīm, Abu 'l-Faraj Muḥammad b. Isḥāq, al-: *The Fihrist of al-Nadīm*, trans. Bayard Dodge, New York and London 1970

Nawawī, Abu 'l-Zakariyyā' Yaḥyā b. Sharaf: *Sharḥ Ṣaḥīḥ Muslim*, 18 parts in 10 vols., ed. Khalīl al-Mays, Beirut 1987

Tahdhīb al-asmā' wa'l-lugha, 3 vols., Beirut n.d. (Idārat al-Ṭibāʿa al-Munīriyya)

Neusner, Jacob: *Studying Classical Judaism. A Primer*, Louisville, Ky. 1991

Nevo, Yehuda D. and Koren, Judith: 'The Origins of the Muslim Descriptions of the Jāhilī Meccan Sanctuary', *JNES*, 49 (1990), 23–44

Nevo, Yehuda D.: *Pagans and Herders*, Israel: IPS Ltd., Negev 84993, 1991

Nielsen, Ditlef: 'Zur altarabischen Religion', chap. 5 of D. Nielsen et al. (eds.), *Handbuch der altarabischen Altertumskunde, I. Die altarabische Kultur*, Copenhagen 1927

Nöldeke, Theodor: review of Wellhausen's *Reste* in *ZDMG*, 41 (1887), 707–26

'Die von Guidi herausgegebene syrische Chronik übersetzt und commentiert', in *Sitzungsberichte der Akademie der Wissenschaften*, Phil.-Hist. Klasse, B 128, Vienna 1893

Neue Beiträge zur semitischen Sprachwissenschaft , Strasburg 1910

Nuʿaym b. Ḥammād al-Marwazī, *Kitāb al-Fitan*, ed. Suhayl Zakkār, Mecca 1991

Nyberg, H. S.: 'Bemerkungen zum 'Buch der Götzenbilder' von Ibn al-Kalbī', in *ΔΡΑΓΜΑ Martino P. Nilsson . . . dedicatum*, Lund 1939, 346–66

Obermann, Julian: 'Islamic Origins: A Study in Background and Foundation', in N. A. Faris (ed.), *The Arab Heritage*, Princeton 1944, 58–120

Paret, Rudi: *Der Koran: Kommentar und Konkordanz*, Stuttgart etc. 1971

Pellat, Charles: 'Ǧāḥiẓiana III', *Arabica*, 3 (1956), 147–8

Peskes, Esther: *Muḥammad b. ʿAbdalwahhāb (1703–92) im Widerstreit*, Beirut 1993

Peters, F. E.: 'The Quest of the Historical Muhammad', *IJMES*, 23 (1991), 291–315

Muhammad and the Origins of Islam, Albany N.Y., 1994

Pines, Shlomo: 'Jāhiliyya and ʿIlm', *JSAI*, 13 (1990), 175–94 (repr. in Sarah Stroumsa (ed.), *Studies in the History of Arabic Philosophy*, Jerusalem 1996, 231–50)

Quinton, Anthony: *Bacon*, Oxford 1980

Qurṭubī, Abū ʿUbayd Allāh Muḥammad b. Aḥmad, al-: *Tafsīr = Al-Jāmiʿ li-aḥkām al-Qur'ān*, 20 vols., Cairo 1935–50

Quṭb, Muḥammad: *Jāhiliyyat al-qarn al-ʿishrīn*, Cairo 1964

Rabin, Chaim: *Qumran Studies*, Oxford 1957

'On the Probability of South Arabian Influence on the Arabic Vocabulary', *JSAI*, 4 (1984), 125–34

Répertoire chronologique d'épigraphie arabe (Publications de l'Institut Français d'Archéologie Orientale du Caire), founding eds. E. Combe, J. Sauvaget and G. Wiet, 17 vols., Cairo 1931–82

Répertoire d'épigraphie sémitique, publié par la Commission du Corpus Inscriptionum Semiticarum, 8 vols., Paris 1900–68

Rippin, Andrew: 'Ibn ʿAbbās's *Al-Lughat fī'l-Qur'ān*', *BSOAS*, 44 (1981), 15–25

'The Methodologies of John Wansbrough', in Richard C. Martin (ed.), *Approaches to Islam in Religious Studies*, Tucson, 1985, 151–63

'The Function of the *asbāb al-nuzūl* in Qur'ānic Exegesis', *BSOAS*, 51 (1988), 1–20

'RḤMNN and the Ḥanīfs', in W. B. Hallaq and D. P. Little (eds.), *Islamic Studies Presented to Charles J. Adams*, Leiden 1991, 153–68
'Studying Early *tafsīr* Texts', *Isl.*, 72 (1995), 310–23
Ritter, Helmuth: 'Studien zur Geschichte der islamischen Frömmigkeit. I. Ḥasan al-Baṣrī', *Isl.*, 21 (1933), 67–82
Robertson, Roland: *The Sociological Interpretation of Religion*, Oxford 1969
Rodinson, Maxime: *Mahomet*, Paris 1961; 2nd English edn, *Muhammad*, Harmondsworth 1996
Rosenthal, Franz: *Knowledge Triumphant*, Leiden 1970
Ruʾba b. al-ʿAjjāj: *Sammlungen alter arabische Dichter. III Der Dīwān des Reğezdichters Rūba Ben El ʾağğāğ*, ed. W. Ahlwardt, Berlin 1903 (*Dīwān . . . El'ağğāğ . . . aus dem Arabischen übersetzt*, trans. W. Ahlwardt, Berlin 1904)
Rubin, Uri: 'Al-Ṣamad', *Isl.*, 61 (1984), 197–217
'Ḥanīfiyya and Kaʿba', *JSAI*, 13 (1990), 85–112
The Eye of the Beholder. The Life of Muḥammad as Viewed by the Early Muslims, Princeton 1995
Ryckmans, Gonzagues: *Les noms propres sud-sémitiques*, 3 vols., Louvain 1934–5
Les religions arabes préislamiques, 2nd edn, Louvain 1951
Ryckmans, Jacques: 'Les inscriptions anciennes de l'arabie du sud: points de vue et problèmes actuels', *Conférence prononcée à la societé 'Oosters Genootschap in Nederland', Le 15 mars 1973*, Leiden 1973, 79–110
Saʿadiya Gaon, *Kitāb al-Āmanāt wa'l-iʿtiqādāt*, trans. S. Rosenblatt as *The Book of Beliefs and Opinions*, New Haven 1948
Sahas, D. J.: *John of Damascus and Islam*, Leiden 1972
Icon and Logos. Sources in Eighth Century Iconoclasm, Toronto 1986
Samhūdī, Nūr al-Dīn ʿAlī b. Aḥmad, al-: *Wafāʾ al-wafā*, ed. Muḥammad Muḥyi ʾl-Dīn ʿAbd al-Ḥamīd, 4 vols., Cairo 1955
Schacht, Joseph: *The Origins of Muhammadan Jurisprudence*, Oxford 1950
Schechter, Solomon: *Aspects of Rabbinic Theology* (1909); repr. New York 1961
Schefer, Charles: 'Notice sur le Kitab Beïan il Edian', in Charles Schefer, *Chrestomathie persane*, vol. I, Paris 1883, 131–203 (text), 132–189 (notes)
Schimmel, Annemarie: 'The Sufis and the *shahāda*', in R. G. Hovannisian and Speros Vryonis Jr. (eds.), *Islam's Understanding of Itself*, Malibu 1983, 103–25
Schoeler, Gregor: *Charakter und Authentie der muslimischen Überlieferung über das Leben Mohammeds*, Berlin 1996
Schoeps, H. J.: *Theologie und Geschichte des Judenchristentums*, Tübingen 1949
Sezgin, Fuat: *Geschichte des arabischen Schrifttums*, vol. I, Leiden 1967
Shahid, Irfan: *Byzantium and the Arabs in the Fifth Century*, Washington D.C. 1989
Shahrastānī, Abu ʾl-Fatḥ Muḥammad b. ʿAbd al-Karīm, al-: *Kitāb al-milal wa'l-niḥal*, ed. Kaylānī, Cairo 1961
Sharpe, Eric J.: *Comparative Religion: A History*, London 1975
Sirriyeh, Elizabeth: 'Modern Muslim Interpretations of *shirk*', *Religion*, 20 (1990), 139–59
Smith, Jonathan Z.: 'The Unknown God: Myth in History', in Jonathan Z. Smith, *Imagining Religion*, Chicago and London 1982, 66–89
Smith, W. Robertson: *The Religion of the Semites*, 2nd edn 1894, repr. New York 1972
Sourdel, Dominique: *Les cultes du Hauran*, Paris 1952

Sourdel, Dominique: (ed. and trans.) 'Un pamphlet musulman anonyme d'époque 'abbāside contre les chrétiens', *REI*, 34 (1966), 1–34
Southern, Richard W.: *Western Views of Islam in the Middle Ages*, Cambridge, Mass. and London 1962 (rev. repr. 1978)
Sozomen: *Historia Ecclesiastica*, ed. J. Bidez and G. C. Hansen, Berlin 1960 (Eng. trans. E. Walford, London 1855)
Sparks, H. F. D. (ed.): *The Apocryphal Old Testament*, Oxford 1984
Sprenger, Aloys: *Das Leben und die Lehre des Moḥammad*, Berlin 1861–5
Stemberger, Günter: *Introduction to the Talmud and Midrash*, Eng. trans., 2nd edn Edinburgh 1996 (*Einleitung in Talmud und Midrasch*, Munich 1992)
Stummer, F.: 'Bemerkungen zum Götzenbuch des Ibn al-Kalbī', *ZDMG*, 98 (1944), 377–94
Surty, Muhammad Ibrahim H.: *The Qur'anic Concept of al-Shirk (Polytheism)*, London 1982
Suyūṭī, Jalāl al-Dīn, al-: *Lubab al-nuqūl fī asbāb al-nuzūl*, Tunis 1981
Ṭabarī, Muḥammad b. Jarīr, al-: *Tafsīr* (Bulaq) = *Jāmiʿ al-bayān fī ta'wīl āy al-Qur'ān*, 30 vols. in 10, Bulāq 1323–8/1905–12
Tafsīr (Cairo) = *Jāmiʿ al-bayān* . . ., 16 vols. to date, ed. M. M. Shākir, Cairo 1954–
Ta'rīkh = *Annales*, ed. M. J. de Goeje et al., 15 vols., Leiden 1879–1901
Teixidor, Javier: 'Arabic Inscriptions of Hatra', *Sumer*, 20 (1964), 77–80
The Pagan God: Popular Religion in the Graeco-Roman Near East, Princeton 1977
Tertullian: *Apologeticus*, ed. and trans. T. R. Glover, Loeb Classical Library, London 1931
Thomas, David (ed. and trans.): *Anti-Christian polemic in early Islam*, Cambridge 1992
Tihrānī, Āgha Buzurg: *Al-Dharīʿa ilā taṣānīf al-shīʿa*, Najaf 1936
Torrey, Charles Cutler: *The Jewish Foundations of Islam*, New York 1933
Tosefta: ed. S. Lieberman, 5 vols., New York 1955–88; Eng. trans., J. Neusner as *The Tosefta Translated from the Hebrew*, 6 vols., New York 1977–86
Urbach, Ephraim E.: *The Sages*, 2nd edn, Eng. trans. Cambridge, Mass. and London, 1979 (Hebrew original, Jerusalem 1969)
van den Branden, A.: *Les Inscriptions thamoudéennes*, Louvain-Heverlé 1950
van Ess, Josef: *Anfänge muslimischer Theologie*, Beirut 1977
Theologie und Gesellschaft im 2. und 3. Jahrhundert Hidschra, 6 vols., Berlin 1992
''Abd al-Malik and the Dome of the Rock. An Analysis of Some Texts', in J. Raby and J. Johns (eds.), *Bayt al-Maqdis: ʿAbd al-Malik's Jerusalem*, part 1, Oxford 1993
Waardenburg, Jacques: 'Un débat coranique contre les polythéistes', *Ex Orbe Religionum: Studia Geo Widengren Oblata*, 2 vols., Leiden 1972
Wansbrough, John: *Quranic Studies*, London 1977
The Sectarian Milieu, London 1978
Wāqidī, Muḥammad b. ʿUmar, al-: *Kitāb al-Maghāzī*, ed. Marsden Jones, 3 vols., London 1966
Watt, William Montgomery: *Muhammad at Mecca*, Oxford 1953
Muhammad at Medina, Oxford 1956
'The "High God" in pre-Islamic Mecca', *Actes du Ve Congrès International d'Arabisants et d'Islamisants*, Brussels 1970, 499–505
'Belief in a "High God" in pre-Islamic Mecca', *JSS*, 16 (1971), 35–40

'Pre-Islamic Arabian Religion', *Islamic Studies*, 15 (1976), 73–9
'The Qur'ān and Belief in a "High God"', *Isl.* 56 (1979), 205–11
Welch, Alford T.: 'Allah and Other Supernatural Beings: The Emergence of the Qur'anic Doctrine of tawhid', *JAAR*, thematic issue, *Studies in Qur'an and Tafsir* (Guest ed. Alford T. Welch), 47 (Dec. 1979), no. 4 S, 733–53
Wellhausen, Julius: *Reste arabischen Heidentums,* 2nd edn, Berlin 1897 (repr. with a new introduction as the 3rd edn, Berlin 1961)
Wensinck, Arthur Jan: *Muhammad and the Jews of Medina*, Eng. trans., 2nd edn Berlin 1982 (= *Mohammed en de Joden te Medina*, Leiden 1908)
'Muhammad und die Propheten', *AO*, 2 (1924), 168–98
Wensinck, Arthur Jan et al.: *Concordance et indices de la tradition musulmane*, 8 vols., Leiden 1936–88
Wieder, Naphtali: *The Judaean Scrolls and Karaism*, London 1962
Wilson, Bryan: *Religion in Sociological Perspective*, Oxford 1982
Winnett, F. W.: *A Study of the Lihyanite and Thamudic Inscriptions*, Toronto 1937
Wolf, Eric R.: 'The Social Organization of Mecca and the Origins of Islam', *SWJA*, 7 (1951), 329–56
Wolfson, Harry Austryn: *Philo*, 2 vols., Cambridge Mass. 1948
Yāqūt b. ʿAbd Allāh al-Ḥamawī: *Muʿjam al-Buldān = Jacut's geographisches Wörterbuch*, ed. F. Wüstenfeld, 6 vols., Leipzig 1866–7
Zabīdī, Muḥammad al-Murtaḍā, al-: *Tāj al- ʿArūs*, ed. Alī Shīrī, 20 vols., Beirut 1994

Index

ʿAbbās, Iḥsān, 140
ʿAbbās b. Mirdās, 70
ʿAbd Allāh b. al-ʿAbbās, 92
ʿAbd al-Malik, caliph, 7 n. 13, 82
ʿAbd Manāf, theophoric, 112
ʿAbd al-Muṭṭalib, 22, 109 n. 64
ʿAbd Ruḍā, theophoric, 112, 118
ʿAbd Wadd (or Wudd) b. Suwāʿ, 114
abjuration ritual, Byzantine, 83–4, 85
Abraham (Ibrāhīm)
  brings monotheism to Arabia, 24–5, 35
  builder of the Kaʿba, 21, 24–5, 38
  Dome of, 39 n. 46
  father of monotheism, 36–8
  in Koran, 55, 107
  religion of (*dīn Ibrāhīm*), 20–1, 36, 40, 43, 81, 90, 94, 101
Abū Bakr al-Jawharī, 91
Abū Bakr al-Shiblī, 79
Abū Lahab, ʿAbd al-ʿUzzā, 27 n. 14
Abu ʾl-Maʿālī, 63 n. 43
Abū Sufyān, 139, 141
Abū Ṭālib, 4, 70
Abū Uḥayḥa, Saʿīd b. al-ʿĀṣ, 27, 126
Aflaḥ b. Naḍr al-Shaybānī, 27 n. 14
agnoia (Greek), ignorance, 2 n. 4, 99
ʿAlī, Jawād, 30
ʿAlī b. Abī Ṭālib, 79, 83, 141
Alilat of Herodotus, 141
Allāh, 21, 22–3, 30
  linguistic theory of origins of, 27, 28, 31
Allāt, 63, 107, 112, 117, 130–49, esp. 138–9, 141
Almohads (al-Muwaḥḥidūn), 80
ʿAmr b. al-ʿĀṣ, 107, 121, 127
ʿAmr b. Luḥayy, 36, 40, 90 n. 7, 103–4, 128, 143
andād, peers of God, 51
Andrae, Tor, 30
angels, angel worship, 4 n. 8, 52, 53, 58, 62, 63, 81, 136, 137, 144–8
  fallen, 103–4
anger, as idolatry, 75
anthropomorphism, as idolatry, 75, 84–5
Aphrodite, *see* Venus
Arabs, descendants of Ishmael, 24, 36–7, 38
asbāb al-nuzūl, *see* occasions of revelation
Aʿshā Hamdān, poet, 71
Aʿshā Maymūn, poet, 70–71
Aʿshā b. Zurāra al-Asadī, 109
Aṣnām, Kitāb al-, 89–110
attributes, divine, 80
ʿavōdāh zārāh (Hebrew)
  idolatry, 74–5, 77
awliyāʾ, patrons, 51, 56, 61–64

Babel, tower of, connected with idolatry, 105
Bacon, Francis, 76
Balkhaʿ, place in Yemen, 116
Bar Kokhba, 73
Becker, Carl Heinrich, 13
Bel and the Dragon, story of, 108
Black Stone of Kaʿba, 85–86, 106
Brockelmann, Carl, 30, 65
Brown, Peter, 32
Burton, John, 134–35
buss, place, sanctuary (?), 139–40
Buwāna, place, idol (?), 121–22

Cain (Qābil), 104
Calder, Norman, 12
children (sons, daughters) of God, 52, 54, 58, 63, 103, 130–49, esp. 145–6
Christians, Christianity, 14–16, 64, 74, 76–7, 82–4, 85–6
clothes, on idols, 102
commemoration, leads to idolatry, 101–3, 128
Crone, Patricia, 10, 12
crosses, *see* icons
cultural change, in pre-Islamic Middle East, 13

Dajjāl, al-, Antichrist, 94
Daniel, Norman, 86
Daws, tribe, 122–5, 128
De Haeresibus, of John of Damascus, 83–4, 85

Index of koranic references

Printed in the United States
15680LVS00001B/221

9 780521 651653